W9-CBM-696

OUTDOOR RECREATION MANAGEMENT

Alan Jubenville

Recreation and Park Administration
University of Wyoming
Laramie, Wyoming

1978
W. B. SAUNDERS COMPANY
Philadelphia, London, Toronto

W. B. Saunders Company: West Washington Square
                           Philadelphia, PA   19105

                           1 St. Anne's Road
                           Eastbourne, East Sussex BN21 3UN, England

                           1 Goldthorne Avenue
                           Toronto, Ontario M8Z 5T9, Canada

Library of Congress Cataloging in Publication Data

Jubenville, Alan.

Outdoor recreation management.

Includes index.

1. Outdoor recreation — Management.   I. Title.
GV191.66.J8   658'.91'79   77–23998
ISBN 0–7216–5230–1

Back end paper is a photograph of vehicle camping yesterday.
Photograph courtesy of the U.S. Forest Service.

Outdoor Recreation Management   ISBN 0-7216-5230-1

Last digit is the print number: 9   8   7   6   5   4   3   2   1

ABOUT THE AUTHOR

Alan Jubenville, originally from southeastern Virginia, has had many varied professional experiences from the Appalachian Mountains and the Midwest to the Northern Rockies and Alaska as well as the northern Canadian Provinces. He has worked with federal and state agencies and a private consulting firm.

Alan has a B.S. in forest management from North Carolina State University (1962), and an M.S. in silviculture-ecology from West Virginia University (1964), and a Ph.D. in wildland recreation from the University of Montana (1970). After receiving the doctoral degree, he became the state outdoor recreation extension specialist at the University of Illinois. He later returned to the West to accept a teaching and research position at the University of Wyoming.

Since that time, Alan has conducted several state and federal research projects and has engaged in several private consulting (planning) opportunities. He teaches outdoor recreation planning and management courses at the graduate and undergraduate levels and has published in a number of professional periodicals. In his earlier textbook, Outdoor Recreation Planning, he developed some basic planning concepts and tried to integrate those concepts into a holistic approach to outdoor recreation planning. This new text complements that effort by focusing on the total management system and its various subsystems.

PREFACE

Outdoor recreation management is a relatively new profession—one that is still evolving. In the past, not much concern was given to problems in this area of management because of the small numbers of participants, the primitive types of outdoor equipment, and the minimum impact on the environment. People spent very little of their time in outdoor activities and therefore required only minimal services. But after World War II, we reached a new level of prosperity in which people had more leisure time and more money to spend in the pursuit of specific activities. Emphasis on these and other new outdoor activities has continued to increase, spiraling faster than the rate at which management science has been able to develop the principles and programs to cope with the increased recreational use of the natural resource base.

The present situation finds us eagerly searching for new ways of managing all sub-systems of the recreation management system—the visitor, the resource, and the services. This is further complicated by laws, political boundaries, and agency philosophies. Yet as complicated as today's situation is, tomorrow's problems will be even more difficult—brought about by a boundless technological change, an increasing urge to escape the problems of the cities, and a continued spiraling of demand for specific opportunities.

Faced with these crises, the manager and the educator have worked together rather harmoniously to research and develop new principles and programs in order to not only cope with the problems but also enhance the experiences of the visitors on a sustained basis. Not all problems have been solved, but great strides have been made and will continue to be made. Those who have contributed to the growth of this new management science can take pride in their accomplishments. Yet it is still an evolving science that will undergo many changes.

The more important concepts that have developed in recent times are concerned with involvement of the public in decision making, management by design, and management zoning. The public has demanded more participation in decision making, and new principles and techniques have been developed to describe, encourage, and maximize that input. Probably the greatest contribution has been made by two of my friends and colleagues, Hans and Annemarie Bleiker, in their new book on citizen participation.* Proper development of citizen participation is essential to obtaining usable input; it is not just a matter of holding a public meeting and trying to analyze the results. It requires analyzing the particular situation and employing the proper technique on a timely basis.

Management by design is a concept that the manager of the future must employ if the overall programs are to be effective. Basically, this means the development of a recreation system (such as a river) so that it becomes self-regulating or self-managing. You first decide on the area objectives, establish measurable criteria for those objectives, and then design the system (access, circulation, site developments, and so forth) to achieve the established criteria.

Zoning for management purposes is a controversial issue because it tends to exclude certain uses or user groups. But as a management tool, it is absolutely essential for

---

*Bleiker, A., and H. Bleiker. 1977. *Citizen Participation Handbook.* Laramie, Wyo.: Institute for Participatory Planning.

v

the future maintenance of specified (in the objectives) recreational experiences and of the environment in which the activity takes place. Most managers have been reluctant to zone for specific uses; consequently, as use has increased, social invasion and succession have taken place where the more primitive forms of participation (hiking, canoeing, bicycling) have been displaced by the more modern forms (trail biking, power-boating, motoring). This type of management may be acceptable as long as there are areas to which the more primitive form could disperse. But we have reached a point where casual dispersal is nearly impossible, and we must face the problem or lessen the chances for the survival of the more primitive species. In sum, by not taking any action, we may be favoring one "species" over another.

Given that introductory philosophy, it is essential that the manager attempt to understand the total outdoor recreation system. That is what Part I of this book does. It focuses on the entire system and the potential interactions. We have to understand the system before we can understand the effects a decision may have on any part of that system.

Parts II and III dissect the system into subsystems and then into the major components or phases of each subsystem. This provides the reader with an opportunity to study each phase in depth and to consider the major decisions one must face in each phase. There are no absolute answers, but it is hoped that the manager will have a better insight into all the variables that must be considered in the development of specific management programs

The last part, Part IV, attempts to focus on specific contemporary management concerns. Sample problems are presented to provide the student with a "free-lance" opportunity to test his knowledge and skills in solving real world problems. No answers are presented, but each problem is solvable. Once you have arrived at a decision, you can test it in the systems model to see if there are any negative systems effects.

In sum, this book presents the major management programs and then carefully guides the reader through each program, step-by-step. Other factors could have been included and possibly more detail provided, but it was my intent to focus on the system and its important components without losing the reader in too much detail.

The challenge of management is there. Success will not come easily, but it is hoped that, armed with a knowledge of the total recreation system, you will experience some success in solving whatever problems you may face!

Alan Jubenville

CONTENTS

PART I

THE MANAGEMENT PROCESS

Management is a great potential social resource in both our country and abroad. To be fully effective, however, the practice of management calls for great skill in fusing many elements into a total design suited to each specific opportunity.

Newman, W. H. 1972. *The Process of Management: Concept, Behavior, and Practice.* Englewood Cliffs, N.J.: Prentice-Hall, Inc.

This section of the book is aimed primarily at providing an overview of management as it pertains to recreation areas and sites—regardless of the particular circumstances. The intent is to provide the conceptual foundation for the succeeding sections. It is here that the roles of the recreation manager, the organization, the resource, and the visitor will be integrated into a systems management approach. This holistic systems theory seems appropriate in today's modern, complex society, so that we can readily see all the basic elements involved and how they relate to one another.

In other words, we must first understand the management systems on a conceptual level so that we can better appreciate what effects our decisions about a single element of the system have on the entire system. In later sections we will dissect the system-based specific management strategy and try to understand the basic element or function singly in addition to the role of each in the total system.

This section does not focus specifically on administrative or organizational management matters such as budgeting, personnel, and fees and charges. That is not the intent of the book. It does focus on resource and visitor management, and it is hoped that this section will provide the framework for a better understanding of the succeeding discussions.

The chapters included in this section are: The Management Situation, which briefly describes the history of outdoor recreation management, the role of the manager, and the possible implications for the future; The Basic Outdoor Recreation Management Model, which systematically builds primary elements, functions, and variables into a fully integrated systems management model; The Problem-Solving Process, which describes a stepwise approach to decision making; and Involvement of the Public in Decision Making, which offers a discussion on the role of and means of involving the public in decision making.

CHAPTER 1

The Management Situation

In order to understand some of the management problems we face today in many of our outdoor recreation areas, we need to look at the situation in a historical context. The evolution of outdoor recreation management has occurred over a relatively short period of time, about 100 years. Thus, many of our mistakes are still here and haunt us daily. Unfortunately, many of the mistakes still go unrecognized by supposedly professional outdoor recreation managers. This chapter will focus on not only what *is*, but also *what should be*!

A BRIEF HISTORY

Although there are earlier instances of outdoor recreation management to focus on, the one significant event that drastically changed the course of history or parks and conservation was the establishment of Yellowstone National Park. It was the embryo stage of outdoor recreation management in a public land context, the ushering in of the Custodial Era.

Custodial Era. The Yellowstone National Park Act of 1872 opened the door for the establishment of large areas of land for public purposes, including recreation. Several additional national parks were created during the late 1800s; also, the western national forest lands were established under the Forest Reserve Act of 1891. Other lands were added later. The important management strategy that evolved during the early period was that the lands were to be held in reserve—to be protected but not necessarily to be utilized. Thus, most public lands were held in custodial state with little access, no recreational facility development, and no sense of urgency for outdoor recreation management (Fig. 1–1).

Even with the establishment of the National Park Service in 1916, there was very little change in public use of public lands and in the need for outdoor recreation management. The Industrial Revolution had brought people to the cities, some of which expanded to large urban spaces; however, long hours of work in the factories, lack of transportation, and low incomes severely limited participation in outdoor recreation.

Some interest in outdoor recreation became apparent in the late 1920s, but even this waned at the onset of the Great Depression. Thus, again there was no urgency for the development of even the most rudimentary management pro-

Figure 1–1   The main problem in outdoor recreation has been the lack of management.

gram. That period did bring transition, however, and ultimately the end of the Custodial Era, in the form of intensive recreation developments and building of access roads and trails by the Civilian Conservation Corps and the Work Projects Administration.

All that was needed to usher in the management eras was an upgrading of the economy. World War II did just that; although not intended, it lifted us from our economic woes and cast us into a period of economic prosperity. More people had more money and time than ever before, and they began to seek pleasurable leisure experiences, particularly in an outdoor setting. This new interest in the out-of-doors caused little concern among the land managers (land custodians), since most of them found it difficult to interpret the real significance of increased recreational participation. The end of World War II marked the end of the Custodial Era and the beginning of the Extensive Management Era.

(**Extensive Management Era.**) Although many people were reluctant to recognize the rise of the new management era, its impact was becoming evident to some concerned people. During the 1950s and 1960s, public land use expanded greatly, and many agencies attempted to increase facilities and access in order to accommodate more people. Examples of these programs were Mission 66 (National Park Service) and Operation Outdoors (National Forest Service).

The main emphasis of the Extensive Management Era was on increasing the supply of recreational opportunities. Although most of the management programs were extensive in nature, certain fundamental outdoor recreation management programs did evolve:

1.   Resource management
    a.   Site protection and maintenance

     b. Silvicultural treatment of overstory vegetation

     c. Integration with other resource management

2. Visitor management

     a. Informational services

     b. Concession services

     c. Expansion of interpretive programs

     d. Public safety

During the late 1960s, some managers saw a need for not only expanding both resource and visitor management programs but also focusing more on small land parcels. By this time, many new kinds of recreational equipment were available on the market, such as snowmobiles, trail bikes, and ATV's (all-terrain vehicles). Thus, there was a need not merely to provide new opportunities and services but also to integrate these on a systems basis for more efficient management. It was insufficient to provide a few varied opportunities and to attempt to reduce possible conflict between visitors. The visitor and his equipment had become sophisticated technologically; this situation required changes in existing management strategy. There was a need to update the program—to provide for total resource management in order to protect the resource base, and to provide for total visitor management in order to maintain a quality experience for the various types of users. The two broad programs needed to be integrated to insure congruous decision making toward providing sustained yield public recreation that would benefit all users.

Intensive Management Era. The Intensive Management Era is difficult to isolate. Some people feel that we have not yet reached that level; others feel that we may never reach it. Yet it appears we are in the beginning of a new era. Many agencies are undertaking the development of management plans to coordinate visitor use with the capabilities of the area and the perceived needs of the visitor. In this era the emphasis is on the need for developing and updating baseline data both on the resource in regard to effects of visitor use and on the style of visitor participation in a particular area, including his or her perception of a quality recreation experience (Fig. 1–2).

This is a new role for many agencies that previously regarded outdoor recreation on our public lands with a certain distaste.

Management by Objectives. One strategy that has risen during this era is management by objectives. With this new strategy, the recreation manager is forced to evaluate baseline data and to develop specific management objectives for each newly planned area. These objectives must be realistic and must fit both resource capability and the needs of the visitor. This, then, becomes the yardstick by which we can measure the appropriateness of new programs and strategies. If the objectives become obsolete, they should be changed to parallel the changes in society.

Beyond Management by Objectives. Batten[1] feels that we desperately need new ideas and recreation managers with increased personal vitality to search for new ways of doing "old" things. His concept is that while we need management objectives, we also need innovative managers to develop new strategies for solving tomorrow's problems today. Positive action is necessary now; one cannot wait for research to solve all of the problems. An individualistic strategy is necessary for coping with outdoor recreation management problems, rather than a strategy based solely on traditional management practices.

Figure 1-2 As use increases, there is a need for more intensive management.

Teamwork Approach. In recreation management, a teamwork approach is necessary for solving many of the more complex problems. The recreation manager should work with other staff specialists to solve specific problems. He cannot be an expert in everything; therefore, he must depend upon engineers, landscape architects, range ecologists, and other specialists to assist as a team in the decision making. It is important that the team members have input into the decision-making process; otherwise, they may not take special interest in the problem, or any interest they have may wane very quickly.

AN UNMANAGED SYSTEM—THE NEED FOR MANAGEMENT

The intent of the next few paragraphs is for the reader to visualize what can happen in an unmanaged recreational experience. Perhaps you can recall a personal experience in which no resource or visitor management action was taken but was needed. Was there conflict, confusion, and other problems of visitor use? Was there a loss of vegetation, soil erosion, and other problems of resource deterioration?

Try to visualize the effects of nonmanagement in the following two hypothetical situations. Perhaps when you get to Chapter 3, you may wish to refer again to these situations in a problem-solving context.

Developed Site. A 100-unit forest campground is located in the heavy clay soils of the Piedmont in North Carolina. The rainy season for the area is from April to the middle of June. The season for recreational use is generally from April 15 to September 30. Almost all ground vegetation has been lost, even between units where use has not been heavy. Sheet erosion is occurring and almost all of the A_1 soil horizon has already been lost. No organic matter can be found in the remaining soil. Siltation is evident in a nearby stream. Some stagheading of the overstory trees is taking place in the mixed hardwood stand, even though it is only 60 years old.

There is obviously a management problem that is receiving very little attention; otherwise the matter would have not reached these proportions. This is an unmanaged situation.

Let's look at another example: There is a small oval lake that is used heavily by water skiers, fishermen, and swimmers from a local resort. The fisherman usually uses the lake early in the morning and late in the afternoon. The water skier and swimmer usually use the lake during the middle of the day. However, conflict often exists between the three groups. The fisherman does not like the water skier's using the lake because he disturbs the water and swamps fishing boats. The water skier does not like the other user groups on the lake because they limit the good skiing and create safety problems for him.

There has never been a serious accident on the lake, but several incidents have occurred in which minor injuries were reported. One swimmer was bruised by a skier as he swung wide of the boat on a turn. Some minor vandalism of boat trailers has occurred, and there have been rumors of other conflicts. Perhaps you have already formulated some simple solutions while reading about this situation. But more important, you should recognize that the situation is a problem that needs to be resolved.

Dispersed-Use Areas.   Too often we hear that dispersed-use areas, including wilderness, should not be managed; however, situations do exist that require management action. To procrastinate in implementing this action is really self-defeating—the situation merely gets worse.

Much of the traffic in the backcountry of the Evergreen Scenic Area, which has 17,000 acres and is roadless, enters through a common point at Sugar Mountain Campground. People travel that trail for a mile or so and then fan out to camp, fish, and relax around the many mountain lakes.

Shorelines around the more accessible lakes are showing severe deterioration, litter is everywhere, and conflicts are even occurring over the better camping and fishing spots. This may be a different type of situation, but even to the casual observer, this is an unmanaged situation that must be reversed.

If we recognize the need for management, then we must also recognize the professional role of the manager in fulfilling this need.

THE ROLE OF THE MANAGER

Most of us are aware of the need for competent personnel, and are aware also that at the present, management is neither very efficient nor effective in most places. There may be reasons for this deficiency; however, a need for a professional manager who will adequately provide recreation services and who will manage those services in a way to maximize the benefits to the user on a sustained basis still exists.

The managerial role in outdoor recreation is very complex—incorporating resource management (effects of the landscape on the visitor and of the visitor on the landscape), visitor management (enhancing the social environment in order to maximize the recreational experience), and service management (offering necessary and desirable services so the user can enjoy both the social and resource environs in which he participates).

This requires a unique type of individual who has the interest, education, and skills to be responsive to the total outdoor recreation system. This means that the manager must have an understanding of the visitor—background, desires for certain types of experiences, and reasons for participating—and of how visitor management strategies may affect, positively or negatively, the social and resource environs (Fig. 1–3). He must also understand the resource in terms of both its durability for recreational use and its perceptual effects on the user's enjoyment of the site. As an example, we may increase the use of family picnic grounds near a large urban area and still have very little effect on the social environment. Yet it may be disastrous in terms of vegetation loss and subsequent erosion, i.e., the physical environment. Let us assume that we could institute a cultural treatment of introducing new ground vegetation with proper fertilization and irrigation that would prevent the deterioration of the site. All of this would be accomplished to the visual satisfaction of the users. Thus, we have enhanced the social environment—maximizing the social benefits to the user while minimizing (by using acceptable strategies) the effects on the physical and visual environment.

The last component of the managerial role is service management, which basically relates to the provisioning of services so that the user can enjoy the social and resource environs. This, perhaps, is one of the more difficult managerial functions to isolate, since "appropriate and desirable services" are often determined by the institutional, fiscal, and legal constraints and not by the recreational experience that is being provided.

Now let's look at the previous example in terms of service management. Perhaps we did not increase the density of individual units in the picnic area because the agency policy states that such areas cannot exceed a given density—an institutional constraint. Maybe the expansion needed to accommodate more users (a basic service) was foregone because of limited available capital.

The management process (and the subsequent role of the manager) may appear to be simplified decisions about each separate subsystem (visitor, resource, and service). In reality, this is not the case—the subsystems are con-

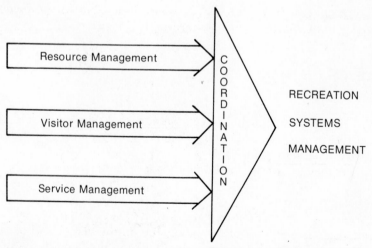

Figure 1–3 General conceptual model of Recreation Systems Management.

stantly interacting with one another. In fact, some decisions on a given subsystem may be made to effect an outcome in another subsystem. We may control a service component, such as the size of a parking area, in order to limit the total number of people participating, or we may implement a rest and rotation system on a multi-loop campground (a form of visitor manipulation) for the purpose of revitalizing worn-out camping units. But we must consider that any change may have a drastic effect on the other subsystems. It is hoped that this system approach will become more understandable in Chapter 2—The Management Model.

THE ORGANIZATION AND MANAGEMENT

How one manages for recreational experiences depends on how one *organizes to manage.* The primary variables associated with the organizational climate of the agency are legislation, organization, and operation.

Legislation. Legislation often dictates the organizational framework of an agency and subsequently how one organizes for management. It often gives an overview of management—at least a general philosophy to guide the future management of the system in general or of a particular park or land unit being added to the system. Not only are some of these mandates very specific, but also they may indicate under whose jurisdiction (management role) that portion of the law is being administered.

Secondary legislation such as the Wilderness Act and the Wild and Scenic Rivers Act tends to further define management goals and roles at the national or state level. These legislative acts are important, since they focus on specific needs and on ways of accomplishing these needs in terms of man-power and appropriations.

Organization. Each legislative act is written in general language so that it is adaptable to changing conditions. Each act is subject to interpretation, even in such areas as how the agency organizes itself for management action. Thus, as stated previously, one manages recreation programs the way one organizes for recreation management. If one organizes the agency in such a way that the decision-making power is held by some central authority, such as a regional office or state office, then the on-site manager may become very disinterested or unmotivated in developing and implementing new outdoor recreation management programs.

On the other hand, if one were to organize the agency under a completely decentralized authority, each manager might develop his own program independently. This may create inconsistencies in program policies, resulting in a total lack of coordination and cooperation—almost organizational anarchy.

A state's Department of Natural Resources that I studied was so hampered by its organization framework that it had lost much of its effectiveness and efficiency. Each major division had separate regional boundaries, yet the agency was expected to operate as a totally integrated, well-coordinated organization. If a park manager wanted to improve the fishery habitat in a lake, which included removing the existing fishery and draining the lake, he may have had to contact the engineer for one district, the fishery biologist for another district, and so on—a complete lack of organizational integrity. The same park manager may have to go to two different districts to obtain the services of a forester for a tree disease problem, depending on whether the problem was in the northern or southern portion of his state park. There has since been a reorganization of this agency into an effective operating organization.

The point is that in order to be effective in your management programs, you must first properly organize to be efficient and effective. Otherwise, subsequent management decisions will also be ineffective and inefficient. There is no magic solution; in fact, an effective organization probably is one that continually reevaluates its organization framework in light of the constantly changing society around it.

Operation. Even with an effective organizational framework, there remain certain organizational variables that the manager must contend with—mission, resources, and staffing.

Mission. The first step in developing the statement of mission is formation of long range goals, which are periodically reviewed and updated. These goals give general direction to the overall management direction of the agency. They are then expanded and interpreted in policy guidelines. Often the guidelines are consolidated into a policy manual or management handbook and are intended simply as guidelines, not decision makers. If we allow the policy manual to make the decision, then we have lost the effectiveness of the on-site manager. The intent of the manual is to establish a framework for the manager's decision, with the realization that each situation is different and must be handled by the person who knows most about the problem.

The decision regarding some local condition is called *specific policy formulation.* It is based on the merits of the specific situation, but within the boundaries of the long range objectives and policy guidelines. To make the objectives or guidelines too specific would create an inflexible approach to management that is neither desirable nor workable for the agency or the using public.

Resources. The resources of an organization include human, fiscal, physical, and natural resources. These are the substance of any outdoor recreation management organization—the essential fabric of any organization. The human resources are both the personnel within the organization and the clientele to be served. There must be an atmosphere of motivation in order for the personnel to work effectively. At the same time, the purpose of the organization is to serve the needs of the users. Too often the management programs become subservient to the needs of management, rather than those of the clientele.

The fiscal and physical resources are the facilitators in the movement toward desirable management. The fiscal resources are funds with which we operate the programs. The physical resources are the manmade developments or capital improvements that provide the media in which various recreational activities take place.

The natural resources really are the foundation for management programs. They are the space where the activity takes place, the source of visitor enjoyment and the base for physical development, and they determine the potential and limitations of the site for various kinds of recreational opportunities.

Staffing. Staffing is an important component of the organization. This discussion could include many facets of staffing; however, two modern concerns should be stressed: functional staffing and interdisciplinary teamwork. Functional staffing means identifying staff functions and management roles within these functions, based on the mission of the organization. If you need an outdoor recreation planner or fishery biologist, you hire a person who has the particular skills for the particular role or function.

All too often, we have hired people who may be suitable in terms of the basic philosophy of management, but who may not have the skills needed to perform specific functions. This creates voids, or at best inefficiencies, in the operation of the organization.

We also need to look at the staff member in terms of his or her effectiveness in a teamwork approach. Problem solving today requires more than a generalist; it demands a team of specialists, each of whom can relate to specific parts of the problem. The specialist should be able to function as an individual and handle any problems peculiar to his own field. However, he also needs to be able to participate as part of the staff interdisciplinary team to solve the larger, major management problems facing the organization.

MODERN MANAGEMENT — SPIRALING DEMAND AND DWINDLING SUPPLY

Participation has increased at an exponential rate since 1960 and should increase at an even higher rate in the future. In fact, the Bureau of Outdoor Recreation projects that the participation in the U.S. should quadruple between the years 1960 and 2000 (Fig. 1–4). The more resource-oriented activities are projected to have the greatest increase. For example, wilderness recreation has the highest rate of increase, with 859 per cent for the period 1946 to 1968.[18]

As stated by Jubenville: "The trend again seems to be toward more self reliant, physical activities, yet in a relatively secure 'recreational setting'."[16] While the participation rates may be low at the present time, we need to give serious consideration to those activities that are receiving increasing participation. A situation that is easy to solve now may be difficult or impossible to solve in the future when the competition becomes more keen for the limited resources. Many management problems occur because we are reluctant to take any action until the problem reaches crisis proportions. The snowmobile was regarded lightly by many managers 15 years ago, but with spiraling increase in demand, it has become one of our primary winter uses. Management programs on snowmobiles are difficult to implement today because we did not follow through with strong, positive action 15 years ago.

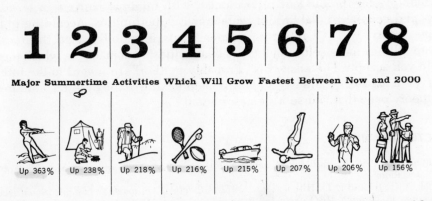

Figure 1–4 Expected rates of growth for the faster growing activities. (From U.S. Bureau of Outdoor Recreation. 1967. *Outdoor Recreation Trends*. Washington, D.C.: U.S. Government Printing Office.)

Demand has always outstripped supply. Perhaps a lag in the development of supply would allow us flexibility for shifting resources to meet changing demands. However, we must also realize that this places an additional burden on the manager to maintain a quality social environment while protecting the landscape from deterioration due to overuse. Instead of planning and creating new opportunities, we should improve the job of managing, maintaining, and perhaps even enhancing the existing opportunities (existing supply).

Too often the planner considers supply to be a one-time addition to facilitate the recreational use of the landscape. However, supply to the manager is a continuous function, which includes good administration and maintenance of the site after development and informational programs for the user.

In order to offer quality outdoor recreational opportunities to the public, we must have innovative, action-oriented managers who realize that the recreational environs and the resource setting must be managed on a continuous basis. With this type of management, we could increase recreational carrying capacity, and consequently the number of people we serve, without adding large acreages to the existing recreation land base.

The problem is often beyond a given agency or manager. Many land use decisions may separately have little effect on the supply of recreational opportunities, yet the cumulative effect can be devastating—our major river systems are prime examples. Pollution in many of these rivers has almost rendered them unusable for providing recreational opportunity. In some places these waters are not only unavailable but also offer health hazards to those who may have the fortitude to use them. Incessant road building in our national forests is another example. This increase in access has caused a loss of many important recreational opportunities and a decrease in the variety of opportunities, which also means a harmful decrease in the existing supply. Unfortunately, many of the substitute opportunities are being lost at the same time; because of this trend, people may eventually not be able to find those activities that are most satisfying to them.

The future for recreation participation may bring great changes. The recreation manager must introduce strategies to meet the needs of new styles of participation. Many managers become technically obsolete because they are unwilling to accept and respond to change.

It is quite possible that the near future will bring a much greater change in leisure lifestyle than the last two decades have. There are two schools of thought concerning the future of recreational activities—the modernistic theory and the antique theory. The modernistic theory predicts high speed, personalized mobility for the outdoor recreationist, with minimal barriers in terms of access and general availabiltiy of recreational opportunities. According to the antique theory, we will return to former levels of mobility, and the recreationist will seek more self-reliant types of activities. As a manager, which theory should you accept? The answer is "Probably neither!" In regard to the future, however, a manager's strategy should remain flexible enough to respond to either theory once that course becomes evident.

SELECTED READINGS

1. Batten, J. D. 1966. *Beyond Management By Objectives.* New York: American Management Association.
2. Beck, A. C., Jr., and E. D. Hillmar (eds.). 1972. *A Practical Approach To Organizational Development Through MBO—Selected Readings.* Reading, Mass.: Addison-Wesley Publishing Co., Inc.

3. Bill, H. L. 1970. "Changing Times in Parks," *Proceedings of Recreation Management Institute.* College Station, Tex.: Texas A & M University.

4. Bittel, L. R. 1972. *The Nine Master Keys of Management.* New York: McGraw-Hill Book Co.

5. Brochman, C. F., Jr., and L. C. Merriam, Jr. 1973. *Recreational Use of Wild Lands.* New York: McGraw-Hill Book Co.

6. Bureau of Outdoor Recreation. 1967. "Outdoor Recreation Trends." Washington, D.C.: U.S. Government Printing Office.

7. Cheek, N. H., Jr. 1976. "The Case for the Increased Regulation of Human Access to Parklands: Established Fact Or Organizational Myth?" *Proceedings of Recreation Management Institute.* College Station, Tex.: Texas A & M University.

8. Cheek, N. H., Jr. 1970. "Today's Park Visitor—Who Is He And What Facilities Does He Need?" *Proceedings of Recreation Management Institute.* College Station, Tex.: Texas A & M University.

9. Clawson, M. 1963. *Land and Water for Recreation.* Chicago: Rand McNally & Co.

10. Clawson, M., and J. L. Knetsch. 1966. *Economics of Outdoor Recreation.* Baltimore: The Johns Hopkins Press.

11. Davis, H. C. 1970. "Technological Change and Recreation Planning," *Elements of Outdoor Recreation Planning.* Ann Arbor, Mich.: The Univeristy of Michigan Press.

12. Dickenson, R. 1974. "Management Challenges for Parks," *Proceedings of Recreation Management Institute.* College Station, Tex.: Texas A & M University.

13. Doell, C. E., and L. F. Twardzik. 1973. *Elements of Park and Recreation Administration.* Minneapolis: Burgess Publishing Co.

14. Douglass, R. W. 1975. *Forest Recreation.* New York: Pergamon Press, Inc.

15. Foss, P. O. (ed.). 1973. *Outdoor Recreation and Environmental Quality.* Ft. Collins, Colo.: Environmental Resource Center, Colorado State University.

16. Jubenville, A. 1976. *Outdoor Recreation Planning.* Philadelphia: W. B. Saunders Co.

17. Koontz, H. (ed.). 1964. *Toward A Unified Theory of Management.* New York: McGraw-Hill Book Co.

18. Lucas, R. C. 1971. "Natural Amenities, Outdoor Recreation, and Wilderness," *Ecology, Economics, Environment.* R. W. Behan and R. M. Weddle (eds.) Missoula, Mont.: Montana Forestry and Conservation Experiment Station, University of Montana.

19. Mordy, W. A. 1970. "Heresy, Hustlers, Hippies, Holism, and Happiness." *Ecology, Economics, Environment.* R. W. Behan and R. M. Weddle (eds.) Missoula, Mont.: Montana Forestry and Conservation Experiment Station, University of Montana.

20. Murphy, J. F. (ed.). 1974. *Concepts of Leisure.* Englewood Cliffs, N.J.: Prentice-Hall, Inc.

21. Satterwaithe, A. 1970. "Some Functions Recreation Will Play for the Individual in the Future," *Elements of Outdoor Recreation Planning.* Ann Arbor, Mich.: The University of Michigan Press.

22. Shafer, E. L., G. H. Moeller, and R. E. Getty. 1974. *Future Leisure Environments.* U.S. Forest Service Research Paper NE-301.

CHAPTER 2

The Basic Outdoor Recreation Management Model

Before we begin a discussion specifically on the outdoor recreation management model, we first need a more general discussion concerning what a model is, why a model is needed in outdoor recreation, and why a holistic, or systems, approach is necessary to the development of an outdoor recreation model. *Webster's New World Dictionary* states that a paradigm is a model or pattern. It is a *copy* made to represent a real object or situation. This representation can come in many forms. It may be a physical model, such as a statue. It can also be a situational model that may include the use of words and charts to describe a particular situation. For recreation management, the situational model is the more appropriate of the two models. The intent of this chapter is, therefore, to show the recreational experience as a situation, but within a management context—i.e., elements, functions, and variables that make up the management environment and that facilitate the movement of the recreationist from a motivation for a leisure experience, to a level of personal satisfaction with the experience, and then, ultimately, to the benefits gained from the leisure experience. We will first describe the elements in a system.

A system is a set of interrelated and interdependent parts, or subsystems, which can react as a total organism under given situations (Fig. 2-1). Each subsystem may have several phases that are also interrelated and interdependent. If one subsystem or phase of a subsystem is altered, then the whole system is affected; therefore, the boundary of a system is flexible so that it can meet both external and internal changes. As a model of a system grows and changes, it also develops a history that will have some predictive value. For example, for a given input, we may reasonably forecast the effects on the entire system.

A system can be either open or closed. A closed system is self-contained. An open system receives certain input from the external environment and returns certain output. By external environment we mean that which lies outside the system's boundary, but directly affects a subphase or subsystem within the boundary.

If the outdoor recreation model is to be effective, it must be presented as an open system model. To describe the total outdoor recreation management situ-

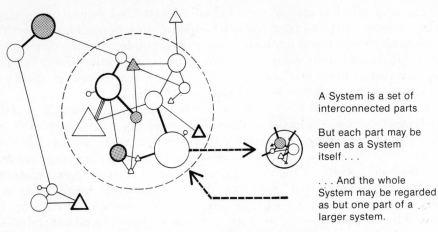

A System is a set of interconnected parts

But each part may be seen as a System itself . . .

. . . And the whole System may be regarded as but one part of a larger system.

Figure 2-1   A General Open System Model.

ation, only a holistic approach can be used. After we get a picture of the total situation, we can dissect the *system* into *subsystems,* and then analyze each subsystem in greater detail. The detailed, complex subsystems can be reintegrated to form a highly complex, fully integrated management system. A fully integrated system should enable us to understand the interrelationship between subsystems. Theoretically, we could predict the effects of manipulating a given variable in a subsystem on other variables within that subsystem or on other subsystems; however, we must also keep in mind that this is an open system where external environmental factors are affecting the internal operations and are constantly changing the composition of the system.

Perhaps we have not yet reached a level of management sophistication in outdoor recreation that would require a complex, open system model; however, this does not mean that we should not strive to build an outdoor recreation model for future use. Even with the limited information we have about certain variables and subsystems, not only could such a model be of benefit to the outdoor recreation manager, but it also could point out the need for baseline information in areas where such voids occur, and the possible priorities for future research where there are real deficiencies in a portion of the overall system.

THE PRIMARY ELEMENTS OF THE SYSTEM

Elements are the basic descriptors of any system. They place boundaries on what is to be included in the systems management model. In outdoor recreation management, there are really three primary elements—the visitor, the natural resource base, and the management. We will focus on the nature of each element, the general relationships of the elements, and the overall concept of the system.

The first and, probably, the most important element in the system to be considered is the visitor (or recreationist), since he or she creates the demand for the recreational experiences that require the other two elements. It is for the visitor that recreational opportunities are planned and managed in our modern society. He generally has special recreational interests and expects the system, which is designed to provide recreational opportunities, to meet his needs. The system usually responds to interests at the user group level—for example, wilderness hikers and auto campers—rather than to individual interests. This means that certain users may not find satisfying experiences, or even good substitutes, among the available recreational opportunities.

The natural resource base is the media in which the activity takes place. This element can be conducive or disruptive in the movement toward visitor satisfaction in a recreational experience. It is important to realize that it is absolutely necessary to have a physical environment in which experiences can take place; however, because of the value systems of many recreation managers, we have often misjudged what really are the environmental needs of recreationists.[9] It is not necessarily what the physical characteristics of the site are, but how they are perceived by the user. Perhaps we have placed too much emphasis on the resource itself, without regard to how it affects the visitor. We have postulated a need for certain types of environmental settings, such as a pristine environment for the hiker, or maximum privacy for the auto camper, when in fact, other environmental settings may be more satisfying. A pristine environment may be satisfying to one hiker group, but appear hostile to another; a modern trailer campground may be very attractive to one camping group, but very unattractive to another. (The importance of this will be discussed in more detail under Primary Functions.)

In many instances, however, the physical characteristics of the resource are a direct indicator of the potential for providing various recreational pursuits. Given the opportunity, the skier will seek environs that offer good skiing conditions over a lengthy season; the sightseer will seek those landscapes that offer maximum aesthetics and unique types of viewing opportunities.

Management is the third of the three elements of a system whose ultimate goal is to provide satisfying experiences for the various user groups. It coordinates the activities and services of the available resource base with the needs of the visitor on a sustained basis. It is the element that protects the integrity of the recreational experience and the resource base.

The interrelationships of the three elements are as follows:

1. The *resource* affects the *visitor*.
2. The *visitor* affects the *resource*.
3. The *resource* situation affects *management* programs.
4. The *management* programs affect the *resource* situation.
5. The *visitor* affects *management* programs.
6. The *management* programs affect the disposition of the *visitor*.

These interrelationships are meaningful only in the context of the type of experience we are trying to offer in a given situation. These relationships will be discussed more thoroughly in other parts of the chapter.

PRIMARY FUNCTIONS

The functions of the system describe the subsystems—visitor management, resource management, and service management. Visitor management is the manipulation of the visitor (either voluntarily or otherwise). This is done in order to obtain a predetermined social environment in which the activity is to take place. Resource management refers to the manipulation of the resource or visitor use of that resource in order to enhance the experience or protect the site from deterioration. Service management refers to the ability to provide certain services based on the location and design of facilities, while also minimizing the queuing problem associated with the use of these facilities. These three subsystems are integrated as shown in Figure 2–2.

As we have already indicated, there are three management subsystems—visitor, resource, and service. Of these three subsystems, the most important input is the visitor, since he is the main reason we need outdoor recreation management. The resource and service capabilities are really the physical and service environments that should facilitate the user's movement toward the "satisfying experience" in the great outdoors. The three subsystems, or primary functions, of outdoor recreation management must be integrated to produce well defined recreation experiences for user groups under given circumstances.

Each of the subsystems is defined by the variables that affect it. Management programs should be aimed at manipulating the variables to achieve certain desired outcomes, since the subsystems must be integrated to produce the ultimate output, the satisfying experience.

VISITOR MANAGEMENT

The function of visitor management is described in Figure 2–3. There are visitor management information and education programs that the manager has at his disposal in order to manipulate visitor use, either voluntarily or otherwise. Information systems are marvelous tools of management; they can help eliminate voids in information to the user so that he can make a rational choice of activities and places that best suit his interests. Many users are "offsite" simply because they had limited information, and consequently chose the best alternative that was available.

In order to be a totally effective information system, there must be a con-

Figure 2–2 Recreation Management Integration Model.

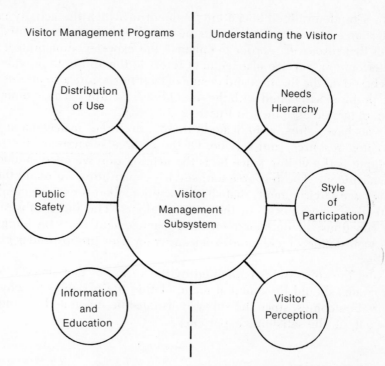

Figure 2–3 Visitor Management Model.

tinuous recycling of information, as shown in Figure 2–5 (p. 20). The user needs the up-to-date information that management provides, but the manager also needs feedback from the user so that he has more current information available to be disseminated for future users. In this way, the user will know not only what is available in terms of activities and facilities but also how these resources are being utilized. If Lake George is already being heavily used, the individual may choose to go to Lake Smith — *if he knows this information in advance.*

Educational programs are important, and should be used to improve both the user's understanding of the landscape and his quality of use. Many of the negative effects for which the user is blamed are often done out of ignorance rather than willful intent. Good educational programs can help to alleviate some of the problems; however, since most educational programs on public lands do not reach a very large segment of the user population, they probably have only a marginal effect in promoting increased understanding of the effects of individual behavior on the landscape and on the experiences of others.

Figure 2–4 Maslow Needs Hierarchy chart. (Adapted from Maslow, A. H. 1970. *Motivation and Personality.* New York: Harper and Row, Publishers.

Also, such programs often have only a temporal effect. The user may feel compelled to abide by the regulations while he is in the recreation area; but he may not feel so obligated once he leaves.

Face-to-face education of the user, when a particular situation occurs, is desirable if you have sufficient staffing: however, it is not a very efficient education system, since it reaches so few. It is difficult to tell what is needed. The current trend is toward environmental education for school children so that they will be better prepared to understand the consequences of their actions, and will choose not to impact the landscape or to diminish the experiences of other recreationists. One other possibility is a target group analysis, which is done to determine who is doing what in terms of education programs. You can then direct specific programs toward specific user groups, creating a dialogue in which the user and manager can attempt to understand each other. There are also variables that the manager should understand but should not try to manipulate to any degree. These variables are needs hierarchy, style of participation, and visitor perception.

Needs Hierarchy. The needs of the individual in terms of what he wants from the recreational experience are important. These needs have been summarized by Maslow[15] in a hierarchical structure (Fig. 2–4, p. 18). Maslow theorized that needs are the primary influences on an individual's behavior. When a particular need emerges, it shapes the individual's behavior in terms of motivations, priorities, and action taken. Thus, motivated behavior is the result of the tension—either pleasant or unpleasant—that is experienced when a need presents itself. The goal of the behavior is the reduction of the tension or discomfort, and the behavior itself will be appropriate for facilitating the satisfaction of the need. Only unsatisfied needs are prime sources of motivation.

As an example, using Maslow's hierarchy, a person may visit a wilderness area with a conservation organization not because of the need for self-actualization but because of the need for belonging, or perhaps even because of the need for safety in terms of group participation. We should try to understand the person and provide desirable experiences for him within the context of a user group that has similar needs, but it is not the role of the manager to attempt to restructure these needs.

Style of Participation. Style of participation is important to the proper management of the recreational experience. There can be great differences in the way people participate in a given activity; for example, Phillips[17] found differences in styles of elk hunting (trophy hunter, meat hunter, and equipment hunter). These are called the macrocharacteristics, or macrobehavioral, patterns of participation. Wagar[24] separated camping into seven styles: transient, central, long term, forest, peak load, backcountry, and wilderness. All activities can be divided into distinct styles of participation, which would help the manager to better structure the management strategies for enhancing macrobehavioral patterns.

The microbehavior is also important, but unfortunately, we do not have many studies that focus on the microbehavior of the participant. The microbehavior of hikers would include, for example, how they travel a wilderness trail, interact with one another, and respond to various environmental stimuli. This type of information could be helpful in the management of the total trail experience by maintaining or enhancing the normal visitor behavior. Also, if it becomes necessary to alter use patterns, a knowledge of the microbehavior can help the manager to better understand the potential effects of these changes.

Visitor Perception. What people perceive as a desirable recreational experience is important to the manager. Management objectives would incorporate the perceptions of the various user groups if they are within the realm of the agency guidelines. By knowing the visitor's perceptions, we should be able to predict the potential effect of a new management policy on the user through deductive reasoning as well as through knowledge of psychological needs and style of participation.

As an example, a study of how floaters on the Snake River perceived a quality floating experience indicated that the commercial floater was very satisfied with every phase of his experience, and that there was almost no feeling of social crowding, except at the common takeout point (Moose Landing). The basic conclusion was that people were satisfied with their experience. There were four significant variables that affected the overall visitor satisfaction. These were: crowding at takeout point, listening to interpretive talk, finding a relaxing atmosphere, and talking with other passengers. Other variables were obviously important, such as seeing wildlife and natural scenery but, in our example, these were rated high and did not vary according to the overall satisfaction rating. The management objectives should incorporate the knowledge that the variables that were consistently rated high are important, and perhaps should direct the program to maintain these variables at their present high quality. The four items that varied directly with the overall perceived satisfaction can be manipulated directly by the manager in order to influence the overall visitor satisfaction. These variables can also be used to influence the type and the level of use that one can expect on the Snake River.

Perhaps there were other variables that could have been utilized in the study, or perhaps the study should have been duplicated elsewhere. The point is that we need baseline data on user perceptions in order to manage the user properly and to better predict what kinds of effects our management strategies are having on the visitor. Without baseline user perception data, we have no way of comparing present conditions to past conditions

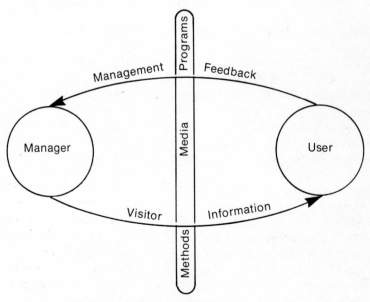

Figure 2–5 The Information Exchange Process.

Resource Management. The resource management subsystem is defined in Figure 2–6. There are two phases in the resource management subsystem: monitoring and programming. Monitoring is done on all major resources. It is essential in the processes of gathering baseline data on each resource an determining the effects of man's activities on the changing of these resources. Monitoring is one important aspect of management that is often forgotten or considered unnecessary, until management plans are to be developed. Sampling techniques are utilized to describe the soil, water, air, flora, and fauna adequately prior to use; they are also used at standard intervals to determine the impact of the user on the site after development. Without the initial data, however, the manager has no basis for comparison to determine change. The programs include:

Site Management. This is the manipulation of the developed site to maintain the quality of the resource setting and to rehabilitate it where necessary. Site management is an intensive program whose functions are to protect the site from overuse by recreationists and to maintain a desirable, aesthetic environment in which the activity is to take place. This may include very intensive and expensive cultural treatments, such as fertilization and irrigation.

Vegetation Management. Primarily, this includes silvicultural practices

Figure 2–6 Resource Management Subsystem.

related to the recreation management of intensive use areas, such as roads and trails, site developments, and around bodies of waters. Many of these practices are initiated prior to any recreational development in order to prepare the site, and they may continue throughout the life of the development. There are also programs that attempt to educate and manipulate the visitor for the purpose of improving the health and vigor of overstory vegetation.

Landscape Management. Landscape management is a program that is designed to assess the visual impact of any manmade development, and where appropriate, to enhance the appeal of the landscape. It is a procedure in which the characteristics of the landscapes are inventoried, analyzed, and classified on ability to absorb the development with minimum visual impact, and one that incorporates the perceptions of the visitor.

We often do not give enough consideration to the visual effect of a development on the other subsystems. Perhaps people lose interest in the site because of the loss of the natural aesthetics after redesigning the facility. The sophisticated public that uses these developments demands that consideration be given to maintaining the aesthetic appeal of the landscape.

Ecosystems Management. Ecosystems management is a broad, all-encompassing title. It includes defining the ecosystems, discussing their boundaries, and determining possible effects of human use. In this book, we will be focusing on the specific controversial areas of concern, as they relate to the fragments of ecosystems that remain. The most controversial management strategy concerning ecosystems has been the suppression of fire for the last 60 to 70 years; thus, the specific discussion will deal with fire management programs.

Hazard Management. Hazard management has just recently become a concept of interest to the outdoor recreation manager. It is concerned with the inventory and subsequent reduction of the natural and manmade hazards that are associated with the recreation use of a given area. We have too often lived with hazards without recognizing them until there was a major accident or catastrophy. Presently, the goal is to seek out potential hazards and eliminate them, or reduce their effects to acceptable limits.

Service Management. Service management is a relatively new term, yet we have been doing this process for decades. It refers to the provisioning of physical site developments, access, and specific services to accommodate the visitor. It is often referred to as "head counts," i.e., how many people can be accommodated with existing facilities, access, and services (Fig. 2–7).

Institutional biases can show up in service management. At times, decisions are made that are not based on the interests of the visitor or on the capability of the resource, but on the goals of the agency. Also, legislation may limit the type of services to be provided. User attitudes that are expressed through pressure group politics may also affect services provided. It is important to recognize these constraints and, where desirable, overcome them. The following are service management programs that are frequently used for a recreation area.

Area and Site Planning. The allocation of the resource base for recreational pursuits is done through *area planning.*[11] In area planning, recreational needs are assessed, and space is allocated for specific sites (camps, marinas, and so on) and for transportation systems (primary access to the sites). Thus, area planning will determine the general kinds of recreational opportunities and related services that will be available at any given resource base.

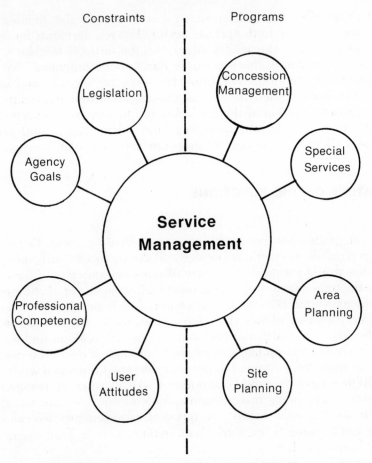

Figure 2–7 Service Management Subsystem.

Site planning determines the specific accommodations to be offered—such as access to the site, numbers of people to be accommodated, and safety guards. These are discussed in more detail in Jubenville.[11] It is important, however, to understand that general and specific requirements—i.e., who is to be accommodated, where, and with what facilities—are determined through area and site planning, respectively.

Special Services. Special services are those management programs designed to enhance the use of facilities in order to make the experience more enjoyable to the user and to increase the efficiency of use of the facility.

Examples of special services are reservation systems, informational service, food service, special facilities (such as Laundromat and swimming pool) and sales. A good example of the need for special services occurs at the transient campground. A camper pulls into the campground at 6:00 P.M., planning to leave by 8:00 A.M. the next morning. His *needs* may be many—a good night's sleep, groceries, gasoline, Laundromat, travel advice, and perhaps reservations for the next night.

Concession Operation. An important decision that should be made in the public sector concerns what is commonly called concession management; this includes what special services are needed, and how they are to be provided. Typically, the public sector has provided the needed services through long-term lease to the private sector. The requirements for service are stated in the lease, and the agency supervises the terms of the lease.

As previously stated, there are only four service programs, two of which focus directly on planning. The other two—special services and concession management—are included in the discussions on visitor management rather than in a separate section of the book devoted to service management. There are usually many constraints, including laws, agency goals, and user preferences, under which the manager must operate service management problems.

INTEGRATION OF THE FUNCTIONS

The integration of the functions is a difficult process because of the number of possible interactions between all the phases in each subsystem. To diagram this would create such a maze of lines that one would have difficulty in tracing the interrelationships. One must realize, however, that there is an interdependence within the system; a decision made in one phase can have a drastic effect on the other phases (Fig. 2–8). Thus, the manager must consider all the ramifications of a particular decision; or one can, with an understanding of these interactions, manipulate one phase to produce a desired outcome in another. As an example, you need to improve site conditions in a wilderness area where outfitters have tended to camp near a lake, causing the resource to deteriorate—this is a resource management problem. Since we are not allowed to manipulate the resource directly (in terms of management), we can either redistribute use voluntarily, or, through an outfitter permit, limit use to allow the site to recover naturally.

A more complex example would be a segment of a major river system that is managed as a wild river, for which the primary activities are scenic floating and fishing. There are only three access points along the portion of the river. The visitor (visitor subsystem) is a novice floater, depending primarily on the commercial outfitters that have concession leases for floating the river. He is attracted to the area by the outstanding scenery, and he regards floating only as a secondary activity. He enjoys the experience and does not perceive any problems (such as crowding, noise, and so on) that would affect the quality of the experience.

Information on floating is available through the agency and through advertisements by the commercial outfitters. A recent study showed that most people found out about floating trips through contact with friends. Education is primarily through natural history interpretation, but other subtle kinds of education can take place because of the surroundings. Each outfitter is required to present a minimum interpretative talk. A self-guiding brochure of the area is being developed by the agency for the private floater.

Use has increased rapidly, especially on the commercial float trips. At certain times of the day, several boating parties must wait to launch their boats. The policy on launching is that the previous boat must be out of sight before the next one can be launched; this is done to reduce any congestion in the water traffic.

Public safety has not been a problem, since most of the use is on a commercial raft under the guidance of a skilled boatman. All craft must meet

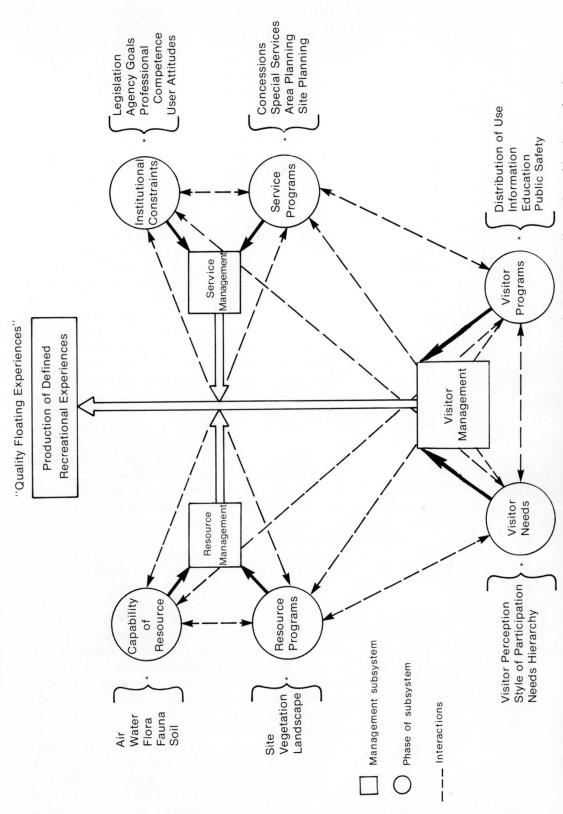

Figure 2–8 The Outdoor Recreation Management Systems Model, showing integration of subsystems and interactions of the phases of each subsystem. An asterisk (*) indicates points where external environment may affect internal parts of the system.

minimum safety standards, and no one is allowed to launch his craft except at the designated access points. The problems in safety have been caused by a few unskilled private floaters who did not appreciate their own limitations on how to maneuver the craft. No serious accidents have occurred.

Resource management problems are minimal, since people are not allowed to stop and get out of their craft. This eliminates environmental impact except at the access points where site deterioration is taking place. No overnight use is allowed.

Service management has probably the greatest effect on the entire system. There are several concessioners who operate on the river who encourage the recreationist to participate in the float trips through advertising. Most outfitters offer a good service that is well received by the commercial floater.

Access to the area is limited by the use of primitive gravel roads leading to the three access points. These roads, in effect, restrict the total amount of use that the river can receive. Total use is limited, in a more formal manner, through a quota system of 75,000 visitors–days of use. Psychological barriers to use of the river by many visitors have been overcome by the presence of a qualified boat operator to handle the trip. Also, the agency uses a river patrol to supervise the policies and increase the visitor's safety on the water.

Obviously, other factors could be mentioned. The purpose here is to delineate the system and indicate how it operates without passing judgment on any phase of it. Now, with our knowledge of the system and how it works, we can better understand the effects that a decision may have on the various subsystems. Each phase may have an effect on every other phase (as was discussed earlier in this chapter). As an example, visitor needs (perception) may affect the type of resource management program that is developed to protect landscape qualities—a one-way action. A visitor management program (information to user) may affect service programs (special services, such as a reservation system); the reservation system, in turn, may require the updating of the information service—a two-way interaction. Multiple interactions are possible just from a simple manipulation of a single phase of any subsystem. Perhaps you can better understand these multiple interactions by tracing the possible interaction paths on Figure 2–8.

SUMMARY

The visitor is the main reason for developing an outdoor recreation systems management model. There is a need for service and resource managements in recreation only if there is a demand for recreation experience. We develop specific visitor management programs to facilitate the movement of the user toward a satisfying experience. The service management subsystem offers basic features, including access, facilities, and accommodations, which are commensurate with institutional constraints, resource limitations, and visitor needs. Resource management programs attempt to maintain the existing resource base within acceptable limits of change (based on either agency goals, visitor perceptions, or both). When use exceeds these limits, feedback through the system may indicate a need to reduce the impact by means of a visitor redistribution program (visitor management), which in turn, should signal a need to adjust area or site planning, number of accommodations, and special services (service management). Another possibility is to manipulate the overused site by using cultural site treatments to increase its durability—as long as the manipulation is acceptable to the user (and the agency) and does not disrupt the activity or the services provided. Even temporary disruption may be permissible if people are willing to accept the temporary inconvenience in order to have a better managed site.

In sum, a systems model can indicate the possibilities for management action and can help predict the potential effects of these possibilities.

SELECTED READINGS

1. Alden, H. R. 1973. "Systems for Analyzing Impacts of Outdoor Recreation Programs on Environmental Quality," *Outdoor Recreation and Environmental Quality*. Foss, P. O. (ed.). Ft. Collins, Colo.: Colorado State University.
2. Beckett, J. A. 1971. *Management Dynamics: The New Synthesis*. New York: McGraw-Hill Book Co.
3. Boulding, K. E. 1956. "General Systems Theory: The Skeleton of Science" *Management Science* 2(3):198.
4. Deutsch, K. 1956. "Mechanism, Organism, and Society," *Toward A Unified Theory of Human Behavior*. New York: Basic Books.
5. Deutsch, K. 1949. "Some Notes On the Roles of Models in the Natural And Social Sciences," *Synthese* 7:506.
6. Driver, B. L., and S. R. Tocher. 1970. "Toward a Behavioral Interpretation of Recreational Engagements, With Implications for Planning," *Elements of Outdoor Recreation Planning* Ann Arbor, Mich.: University of Michigan Press.
7. Frissell, S., and G. H. Stankey, 1972. "Wilderness Environmental Quality: Search for Social and Ecological Harmony," *Proceedings of Society of American Foresters*.
8. Hellriegel, D., and J. W. Slocum, Jr. 1974. *Management: A Contingency Approach*. Reading, Mass.: Addison-Wesley Publishing Co.
9. Hendee, J. C., and R. W. Harris. 1970. "Forester's Perception of Wilderness User Attitudes and Preferences," Journal of Forestry 68(12):759.
10. Johnson, R. A., F. Kost, and J. E. Rosenzweig. 1967. *The Theory and Management of Systems*. New York: McGraw-Hill Book Co.
11. Jubenville, A. 1976. *Outdoor Recreation Planning*. Philadelphia: W. B. Saunders Co.
12. Lange, O. 1965. *Wholes and Parts: A General Theory of System Behavior*. Oxford: Pergamon Press.
13. Lucas, R. C. 1964. *The Recreational Capacity of the Quetico-Superior Area*. U.S. Forest Service Research Paper LS-8. Washington, D.C.: U.S. Government Printing Office.
14. Maier, N. R. F., and L. R. Hoffman. 1961. "Organization and Creative Problem-Solving," *Journal of Applied Psychology* 45(4): 277.
15. Maslow, A. H. 1970. *Motivation and Personality*. New York: Harper & Row, Publishers, Inc.
16. National Park Service. 1975. *Planning Process Guideline*. Washington, D.C.: National Park Service, U.S. Government Printing Office.
17. Phillips, C. 1976. *Preliminary Results of Hunter Attitude Study*. Laramie, Wyo.: Water Resources Research Institute, University of Wyoming.
18. Reid, L. M. 1967. "Sociopsychological Aspects of Outdoor Recreation," *Proceedings of Recreation Management Institute*. College Station, Tex.: Texas A & M University.
19. Schoderbek, P. P. 1971. *Management Systems*. New York: John Wiley & Sons, Inc.
20. Smith, C. H. 1968. "Systems Theory as an Approach to Accounting Theory," Ph.D. Dissertation (Unpublished), Pennsylvania State University.
21. Stankey, G. H. 1974. "Criteria for the Determination of Recreational Carrying Capacity in the Colorado River Basin," *Environmental Management in the Colorado River Basin*. Crawford, A. B., and D. F. Peterson (eds.). Logan, Utah: Utah State University Press.
22. Stankey, G. H. 1972. "A Strategy for the Definition and Management of Wilderness Quality," *Natural Environments: Studies in Theoretical and Applied Analysis*. Baltimore: The Johns Hopkins Press.
23. U.S. Forest Service, Eastern Division. 1969. *Management Handbook: Boundary Waters Canoe Area*. Washington, D.C.: U.S. Government Printing Office.
24. Wagar, J. A. 1969. "Nonconsumptive Uses of Coniferous Forest, with Special Relation to Consumptive Uses," *Proceedings, Coniferous Forests of Northern Rocky Mountains*. University of Montana.
25. Warder, D. S., and A. Jubenville. 1976. *Perceptions and Management Preferences of Users As A Result of the Commercial Floating Experience On the Snake River, Grand Teton National Park, 1975*. Laramie, Wyo.: Recreation and Park Administration, University of Wyoming.

CHAPTER 3

The Problem-Solving Process

From our reading prior to this chapter, we know that an agency attempts to provide a given output (e.g., the production of recreational experiences) through the utilization of a system, which is described in the management model; however, we also need to know how decisions are made within the context of the system.

The term "decision making" suggests the process of choosing specific courses of action to accomplish stated objectives. The basic model for this procedure is shown in Figure 3–1. In each step of the decision-making process, decisions are made that are affected by organizational inputs, public inputs, situational antecedents, and unknown factors.

Organizational inputs include _basic agency policy_, _management philosophy_, and _dispositions of the decision maker_. Basic agency policy is outlined in official policy manuals. Management philosophy is often unwritten and has no formal routing procedure; nevertheless, it seems to filter down through an organization to shape decisions. The dispositions of the decision maker refer to the person's background (previous experiences) and loyalty toward the organization. Public inputs are data that are relevant to the needs, interests, and aspirations of the public. For example, the outdoor recreation system's public inputs include data from the _using public_, along with data from research-related to public needs, from monitored existing use patterns, and through the public-

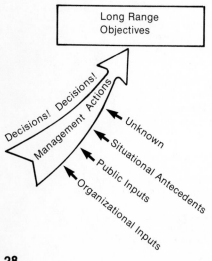

Figure 3–1   The Primary Decision-making Model.

hearing process. The public hearing process is especially significant because it demonstrates both public interest in decision making for specific situations and demand for a direct avenue of public input (see Chapter 4).

Situational antecedents are those factors that either cause or describe a given situation. They are the real data that we must collect, analyze, and incorporate into the final decision. They are also the variables that we must consider in order to avoid making stereotyped decisions that do not reflect specific local conditions.

The unknown has always been a part of decision making. In outdoor recreation, we often have limited baseline data to utilize in our decision. The uncertainty caused by the lack of information on a specific situation results in the risk that a decision may not be the most desirable one. Decisions made under that type of uncertainty and risk—a situation that frequently arises in outdoor recreation—may ultimately lead to failure in accomplishing objectives.

The decision making process is commonly described by the terms *normative decision theory*[20] or the *logic of deliberate choice under uncertainty*. These terms imply a formal and deliberate attempt to evaluate all circumstances, to formulate viable alternatives, and to choose a given alternative that will satisfy broad, well-defined objectives. (For most day-to-day decisions, however, we do not use either a formal model or a formal process such as the normative decision theory, though we may follow a process subconsciously.) A problem arises when this orderly process of moving toward the accomplishment of objectives is disrupted.[1] This chapter focuses on the problem-solving process, which can be described as the process that is used to overcome disruptions and to reunite movement toward achievement of stated long range objectives. By understanding the problem-solving model, the manager can keep specific actions directed toward accomplishing goals and can also minimize the effects of problems, i.e., disruptions.

LEVELS OF DECISION MAKING

Decision making should be viewed in an organizational context in order to fully understand the types and levels of decisions that are to be made. In outdoor recreation management, there are four levels of decision making; consequently, there are four types of decisions, which vary in degree of importance from the long range, *primary* decisions to the day-to-day, *reflex* decisions.

Primary Decisions. They are the strategic decisions made in determining long range direction the agency will follow. These may involve the integration of programs to give direction to the organization or other types of general mandates.

Problem-oriented Decisions. These decisions are arrived at through careful analysis of specific problems. These decisions are used to correct problems in order to move the floundering program toward accomplishing long range objectives.

Task-oriented Decisions. These decisions are made in the lower echelons of management so that a higher-level decision, either primary or problem-oriented, can be implemented. Some people refer to task-oriented decisions in the context of *operational plans*, since operational plans are those detailed plans used to implement some decision made at higher echelons.

Reflex Decisions. These are the routine decisions that are made daily in the operation of the outdoor recreation system. This is considered to be the lowest level of decision making, since a reflex decision is usually an automatic or a habitual type of response that requires very little conscious thought.

PROBLEM SOLVING

For most of the important management decisions, problem solving requires four elements: models, concepts, analytical process, and data.

Models. Before someone attempts to solve a problem, he must first understand the total system—subsystems, phases, and interrelationships—with which he is working (see Chapter 2). One has to understand the potential effects that a problem-oriented decision may have on other parts of the system. A model, if constructed properly, can give the manager a means of systematically and realistically viewing a decision in terms of its effects without using the "trial and error" process.

Concepts. The manager must work within a relevant conceptual framework. These are the concepts specific to the various phases of the outdoor recreation management model (such as vegetation management, concession management, and so forth), which may have either been learned during formal education, then modified through personal observation and ultimately molded by the specific agency guidelines or were acquired through personal research. Regardless of what the concepts' origins may be, they are the generalizations and aggregations that the individual manager has synthesized, over a period of time, through education and personal experience; they are the concepts that work for him. Most of these concepts that are related to management are employed subconsciously in daily operations. Without his personal generalizations of the real world the manager would be so overwhelmed by details that he would be unable to respond to most problem situations, some of which may require an immediate response.

Analytical Process. When a manager is confronted with a problem, he needs not only a conceptual framework (from which to approach the problem) and a model (to show relationships) but also an *analytical process* (to organize the attack on the problem). From the proper statement of the problem, the analytical process should lead the manager to the development and evaluation of alternative solutions. (This will be further discussed in the section on the Problem-Solving Model (Fig. 3–2).

Data. Finally, data are needed about specific problems in order to make a problem-solving model operational. One cannot arrive at outdoor recreation decisions without having baseline data on factors such as travel behavior, use patterns, and resource stability. There is no way the problem-solver can really function without data; yet, we do this all the time. Too often, the manager stereotypes a situation and makes his decisions based on this stereotype, without utilizing data specific to the problem.

THE MODEL

The problem-solving model, which is a synthesis of several potential models, shows the logical flow of events from the initial identification of a

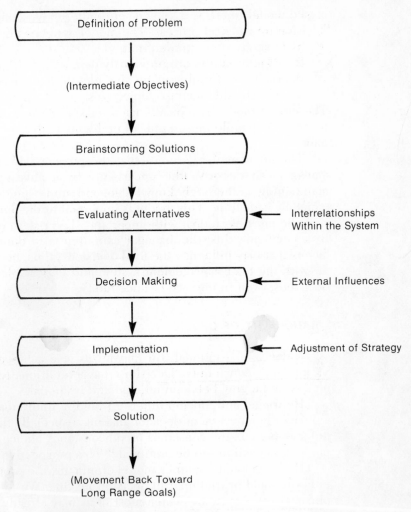

Figure 3–2 Problem-solving Model.

problem to the implementation of a course of action.[1, 5, 7, 12, 13, 20, 24] It is commonly called a *sequential model* because it is the *sequence* of events that leads to a possible solution—not any single event. After determining that a problem exists, the next step is a statement of the exact problem. The outcome of the whole process depends upon a proper statement of the problem. Brainstorming ideas, which is the next step, should allow maximum freedom of thought without constraints so that a continuum of possible solutions can be developed. Next, the various alternatives are examined and evaluated, with the realization that external influences can affect the success of any given alternative. Choosing the best alternative and developing a program to implement the desired course of action are the last two steps. This course of action will move our ship back into the mainstream of decision making and propel it steadily toward the originally stated long range objectives.

CLOSED-END VERSUS OPEN-END MODEL

The open-end model vary in the degree of openness in terms of the effect of influences (many of which are presently unknown) on the final decision. In a closed model, there is a known set of alternatives, and the manager reaches a decision by a logical process. The model assumes the following:

1. Objectives are predetermined.
2. All alternatives are previously defined.
3. Analyses of problems involve identifying and ranking alternatives.
4. One should maximize objectives.

The closed model is typically used for solving routine problems. It helps the manager to handle these kinds of problems with a minimum input of time and effort.

The open model assumes that the process will contain uncertainty. The manager can decrease the uncertainty by evaluating all influences and by maintaining a thorough knowledge and understanding of the system with which he is dealing. This model is important to the outdoor recreation manager since he must often deal with uncertainty and risk in choosing his alternatives. By recognizing this, the manager can attempt to enumerate and evaluate the factors that may influence the final decisions; thus, he will become more familiar with the total management system and better able to predict the effects of decisions, even in the face of uncertainty.

RATIONALITY OF CHOICE

A decision is rational if it maximizes goal achievement within certain environmental constraints. Decisions have traditionally been viewed as being on a scale ranging between rational and irrational.

Hellriegel and Slocum differed from the traditional view; they considered a broader perspective of decision making, especially that which involved value judgments—i.e., the conscious or subconscious choice of values by an individual or organization—to be arational.[15] This perspective is shown in Figure 3–3.

Hellriegel and Slocum's model eliminates the problem of our having to be either rational or irrational in decision making. We may respond based on our personal value systems, which most of us may already be guilty of doing. Irrationality is generally not accepted as a typical characteristic of decision making; however, many people could not function in the role of decision maker if they were not allowed to have some freedom of choice or to be able to let their own personality enter into the decision. Thus, all decisions are, to a certain degree, arational. In order to reduce arationality and to improve the level of decision making, one must follow a logical, systematic process for arriving at a decision, with the realization that value judgments may ultimately have to be made.

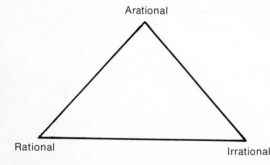

Figure 3–3 Hellreigel and Slocum Decision-making Model.

Complete rationality may not always be the best approach, however, according to Simon:

> One of the reasons for the conflicts and differences in decisions arrived at by individuals, even when confronted with the same information, can be partially explained through the concept of bounded rationality.[22]

Bounded rationality is what most people perceive as being the rational process. It is based on the following three elements:

1. Instead of seeking a single optimum action for solving a problem, an individual might establish a very limited range of outcomes that would be satisfactory.
2. An individual, to obtain the specified outcome, undertakes only a very limited search for possible alternatives.
3. Some factors outside the control of the decision maker will affect the outcome of his decision. This further supports the precept that rationality is generally tied to a limited frame of reference, from the individual or organization. In complete rationality, the manager would attempt to identify all factors or variables that affect the ultimate outcome and incorporates them into the decision.

SYSTEM EFFECTS

For most problem-solving that occurs in outdoor recreation management, we must concern ourselves with the effects of our decisions on the total system—i.e., the systems effects. It is not a simple input/output relation; a decision that alters a given portion of the system may, in turn, have drastic effects on other portions of the system.

For example, a manager may increase the service capacity of a large campground by adding more facilities. The increase in "head count" is based on both an increase in demand and user perceptions, which indicate that it would still be possible to have an enjoyable experience—even with the addition of more people to the camping area.

Suppose the poorly designed new facilities disrupted the visual harmony of the entire site, so that the user rebelled at the decision to expand service capacity. Suppose the increase in service capacity at the campground caused an overloading on the adjacent small lake, which then caused increased user conflict—even safety hazards for certain users. Suppose the increased capacity resulted in an accelerated rate of deterioration for the vegetation on the adjacent sand dunes, which caused the closure of the dunes to all recreationists. This in turn caused a decrease in attendance, since the dunes were one of the primary attractions for the camper. This type of vicious circle is a potential consequence of decisions; however, a knowledge of the systems model as applied to a specific situation can help to understand the potential consequence *before* the decision is implemented.

DEFINITION OF THE PROBLEM

Before we can solve a problem, we must first define it. According to Bannon, the simplest definition of problem is "something is wrong."[1] Thus, a *problem* is a deviation from the normal, expected, or desired outcome for a given situation; however, it only becomes meaningful when the manager recognizes the problem and wishes to take corrective action to remedy it.

The first step in problem definition is recognition of the problem—i.e., there is a deviation from the normal situation, and we must identify what is wrong in the system.

The second step is to isolate the specific problem. To do this, we must gather as much information as possible, sort the data, eliminate the insignificant variables, and then try to fit the significant ones together to determine the problem. Isolating the specific problem can sometimes be so complicated that it requires a team of specialists. If the problem is not isolated, however, the manager cannot deal with it effectively by using specific actions. His best efforts become a trial-and-error process. The situation is analogous to changing parts on a car, hoping that something will work to make it run better.

In isolating the problem, we must compile all the symptoms that indicate parts of the problem. These are commonly called subproblems.

Symptoms $\longrightarrow$ Subproblems $\longrightarrow$ Real Problem

The real problem may continue or even get worse if we only attack the symptoms or subproblems.

In the example of the sand dunes (see p. 33), a problem occurred when the loss of stabilizing vegetation on the dunes created the necessity of closing them to public use. We are assuming that the dunes are unique; the long range goals are to maximize recreational and esthetic potentials of the dunes while maintaining the fragile ecosystem. The loss of vegetation is symptomatic of the underlying problem. We can make our decision based only on symptoms, and then attempt to re-establish vegetation; but this attempt is doomed to fail simply because the cause of the vegetation deterioration is still present—i.e., overuse.

So we step back one level and look at the overuse problem. Overuse caused the vegetation loss; thus, if we control overuse, coupled with the program to re-establish vegetation, our problem should be solved. Right? Probably not! Overuse should realistically be viewed as a subproblem. Remember that there was no deterioration of the vegetation until we expanded the campground to meet the increased demand for camping. Then perhaps the real problem is the expansion of the campground, which caused the overuse.

I would even suggest that the real problem is in the area plan, which allocates space for specific recreational opportunities. If there is a growing demand for both "duning" and camping, the manager may want to separate the two activities, yet have each of them reasonably available. In the long run, we may be causing or greatly contributing to the site deterioration of the magnificent dunes by allowing camping immediately adjacent to the dunes. We encourage much use by the casual camper merely through location, access, and attractiveness. This may reduce the availability of the dunes for those who are actually seeking such an experience. If we have not recognized this, we may further complicate the malady by increasing the camping opportunities adjacent to the dunes while trying to re-establish the dune vegetation.

The third step in problem definition is articulating the symptoms, subproblems, and the real problem. We must be able not only to isolate the real problem but also to describe it in terms of present form, causes, and significant historical data involved. Without this articulation, the manager and his staff may not be able to reduce or eliminate the causes and will simply revert to the "trial-and-error" process to solve the problem.

We must establish some intermediate goals to resolve the problem once it has been isolated and articulated. We can then put the entire system back on course, moving toward the long range objectives. This could be compared to a sailor who sets sail for a distant island. He was right on course when the rudder broke. First, he had to isolate the problem—the broken rudder. His intermediate objective was to fix the rudder (eliminate the cause of the malfunction). Once the problem was solved, he regained his original course and continued toward his long range objective. The example is oversimplified, but it does show the proper sequence.

INTERMEDIATE OBJECTIVES

Setting goals in the leisure services is very different from setting them in a business or industrial organization, where a better product, and its concomitant profit, can be visibly measured and decided on. This is not to simplify the crucial aspects and complications of business decision making, but to highlight the basic difference between the more pragmatic and internal pressures of business and the value-laden and more social concerns of the leisure services. Many times our objectives are not as clear-cut as those of business organizations, especially when we seek to cope with the dynamic social pressures felt recently in the leisure-service fields.[1]

Once we have isolated and articulated the problem, we need to establish some intermediate objectives to get the system back to normal operating conditions. The intermediate objectives are really statements of desired outcomes— what you want to happen after implementation in order to ultimately obtain the long range goals. It is hoped that we would know enough about the system to predict certain outcomes, perhaps even to a given level of probability. Thus, even after we have adequately defined the problem, we must properly formulate the intermediate objectives in solving the problem. The key is to "be as specific in our formulation of objectives" as we were in the definition of the problem.[1] At this point, it is essential that the objectives be stated so that the problem solving has some direction. They should be specific and lead to the best possible solution; however, the manager must remain flexible and willing to modify the intermediate objectives, if necessary.

Determining intermediate objectives is often difficult unless the problem solver has faced similar situations in the past, or unless most of the parameters are known. If we have considerable constraints on the problem definition, such as the lack of baseline data, then we will have difficulty in attempting to define the desired outcome. The objectives are the means by which we judge the success or failure of problem solving, and they are necessary to the formulation of possible solutions, which is the next step. The possible solutions are directed toward the achievement of the intermediate objectives. The problem solver must recognize the constraints with which he must work in order to understand whether the solutions are potentially temporary or lasting in nature. If existing management strategies are not adequate enough to handle a new situation that you have encountered, then view the solution as temporary, attempt to continue to monitor the situation, and at the same time, seek new baseline information and new strategies for attacking the problem. You should go through the process of defining the "new" problem and intermediate objectives if you decide to try new, more permanent kinds of solutions in the future.

In sum, we must have a clear idea of desired outcome for the problem. The desired outcome (intermediate objective) must conform to the resources available or resources that could be made available (fiscal, manpower, equipment, and so forth) to achieve the objectives. If we state unachievable objectives, the problem solving is blocked or is ineffective in the process of obtaining a lasting solution.

BRAINSTORMING SOLUTIONS

Brainstorming solutions is often equated with creative thinking. It is a process in which the individual or group is encouraged to give unrestrained ideas about solving the problem, without regard to the appropriateness of the proposed solution. This is where the problem solver allows himself the freedom to conjure up new alternatives for solving a problem, without any social, legal, or organizational constraints. Its importance is to encourage new ideas without any overt judgments being made on their quality. Too often, we mentally evaluate an alternative and summarily dismiss it because it is too "far-out." Brainstorming is a separate process from evaluation and should be directed to bring out new ideas—the "farther-out," the better.

It works like this: The problem solver and his staff are seated around a conference table. The definition of the specific problem is presented to the team. Everyone is given an opportunity to respond with a solution, which is usually in general terms (though more specific terms are preferred). No judgments are passed on the ideas. When a judgment is deferred, there tends to be a maximum output of ideas, both in number and quality. This continues until a reasonable number of ideas are received. Ideally,

> Offbeat approaches, silly solutions, and zany notions are the raw material of a brainstorm. Everyone participating is encouraged to join into (hitchhike) other people's ideas. The successful problem-solver is one who can make the seemingly irrelevant or wild idea become relevant and productive in terms of the problem.[1]

Brainstorming encourages individual thinking. Too often, it is viewed as an undisciplined, disorganized rap session by a group of organizational misfits. It is not felt to be logical. This type of criticism arises from the bounded rationality with which most problem solvers surround themselves. This does not mean that we will accept any far-out idea as a problem solution; however, it does mean that we should continue both to search for new ideas to solve problems better and also to break away from the bounded rationality. Without new ideas, we would stagnate, and brainstorming is one way of reaching out for new, creative approaches to problem solving.

In reality, brainstorming is not something that can be done well without training and practice. It may seem so simple on the surface, but it is difficult to actually do. Most people feel strange in their first session; they are inhibited in formulating far-out ideas because of their education, professional training, and associations. It is hoped that with time and effort the problem solver can discard bounded rationality and search for new ideas to solve the problems that plague us. If this type of approach to problem solving can be developed through training and practice, there is hope that in the future we will be able to face difficult problems and solve them.

EVALUATING ALTERNATIVES

Evaluation of alternatives should be viewed as reduction or elimination of the worst alternatives and re-examination of the better ones. It is not simply a perusal of a few alternatives and a selection of the best one. It is a concentrated effort in which the problem solver seeks all available information about each alternative, attempts to sort the information based on pertinence to the problem, eliminates undesirable alternatives, and then ranks the better ones. No attempt is made, at this point, to reach a decision.

Judging the alternatives that were developed during the brainstorming has been deferred to this step. No alternative should be either dismissed summarily or evaluated superficially. The first step is to single out these alternatives that cannot be handled by existing resources; however, do not discard them. We may later need to re-evaluate them and seek ways to implement them if the other alternatives do not solve the problem.

After evaluating the alternatives, we should also set aside those which do not fit the intermediate objectives. At this point in the problem-solving process, the old-fashioned problem solver will often dismiss new ideas or alternatives with objections such as they will not work, they are too expensive, or they do not meet objectives, but this is a "cop-out." He is merely reverting to bounded rationality, which evokes an attitude of "Why bother? He is going to do what he wanted to do in the first place." We have to be in tune with the whole process if we are really going to solve today's problems *today*.

Next, we begin to screen and classify the more viable alternatives. They should be critically evaluated in relation to the established objective. The evaluation should be just as judicious and creative as the developmental phase has been up to this point. In all cases, the effort extended should be equal to the complexity of the problem. Problems having obvious solutions would not require many steps in the problem-solving process; this is the closed model of problem solving. Thus, one does not need to spend a great deal of time and effort to arrive at a solution; for the more complex problems, we should employ the open model. In this way, we can search for new ideas, then spend an appropriate amount of time in the evaluation of each idea.

The ideas are then sorted and classified into lists according to "similarity, relatedness, and applicability."[1] Some ideas can be handled as a group if they are similar enough. All the information that has been gathered must be filtered through to determine its relevance to the particular alternative. The problem solver cannot simply choose the best alternative without using baseline data, which should be continuously collected; however, he must choose the data that are pertinent to his problem and to the alternative that he is evaluating. These are the *interrelated factors* of the model. It is absolutely essential for us to understand the outdoor recreation management system and to have information or facts about each phase and subsystem. Then we would not only understand the direction of change but also the magnitude of change caused by a problem.

Conversely, if we expect to manipulate part of the system to solve the problem, we should also have some understanding of the direction and magnitude of expected change based on the particular alternative.

In the dune problem, interrelated factors would include the following: information about the resource system (the dune ecosystem and the effects of visitor use, i.e., where the problem was first recognized); the visitor subsystem, including types of behavioral patterns, visitors' perceptions of the recreational experience, and social impact; and the service subsystem. Questions concerning how the entire area was planned, why the particular campground was expanded, and what effects different decisions have had on the existing use patterns must be answered before we can determine, at least hypothetically, what the effects of a particular alternative will be—given the immediate objective of stabilizing the dune system and the long range objective of offering a quality hiking experience in the unique dune formation. It is hoped that the final decision will reflect a combination of alternatives, which will best satisfy the problem at hand and which will consider the interrelated factors of the management system, the agency constraints of fiscal resources, the public interest, and the available information. Perhaps in the future, more and better information will be available for decision making; this would be one way to reduce uncertainty and to improve decisions. We cannot simply wait for this information to arrive; we must still make decisions today. There will always be problems in decision making, since we are dealing with uncertainty and risk. But look at it from this point of view: This is what you were hired for—to do the best that you can, under existing circumstances; otherwise, they would not need you.

Synthesis of the final alternative or decision is based on evaluating individual alternatives, choosing the better parts of the various alternatives, integrating them, and mentally testing the potential effects in the management system; this should improve decision making. The synthesis of the final alternative can be facilitated by ranking the various alternatives, and if possible, weighting these according to the available qualitative and quantitative information. One should also explain the reasons for ranking and weighting. We would then have a means of facilitating the synthesis process by deciding which alternatives are considered the best—or which part of the alternatives best fit the problem—and why these were chosen.

DECISION MAKING

The problem solver and the decision maker may be the same person, or the information, analysis, and alternatives (including a priority listing) may be turned over to the manager or decision maker by the specialist who has handled the problem. How this is handled will be determined by size and organization of a particular agency and the extent of the problem itself. As was indicated in the beginning of this chapter, many decisions are task-oriented and do not pertain to problem solving or to long range objectives. The decisions made at each step to solve a problem will ultimately determine the outcome; thus, every step leading to the decision must be given careful attention. The decision maker must be made aware of the potential effects of all the alternatives, so that when the decision is made, the results can be predicted reasonably well.

The final decision making generally is influenced by external factors; thus, we are dealing with an open model. The external factors may include pressure group politics, legislative mandate, time constraints, budgeting process, trade-offs in other areas of operation, and so forth. On the dune problem, external factors that affect the decision may include pressure group politics, such as a conservation organization using the newspaper and television media to present arguments for handling the problem in a particular manner. Perhaps even a special envoy is sent from a conservation organization's national headquarters to persuade the managing agency to permanently close the dunes to recreational use. To counteract this, the state businessmen's organization may claim that there is no problem and that all that the agency is trying to do is to drive them out of business. Then Senator Smith calls you on the phone and says that he wants to hold a special hearing; existing laws do permit this type of hearing, but it is not mandatory. After reflecting on the existing situation, you may decide that an environment assessment report is necessary before you can proceed with the decision.

Has the situation gotten out of control? Has it been blown out of proportion? Probably not! There are other external factors to be considered — environmental effects beyond the immediate area, regional economies, national goals, legal requirements, reduction of other programs to concentrate on this one — the list may be almost unlimited. Perhaps this is one justification for separating problem analysis from decision making. Thus, the problem solver would actually be two people, each with a distinct role. The problem analyzer (probably a staff person) would bring the process up to the point of decision making. Then the manager or decision maker would integrate the data with the known information on the external factors, which is being continuously received, sorted, and analyzed. Finally, he arrives at a decision. The decision, therefore, is based on known conditions at that point in time. This may be re-evaluated in the future as conditions change or as more information becomes available.

As part of the problem-solving procedure, some managers choose to have a review of data by each major staff person; this is commonly called *jurying*. It provides an opportunity for a specialist to weigh the information that is related to his own area of expertise and to make certain recommendations which are based on this knowledge. Theoretically, jurying should serve two purposes. First, it can create a better, more widely accepted decision because of the quality of the individual input. Secondly, it can create a more congenial atmosphere in which the final decision can be supported and implemented.

IMPLEMENTATION

The decision can really only be as effective as the implementation. Thus we must develop detailed strategies on how to implement the decision. These strategies should include how we will accomplish it, when it will occur (time schedule), who will be involved (personnel resources), and what will be needed (commitment of other resources). These involve task-oriented decisions, which were discussed earlier in the chapter.

Too often, failure of a decision is blamed on errors in the problem-solving phase; in fact, most problem-oriented decisions that have been well-thought out fail in the implementation phase for reasons such as the following: the staff may not choose to support the decision; the manager may not be willing to commit the necessary resources; and the time framework in which to implement the decision may be inadequate.

Nothing important ever happens in a hurry in problem-oriented decision making. Its success depends upon both a decision, which is well-conceived and relevant to the specific problem, and an implementation plan, which is given a sufficient amount of staff support, resources, and time. Many problems have evolved over years of neglect; it may take many more years to solve them properly. In general, the public has to be receptive to the limitation. Often, certain phases of the decision must be accomplished before the other phases can be implemented. If we proceed too rapidly, we may skip a step and doom the problem-oriented decision to failure.

In the case of the dune ecosystem, it may take years to fully re-establish the vegetation, even though use has been either eliminated or restricted to certain paths. If use is allowed to continue at low levels over the entire area with reasonable controls, it may still take 10 to 15 years to revegetate. These task-oriented decisions are difficult to make but necessary in order to effectively implement the problem-oriented decision.

For a long implementation period, it is necessary to monitor the results of each phase, possibly changing strategy to better implement the problem-oriented decision. This final phase of problem solving is one of developing strategies, making task-oriented decisions, adjusting strategy, and supervising work needed to fully implement the decision that was reached through problem analysis. We wish to put the program back on course, proceeding ultimately toward long range goals; but the problem solving is not complete until we have fully implemented the decision and have returned the errant program to the originally charted course.

SELECTED READINGS

1. Bannon, J. J. 1972. *Problem Solving in Recreation and Parks.* Englewood Cliffs, N.J.: Prentice-Hall, Inc.
2. Blake, R. R., and J. S. Mouton. 1961. *Group Dynamics—Key To Decision Making.* Houston: Gulf Publishing Co.
3. Braybrooke, D., and C. E. Lindblom. 1963. *A Strategy of Decision.* New York: The Free Press.
4. Brinkers, H. S. 1972. *Decision-Making: Creativity, Judgement, and Systems.* Columbus, Ohio: Ohio State University Press.
5. Bury, R. L. 1967. "Wilderness Problems of the Forest Service," *Trends,* 4 (10):25.
6. Collins, B. E., and H. Guetzkow. 1964. *A Social Psychology of Group Processes for Decision-Making.* New York: John Wiley & Sons, Inc.
7. Cooper, D. C. 1961. *The Art of Decision-Making.* Garden City, N.Y.: Doubleday & Co., Inc.
8. Driver, B. L. 1970. "Some Thoughts on Planning, The Planning Process and Related Decision Processes", *Elements of Outdoor Recreation Planning.* Driver, B. L. (ed.). Ann Arbor, Mich.: University of Michigan Press.
9. Festinger, L. 1964. *Conflict, Decision, and Dissonance.* Stanford, Calif.: Stanford University Press.
10. Fox, I. K. 1970. "The Nature of Planning Decisions in a Democratic Society," *Elements of Outdoor Recreation Planning.* Driver, B. L. (ed.). Ann Arbor, Mich.: University of Michigan Press.
11. Frissell, S. S., Jr., and G. H. Stankey. 1972. "Wilderness Environmental Quality: Search for Social and Ecological Harmony," *Proceedings, Annual Meeting of the Society of American Foresters, Columbia River Section,* Portland, Ore.: Society of American Foresters, p. 170.
12. Gordon, P. S. 1962. "Heuristic Problem-Solving," *Business Horizons.* 5:43.
13. Gore, W. J. 1964. *Administrative Decision-Making: A Heuristic Model.* New York: John Wiley & Sons, Inc.
14. Hammond, J. S., III. 1967. "Better Decisions with Preference Theory," *Harvard Business Review,* 45:123.

15. Hellriegel, D., and J. W. Slocum, Jr. 1974. *Management: A Contingency Approach.* Reading, Mass.: Addison-Wesley Publishing Co.
16. Kassauf, S. 1970. *Normative Decision-Making.* Englewood Cliffs, N.J.: Prentice-Hall, Inc.
17. Kepner, C. H., and B. B. Tregoe. 1965. *The Rational Manager.* New York: McGraw-Hill Book Co.
18. Koontz, H. (ed.). 1964. *Toward A Unified Theory of Management.* New York: McGraw-Hill Book Co.
19. Luce, R. D., and H. Raiffa. 1957. *Games and Decisions.* New York: John Wiley & Sons, Inc.
20. Morris, W. T. 1972. *Management for Action: Psychotechnical Decision-Making.* Reston, Va.: Reston Publishing Co.
21. Schlaifer, R. O. 1969. *Analysis of Decisions Under Uncertainty.* New York: McGraw-Hill Book Co.
22. Simon, H. A. 1965. *Administrative Behavior.* New York: The Free Press.
23. Warder, D. S., and A. Jubenville. 1975. "An Analysis of the U.S.D.A. Forest Service Environmental Statement for Relocation of the Ryan Park Winter Sports Site," Laramie, Wyo.: J & W Planning and Research Institute.
24. Wickelgren, G. 1974. *How to Solve Problems.* San Francisco: W. H. Freeman & Co.

CHAPTER 4

Involvement of the Public in Decision Making

In the past, public involvement in decision making has been minimized. The agencies seemed to prefer this arrangement because it meant little interference with what they wanted to do. It was almost as if the agency were using their own value system for that of society. Public apathy probably contributed greatly to the situation. This certainly made decision making much easier. Both good and bad decisions were made, and the future will probably bring a similar mixture of successes and failures. Unfortunately, many of the "good" decisions about allocation of resources have been made for all the wrong reasons, often without consultation with the public, evaluation of public needs, or any other direct public input.

Today, the public is intelligent and often well versed on local issues. More people are demanding the right to participate in decision making and the right to express their feelings. The true feelings, however, are sometimes masked by the game playing that occurs in public meetings. People may present polarized views in the hope that a compromise decision will be reached in their favor, or they may use the public meeting as an opportunity to antagonize. In such cases, the input often is not viable, and nothing is really accomplished. Thus, the agency has two major responsibilities—education of the public and communication of ideas.

Education of Public. The public is often armed with misleading information. There is a need to correct misinformation, to present objective data about the assets and the limitations of the area, and to interpret for the public the potential effects of a given decision. Public input is only valuable if the public has pertinent information on which to base a decision and each individual is willing to follow a rational process in his personal decision making.

Communication of Ideas. Somehow the agency needs to develop a medium in which an honest exchange of ideas can take place. The medium must be able to remove the pseudo-attitudes of indifference toward other views and open up a new world of communication in which people will express themselves freely. If this type of interchange can take place, we can remove the facade of polarization that occurs in public meetings and focus on the common points of view as well as the *real* differences. The people themselves, as well as the manager, must be reconciled to the possibility that all facets of a decision will not be equally acceptable to all people.

THE INVOLVEMENT PROCESS

The involvement process is becoming more sophisticated in its encouragement and analysis of public opinion. Before we examine the process, we should define *public opinion,* the expected kinds of input. According to *Webster's New World Dictionary,* it is "the opinion of the people generally as a force in determining social and political action." This opinion itself is important, but probably more important is the way it is utilized in decision making. Basically, it is not just a popularity contest in terms of voting; it is the balance of opinion and the rationale used in formulating the opinion. This reflects the need for information and education that will enable the individual to better construct a rationale for personal decision making. The public also needs to be made aware of how its input is used. With these needs in mind, it is imperative that we now look at the entire public involvement process, which is described by the following model (Fig. 4–1).

THE PUBLIC INVOLVEMENT MODEL

This model presents the ideal situation in terms of both the manager and the user. Altogether, there are three phases:

Identification and enumeration of the issue. The public issue is identified, investigated, and reported to the public through various media.

Formulation of public opinion. The individual filters the information, integrates it with his own beliefs, and arrives at an opinion.

Integration of public input into decision making. This phase will be treated in detail later in the chapter.

Factors behind the identification of an issue (for a particular area) may be anticipation of need by the agency, response from the public, or legal requirement such as the roadless area review conducted by the U.S. Forest Service. Regardless of how the issue is initiated, the agency must recognize and properly identify it by using the problem-solving model described in Chapter 3.

Once the issue has been isolated, the agency then must formally initiate the involvement process so that it can obtain the most useful input from the public. This requires a tremendous work force to gather all the pertinent information. All available information first should be collected and then assimilated and verified before field data collection is begun. In this way, the field data can be used to verify existing data or to fill in any gaps in the available information. Too often, we duplicate our efforts by initiating field data collection before considering what information is already available. In our haste, we may either collect too much data or require a greater degree of precision in our data than is really necessary.

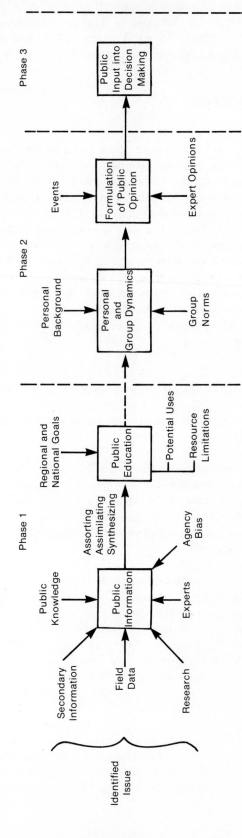

Figure 4–1 Model for formulation and integration of public opinion into management decision making.

The data should be made available to the public in some useful form so that they also have the pertinent information on which to base their opinions. A majority of interested "publics" today are sophisticated enough to understand the information if it is being presented in a suitable manner. Some assistance may be needed in the interpretation of data. This openness about the issue and related data can help in obtaining better public input and reducing public suspicion about "closed-shop" decision making.

The manager must also educate the public, through interpretation of data, about the potential and the limitations of the area for certain kinds of recreational opportunities. In this way, public input could be based on real knowledge and rational judgment. Furthermore, the public needs to understand trade-offs if such a course of action is to be implemented. Trade-offs are the opportunities (recreational), goods, and services that must be relinquished in order to develop a particular recreation management plan.

The need for education as well as its potential results has been misunderstood. Some have felt that public opinion should not be "manipulated"; yet input received has often been unusable because there was no reason given for the opinion or it was based on misinformation. Educational sessions can help to reduce the *aura of misinformation, misunderstanding, and misjudgment.* As a result, the quality of rational public input may improve, and the quantity may increase because of greater confidence in the agency. Even so, there are limitations. Each person has a unique personality and, in his own way, filters the information in order to arrive at an opinion. Everyone has biases related to specific situations or objects. We cannot eliminate these biases, nor should we try; but we can hope that each individual will be better prepared to make a more rational, personal choice and will better understand his reasons for making that choice.

The information and education process completes Phase 1. Phase 2 involves personal decision making in which the individual, having a free choice to make, will attempt to formulate his own opinions on the issue. There are actually two parts to this phase — personal and group dynamics. The individual probes his own background, personal beliefs, and biases when attempting to sort the information. The individual may also respond as a member of a group — for example, as a conservation club member, a snowmobiler, or a hiker. He may then incorporate group norms and social expectations into his opinion. His decision may be further tempered by events or the opinions of experts in whom the individual has confidence. (This is why the television networks were requested to stop issuing election returns until the polls had closed. The networks were, in fact, influencing the final vote.)

LAWS AND PRINCIPLES OF PUBLIC OPINION

In order to better understand how public input is related to the decision-making, we must first understand public opinion in terms of how it is formed, why it is formed, and what it responds to. Public opinion has been summarized by Newsom into the following four principles:

1. *Identification Principle.* People will ignore an idea, an opinion, or a point of view unless they can see clearly that it affects their personal fears, desires, hopes, or aspirations. Your message must be stated in terms of the interest of your audience.

2. *Action Principle.* People do not buy ideas that lack action. This may be either action taken (or about to be taken) by the sponsor of the idea or action that can be conveniently taken by the people to prove the merit of the idea. Unless a means of action is provided, people tend to shrug off appeals.

3. *Principle of Familiarity and Trust.* We buy ideas only from those we trust; we are influenced by or adopt only those opinions and points of view espoused by individuals, corporations, or institutions in whom we have confidence. A person is not likely to listen to or believe someone unless he has confidence in the speaker.

4. *Clarity Principle.* The situation must be clear to us — not confusing. Information we observe, read, see, or hear must be *clear* — not subject to several interpretations. To communicate, one must employ words, symbols, or stereotypes that the receiver can understand and comprehend.

These principles present some interesting characteristics of public opinion. If the public is to respond, the information and ideas must affect the well-being of the individual; i.e., his self-interest is involved. This self-interest may be based on economic, aesthetic, or other concerns of the individual. An issue, to have meaning for the individual and to cause him to actively respond (get involved), must be of great personal importance. The individual may feel he cannot tolerate the situation or contemplated action of the agency, or he may feel compelled by the group norms of an organization. Even though the individual involves himself in organizational action, he still must feel a personal commitment in relation to the issue.

None of this may take place unless the issue is clear, the public understands it, and they can relate personally to the problem. The general public will then respond according to the self-interest and the sense of urgency involved in formulating a personal course of action. For any given issue, only a small portion of the population will become involved. The remaining people simply do not feel the need or are already involved in more important issues. Today as never before, we lead socially complex life styles — at work, at home, and during leisure. Already, we have overcommitted our time and personal energy. If important social issues are to be faced, the individual must first reorient his priorities. At best, he must carefully select the issues that he will become involved in — and there are hundreds of issues to choose from. It is easy to narrow down our list of issues, but we still must structure our priorities within that list.

Finally, we must consider that the source of information drastically affects how people will respond. If we have confidence in the source, we may be more willing to respond in a positive, aggressive way. Otherwise, we may choose to ignore the issue or to respond negatively.

In sum, public opinion is somewhat like good communication in which the message must be clear, identify the issue, give cause for action, and come from a reliable source. Nevertheless, only a limited number of people will become involved. It is hoped that we can, in some way, dissect this problem to find out not only what the public opinion is but also how people arrived at that conclusion.

Based on a research study of the public opinion trends over a decade, Cantril formed the following *Laws of Public Opinion*[10]:

1. Opinion is highly sensitive to important events.

2. Events of unusual magnitude are likely to swing public opinion temporarily from one extreme to another. Opinion does not become stabilized until the implications of events are seen with some perspective.

3. Opinion is generally determined more by events than by words — unless those words are themselves interpreted as an "event."

4. Verbal statements and outlines of courses of actions have maximum importance when opinion is unstructured and people are seeking some interpretation from a reliable source.

5. By and large, public opinion does not anticipate emergencies; it only reacts to them.

6. Psychologically, opinion is basically determined by self-interest. Events, words, and other stimuli affect opinion only insofar as their relationship to self-interest.

7. Opinion does not remain aroused for any long period of time unless people feel the issue acutely involves their self-interest or unless the opinion — aroused by words — is sustained by events.

8. Once self-interest is involved, opinions are not easily changed.

9. In a democracy, public opinion is likely to be ahead of official policy when it involves self-interest.

10. When an opinion is held by a slight majority or it is not solidly structured, an acknowledged fact tends to shift opinion in the direction of acceptance.

11. At critical times, people become more sensitive to the adequacy of their leadership — if they have confidence in it, they are willing to delegate greater responsibility; if they lack confidence in it, they become less tolerant.

12. People are less reluctant to have critical decisions made by their leaders if they feel that somehow they, the people, are taking some part in the decisions.

13. People have more opinions and are able to form opinions more easily with respect to goals than with respect to methods necessary to reach those goals.

14. Public opinion, like individual opinion, is colored by desire, and when opinion is based chiefly on desire rather than on information, it is likely to fluctuate sharply with events.

15. By and large, if people in a democracy are provided educational opportunities and ready access to information, public opinion reveals a hardheaded common sense. The more enlightened people are to the implications of events and proposals for their own self-interest, the more likely they are to agree with the objective opinions of realistic experts.

These laws summarize public opinion and how it is formed. Public opinion *reacts* to identified issues. These reactions are caused more by *events* than by words and are generally determined by the level of *self-interest*. If the public is able to participate in decision making, the intensity of the reaction will be based, to a certain degree, on the level of confidence concerning leadership. People are better able to form decisions about *goals* than about methods of reaching these goals. The professional's job is to develop methods to accomplish these goals. Too often, we have sought public input on methods rather than goals. Finally, people should have *access* to information and *interpretation* of the information so that they can formulate a common-sense response to the issue.

PRINCIPLES OF PERSUASION

The principles of persuasion are presented in the context of understanding the communications between the agency and the public rather than in terms of the agency assuming an advocacy role. Certain roles are assumed; certain influences are exerted; and certain behaviors are expected. Thus, the following principles of persuasion will help us to understand some of the cause-effect relationships in the public involvement process[14]:

1. To accomplish attitude change, a suggestion for change must first be received and accepted. "Acceptance of the message" is a critical factor in persuasive communication.
2. The suggestion is more likely to be accepted if it meets existing personality needs and drives.
3. The suggestion is more likely to be accepted if it is in harmony with group norms and loyalties.
4. The suggestion is more likely to be accepted if the source is perceived as being trustworthy or expert.
5. All things being equal, a suggestion that is carried in the mass media, coupled with face-to-face reinforcement, is more likely to be accepted than a suggestion carried by either method alone.
6. Change in attitude is more likely to occur if the suggestion is accompanied by other factors underlying belief and attitude. This refers to a changed environment that makes acceptance easier.
7. There probably will be more of an opinion change in the desired direction if conclusions are explicitly stated than if the audience is left to draw its own conclusions.
8. When the audience is receptive, when only one position will be presented, or when an immediate but temporary change of opinion is desired, it is more effective to give only one side of the argument.
9. When the audience disagrees or when it is probable that it will hear the other side from another source, it is more effective to present both sides of the argument.
10. When equally attractive opposing views are presented in succession, the last one will probably be more effective.
11. Sometimes emotional appeals are more influential; sometimes factual ones are. It depends on the kind of message and kind of audience.
12. A strong threat is generally less effective than a mild threat in inducing desired opinion change.
13. The desired opinion change may be more measurable some time after exposure to the communication than right after exposure.
14. The people you most want to be in your audience are least likely to be there. This principle goes back to the censorship of attention that the individual invokes. Thus, the people who may be most affected by a particular decision may not show much concern until after it is implemented simply because they focused their attention on what was perceived as a more important problem.
15. There is a "sleeper effect" on communications received from sources that the listener regards as having low credibility. Some tests show that in time the distrusted source is forgotten but the information is retained.

MEDIA OF PUBLIC INVOLVEMENT

The following are the various media through which public involvement is encouraged. No one approach is completely satisfactory; each one may be applicable for specific situations. Thus, an agency may be using all these media at any one time.

Public Hearings.   Public hearings are a formal type of public meeting in which testimony is given to a panel or group about a particular issue. The panel is then expected to make a decision or a recommendation. Generally, presentations must be prescheduled and written copies distributed to the panel for their review. Often, polarized views are presented in the hope of obtaining a better position in the compromise decision.

Public Workshops.   Public workshops are scheduled meetings that are less formal, but require more intensive input by each participant. In the workshop format, the participants are presented with certain information about an issue and then are segregated into small groups for discussing and formulating a course of action. In the final step the groups interact with one another so that each has the opportunity to understand the other's position as well as to advocate its own. Theoretically, then, each position is based on some cognitive justification rather than its relation to the final decision. Often conflict can be worked out without polarized views.

Solicitation.   Solicitation of comments on public issues allows the individual to respond in writing to some prepared statement on the issue. It is a general solicitation to encourage feedback from the public. Often this is done in conjunction with a public hearing, public workshop, or a prepared statement by the agency.

Surveys.   Surveys of public opinion on an issue, planning task, and management policy can give insight into visitor perceptions of both the problem and possible solutions. These can help in making judgments concerning the effects of particular management strategies on the user. Each issue cannot be surveyed nor should it be.

Advisory Committees.   These committees advise the manager in general policy formulation or on specific issues. Each major administrative unit or program probably should have an advisory committee, representing major segments of the public, through which input can be solicited. This opens a continuous channel for public-management interactions but does not eliminate the need for general public input.

Continual Contacts.   If there are groups or associations of interested public, continual contact with these groups can maintain an open channel of communication. A manager who is selective in his group contacts may also minimize effective input.

Expert Opinion.   Expert opinion can be solicited on specific issues in relation to technical aspects — behavioral modeling, resource damage, and so forth — however, it is still up to the manager to make the decision by weighing the evidence and the public opinion.

PUBLIC MEETINGS

Historical Approach.   Traditionally, public meetings on controversial issues have been formal public hearings that were conducted according to a predetermined scenario—certain things were to happen at certain times, with a reasonably predictable outcome. The atmosphere was stifling because the scenario did not allow for much open discussion or even for clarification of testimony. The input was limited by restricting the number of speakers and the length of presentations and by maintaining a "necessary" balance between the *pros* and the *cons*. A potentate controlled the discussion so that it would "not get out of hand." What had started out as a means of obtaining public input actually created an atmosphere of ignorance in which people were confused by conflicting testimony and no attempt was made to clear up misinformation or misinterpretation. Such meetings often degenerated into popularity contests based on polarized views. Most of the people had little confidence in testimony presented in such an atmosphere and therefore would adhere more firmly to the group ideals of people who agreed with them. If people were not polarized before the meeting, they were afterward. Each party perceived the other to be the villain. The typical meeting would proceed like this.

After the leader calls the meeting to order, a subordinate reads the ground rules. The agency then informs the public of all facets of the issue; often using technical and bureaucratic jargon. Next, testimony is heard from each interested party, who must have scheduled the appearance prior to the meeting and have prepared a formal statement, which is read, and then submitted to the leader. There are no opportunities for discussion of critical points. Each presentation is made within a prescribed time limit. After the final presentation, the meeting is adjourned.

Either by design or by accident, this created a situation that permitted the agency to choose almost any management direction it so desired. The testimony was evenly divided; confusion existed; ignorance was rampant; and factions were fighting each other instead of debating the issue. No feedback was given to the public on either the nature or the purpose of the decision. It simply was implemented by the agency, and the public was expected to comply. (Interestingly enough, the agency could not understand the public's lack of confidence in its ability to manage these precious resources.)

Rather than dwell on past history, we must look to the present and try to initiate a positive approach to involving people in decisions about public policy.

A PLAUSIBLE APPROACH—THE WORKSHOP

Soliciting and analyzing public opinion are formidable tasks for which there are no simple approaches. An approach that is too difficult may cause people not to respond, but one that is too simple may result in input that is not usable. The public workshop can offer a balanced approach that encourages maximum public input while obtaining useful inputs; this fits the basic model (Fig. 4–1). To produce the workshop model (Fig. 4–2), one additional phase is needed—the interphase, which is between Phase 1 (Identification and Enumeration) and Phase 2 (Formulation of Public Opinion).

Small group communications characterize the workshop model. People are divided into small groups in which to discuss the information they have received. Each group, through discussion, should arrive at a compromise solution about the issue. Each member must listen to and assess the discussion of others, express his own feelings, and justify his opinion of the issue. The summary of all the groups, including justifications, should reflect the sentiment of those

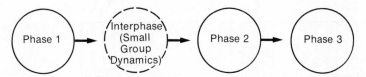

Figure 4–2   The Workshop Model of public involvement in decision making.

people present. Under these circumstances, pseudopolarization diminishes, and the real conflict of the issue is isolated. The issue is reduced in scope, specific details are refined and re-formed into a more practical, manageable problem. The input received therefore focuses on the real problem rather than on a collection of "problems" that are often alluded to in typical public hearings or in "gripe sessions."

Basic Management Functions.   Information and education are the two basic management functions that must be accomplished in order for the workshop approach to work. The information session should focus—without using highly technical language—on the visitor, the resource, competing land uses, and both national and regional public inputs.

The education session may be held directly following the information session; for more complex issues involving much information, the session may be held after some time so that people can assimilate the material presented. The three factors considered in the interpretation of information are as follows: potential of the resource for certain uses, limitations of resource for desired activities, and the associated trade-offs.

Potential of the resource can be evaluated in two ways: by what it can sustain without suffering permanent physical deterioration, and by what it can be used for. Both factors should be discussed so that people understand the available options and the potential effects of a given option.

The trade-offs are difficult to handle even with a knowledge of the interrelationships between various elements of the resource, and the difficulty increases when the element of people-use is added. Trade-offs, however, are essential in understanding the potential effects of choosing a given management option (a goal or mixture of goals) and in interpreting these effects for the public. Even if one cannot attach an absolute value to the trade-offs, one should still be able to predict, with the assistance of the technical staff, the relative value (concerning changes) of a given option. An example using this technique is the summary sheet for the Encampment River (Fig. 4–3).

Public Functions Through Small Group Dynamics.   The small group dynamics is accomplished by dividing the larger body of people into groups that are small enough for people to feel comfortable in informal interactions. There are six basic factors that must be considered in order to ensure the success of small group dynamics:

1. *Size.*   The size of the group may vary, but it generally is recommended for a maximum of 8 to 10 people. In a larger group, most people tend to make fewer interactions, allowing a few individuals to dominate the discussion.

2. *Heterogeneity.*   It is important that people with different views on the issue discuss these openly. If people with the same view (homogeneity) are in the discussion group, very little critical analysis of the issue is accomplished. The people in the group merely agree with one another

ENCAMPMENT RIVER PLANNING UNIT

POTENTIAL EFFECTS BY SELECTED ALTERNATIVES AS COMPARED TO THE PRESENT SITUATION

Resource	Specific Elements	A	B	C	D	E	Present Situation
Wildlands	Wilderness Acres Available	28,930	35,820	41,200	39,470	41,300	7,490[1]
	Back Country Acres Available	21,440	38,950	41,350	44,120	62,000	12,450[2]
	Scenic Rivers Acres Available	0	10,620	7,640	12,120	8,190	6,760[3]
	Recreation River Acres Available	-	/	-	960	-	/
Recreation	Potential for Developed Area Use	/	/	/	/	/	/
	High Density (Class I) (Ski Area)	0	+2	+2	+3	0	0
	Intermediate Density (Class II)	+5	+3	+4	+2	+1	0
	Low Density (Class III)	+5	+6	+5	+3	+1	0
	Potential for Undeveloped Area Use	+2	+4	+5	+6	+8	0
	Dispersed (Class IV) (Motor Vehicles Allowed)	+3	+1	-1	-1	-2	0
	Back Country (Class V)(Motor Vehicles Not Allowed)	-2	+1	+2	+1	+4	0
	Wilderness (Class VI)(Motor Vehicles Not Allowed)	0	0	0	0	0	0
Esthetics	Quality	-1	-1	-1	-1	0	0
Wildlife	Big Game	+2	+2	+1	+1	0	0
	Small Game Animals and Birds	+2	+2	+1	+1	0	0
	Small Animals and Birds	+1	+1	+1	+1	0	0
	Fishery	+1	+1	+1	+1	+1	0
Range	Usable Range Acres	12,995	11,980	12,965	10,535	10,370	12,995
	Livestock Carrying Capacity (Cattle)	4,445	3,530	4,095	2,970	2,820	4,105
Fire	Risk (Chance of Fire Starting)	-3	-2	-1	-1	-1	0
	Hazard (Chance of Fire Buildup after Started)	+4	+3	+2	+2	-2	0
Insect & Disease	Epidemic Potential	+5	+4	+4	+3	0	0
Soils	On-Site Erosion (Natural Conditions)	-3	-2	-2	-2	-1	0
	Mass Movement Risk	0	0	0	0	0	0
Water	Quality	-3	-3	-2	-2	-1	0
	Average Annual Yield (Acre-Feet)[4]	165,180	165,060	165,050	164,950	164,290	165,060
	Increase Due to Timber Harvest (Acre-Feet)[4]	2,580	2,460	2,450	2,350	1,690	2,460
Timber	Total Available Volume (MMBF/MMCF)	506/171	433/150	409/144	398/138	291/99	447/152
	Estimated Annual Sustained Yield (MMBF/MMCF)	7.1/2.4	5.8/2.0	5.2/1.8	5.3/1.8	3.3/1.1	5.7/2
	Estimated Harvest Next 20 Years (MMBF/MMCF)	142/48	116/40	104/36	106/36	66/22	114/40
Transportation	Potential Additional Roads (Miles)	115	96	111	100	60	0(132)
	Potential Additional Trails (Miles)	5	22	30	35	25	0(199)

Explanation Graph of Effect Ratings   -10   -5   0   +5   +10

Adverse   No Change   Favorable

1/ Mount Zirkel
2/ Present Multiple Use Zones I-7 (Encampment River) and I-17 and C-2 (Houston Park)
3/ Present Multiple Use Zone I-7 (Encampment River)
4/ One Acre-Foot equals 325,900 Gallons

Figure 4-3 Sample Summary Sheet, showing trade-off of effects for various management options.
Taken from the *Preliminary Plan for the Encampment River Unit*, Medicine Bow National Forest, Wyoming.

without attempting to identify the real issues, to formulate a logical response to the issue, or even to understand their own stance. Heterogeneity does cause some personal tension; however, this is beneficial because it tends to cause each individual to *think* about the issue, his feelings about it, and verbalize these feelings.

There are several ways to obtain heterogeneity. One of the more popular ways is to have agenda sheets that are coded by color or by number passed out on a random basis as people enter the meeting room. Individuals can then be assigned to a certain group number or color. One has to have a technique for doing this; otherwise, the groups will be homogeneous.

3. *Leadership.* Leadership is difficult to handle because of the potential effect a leader can have on the group decision. Observation has indicated that group leaders from the agency tend to create more tension, which then reduces the effectiveness of the discussion and the final choice of options. Apparently their presence casts suspicion on the whole process.

There are two other possibilities — hire professional leaders who are not agency people but who have the ability to get people involved in the discussions, or allow the leadership to evolve or to be selected from each group. This generally works well, since in such a small group most participants will not allow the leadership to dominate the conclusions. Some theoreticians feel that one way to eliminate the air of dominance is to omit a table (where people can establish positions of dominance) and to arrange the chairs in a small circle.

4. *Deciding on Goals.* The participants should understand that they are to focus on those goals which they feel are desirable and obtainable. As was shown earlier in the chapter, people are more able to decide on goals than on methods of obtaining those goals. Since the agency will be seeking specific kinds of input on the issue, they might develop a set of open-ended questions, which people could respond to.

5. *Reporting.* Each small group then should report their findings and the reasons for the findings to the whole assembly. They should also report gaps in information or inaccurate data associated with the decisions. This may help the agency in its deliberations and preparations for future workshops. Opportunities should be given for minority reports if people disagree with the small group conclusions or if they feel that a single individual dominated the discussion.

6. *Information and Education.* Desirable small group dynamics is predicated on information and education sessions. These are not designed to eliminate personal bias. It is hoped that it will give the individual a better informational base and will make him more aware of all the ramifications of the issue.

INTEGRATION OF PUBLIC INPUT INTO THE
DECISION-MAKING PROCESS

There is a need to effectively and objectively analyze public input on an issue so that the manager can evaluate the input and integrate it into the final decision. This has been the greatest shortcoming to proper utilization of public input.[11] There are four steps in the integration of public input into a decision.

Analysis. "The analysis process summarizes and displays the nature, content, and extent of input received."[11] Its objective should be to relay the public messages to the decision maker with minimal distortion and loss of detail.[10] No judgment should be made on its value or its applicability. Clark and Stankey recommend an applied content analysis approach to sort the information relay in a manner useful to the manager.[11] It is desirable to know not only what was said and who said it but also how it was said. As input, form letters are generally considered to be less important than personal letters since they usually represent the ideas of only one individual with little personal thought on the part of the sender in regard to the total issue.

Evaluation. Unlike analysis, evaluation is subjective in that the information is filtered and interpreted in relation to the issue; it should follow, however, a logical and objective process (as shown in Chapter 3) in order to arrive at some conclusions about the input and to incorporate these conclusions into the final decision. Considering the principles of public opinion, it seems desirable to interpret the input into specific objectives. Sometimes various specific objectives can be compatible and accommodated within some overall objective for the area.

It is important in the analysis process to determine local, regional, and national public inputs, since the nature of the decision may cause a weighing of inputs in the evaluation step. Some issues may reflect broad national and regional concerns; others may more directly affect local conditions within some minimal regional concerns.

In sum, evaluation is an interpretation of the validity and significance of public comments and an examination of these comments in relation to the particular issue. It is not a counting of votes. It should "follow the rule of reason rather than rule of number."[34] Knowing both the balance of opinion and the supporting rationale is critical; these elements define public values on any issue.

Integrating. Integrating requires consideration of public input, as evaluated by the manager, along with the other factors such as legal responsibility, fiscal constraints, resource capability, environmental effects, and related social and economic conditions to arrive at a decision. It is important to understand that the public input is one of the many inputs that must be considered by the manager making a decision. The manager must also realize that these are the expressed opinions of the public in relation to goals and that he should neither summarily dismiss them nor relinquish his own goals for those of society. The decision concerns formulation of long range goals rather than specific management strategies. (For further discussion, see sections on Primary Decisions in Chapter 3, and on the Management Model in Chapter 2.)

Implementation. Implementation requires the development of operational objectives to redefine the long range goals so that the manager can then formulate specific management strategies to implement these goals. For example, suppose the long range goals for managing the Upper North Platte River, based on all the inputs, are to maximize recreational use, reduce social encounters on the water, and maintain minimal environmental impact. These goals seem to be challenging, perhaps even conflicting. What needs to be done is to formulate them into specific objectives, which should then be the basis for specific management strategies. Perhaps the operational objectives might be as follows:

1. Goal. Maximize on-water recreation use.
    a. *Objective.* Offer medium density floating experience, which would emphasize the active recreational aspects of river floating without the need for a pristine environment and solitude.
    b. *Objective.* Make the potential visitor aware of the type of experience being offered.
    c. *Objective.* Coordinate with regional plans in order to offer a variety of floating experiences.
    d. *Objective.* Minimize safety hazards.
2. Goal. Reduce social encounters.
    a. *Objective.* Limit access to the river.
    b. *Objective.* Limit use to day use only in the river corridors.
    c. *Objective.* Design the recreational system so it is self-regulating, i.e., manages itself with minimum field supervision.
3. Goal. Maintain minimal environmental impact.
    a. *Objective.* Maintain water quality at its existing level.
    b. *Objective.* Eliminate silt caused by manmade erosion.
    c. *Objective.* Reduce access to the river.
    d. *Objective.* Maintain natural aesthetics.

All these objectives will still allow the manager to have the opportunity for individuality in choosing strategies for managing the Upper North Platte River system, under the guidance offered by the operationalized long range goals. One example of a possible innovative management strategy is to allow the camping to occur in conjunction with floating but to build the campgrounds away from the narrow river corridor and to require the camper to remove his lightweight craft out of sight. Other strategies should be brainstormed before one begins to evaluate and implement selected ones.

SUMMARY

Public involvement is a necessary and desirable input into public decision making. People demand that their feelings be considered in any major decision on the use of public lands. However, the input should be solicited in terms of long range goals, rather than methods of implementing goals. It is the role of the manager to implement these goals by using selected strategies.

The agency has certain responsibilities in the public involvement process: information, education, solicitation of input, objective analysis, evaluation and integration of all inputs into the final decision. Then the agency should give feedback to the public concerning the nature of the final decision and the reason for it.

SELECTED READINGS

1. Alston, R. M. 1972. *Goals and Decisionmaking in the Forest Service.* U.S. Forest Service Research Paper INT-128.
2. Alston, R. M., and D. M. Freeman. 1975. "The Natural Resource Decision-maker as a Political and Economic Man: Toward a Synthesis," *Journal of Environmental Management,* 3:1.
3. Arrow, K. 1951. *Social Choice and Individual Values.* New York: John Wiley & Sons, Inc.
4. Bales, R. F. 1970. *Personality and Interpersonal Behavior.* New York: Holt, Rinehart & Winston, Inc.
5. Bishop, B. A. 1970. "Public Participation in Water Resource Planning." Washington, D. C.: U.S. Army Corps of Engineers.

6. Bleiker, H. 1976. "The Role of Values in Environmental Decision-Making and in Environmental Education," Fifth Annual Conference, National Association for Environmental Education, Atlanta, Ga.

6a. Bleiker, A., and H. Bleiker. 1977. *Citizen Participation Handbook.* Laramie, Wyo.: Institute for Participatory Planning.

7. Borton, T. E., and K. P. Warner. 1971. "Involving Citizens in Water Resource Planning: The Communication-Participation Experiment in the Susquehanna River Basin," *Environment and Behavior,* 3(9):284.

8. Buchanan, J. M., and G. Tullock. 1965. *The Calculus of Consent.* Ann Arbor, Mich.: Ann Arbor Paperbacks.

9. Callen, J. 1973. "The Effects of Seating Arrangement on Verbal Interaction Patterns in Small Groups," Masters thesis (unpublished). University of Wyoming.

10. Excerpts from Hadley Cantril, *Gauging Public Opinion* (copyright © 1944 by Princeton University Press, copyright © renewed 1972 by Princeton University Press), pp. 226–230. Reprinted by permission of Princeton University Press.

11. Clark, R. N., and G. H. Stankey. 1976. "Analyzing Public Input to Resource Decisions: Criteria, Principles, and Case Examples of the Codinvolve System." *Natural Resources Journal,* 16(1):213.

12. Clark, R. N., G. H. Stankey, and J. C. Hendee. 1974. "An Introduction to CODINVOLVE: A System for Analyzing, Storing, and Retrieving Public Input to Resource Decisions," U.S. Forest Service Research Note PNW-223.

13. Creighton, J. L. 1973. *Snergy—Citizen Participation/Public Involvement Skills Work.* Los Gatos, Calif.: Snergy, Inc.

14. Cutlip, S. M., and A. H. Center. 1971. Effective Public Relations (2nd ed.). Englewood Cliffs, N.J.: Prentice-Hall, Inc.

15. Giff, J. R., G. N. Platts, and L. F. Miller (eds.). 1951. *Dynamics of Participative Groups.* Chicago: John S. Swift Co.

16. Gilbert, D. L. 1970. "Public Relations and Parks," *Proceedings of the Third Recreation Management Institute.* College Station, Tex.: Texas A&M University.

17. Hendee, J. C., R. N. Clark, and H. Stankey. 1974. "A Framework for Agency Use of Public Input in Resource Decision-Making," *Journal of Soil and Water Conservation,* 29(2):60.

18. Hendee, J. C., R. C. Lucas, R. H. Tracy, Jr., Tony Staed, R. N. Clark, G. H. Stankey, and R. A. Yarnell. 1973. *Public Involvement and the Forest Service: Experience Effectiveness, and Suggested Direction.* Washington, D.C.: U.S. Forest Service.

19. Hornback, K. E. 1975. "Overcoming Obstacles to Agency and Public Involvement." *Environmental Design Research Association Annual Proceedings.* Lawrence, Kan.

20. Kedder, L. H., and V. M. Stewart. 1975. *The Psychology of Intergroup Relations: Conflict and Consciousness.* New York: McGraw-Hill Book Co.

21. Kulas, R. E. 1973. "Group Size: A Comparison of Decisions Made by Six and Twelve Member Problem Solving Groups," Masters thesis (unpublished). University of Wyoming.

22. Lundblad, D. 1972. "Community Workshop—An Experiment in Public Involvement," *The Grass Roots and Water Resource Management.* McKenzie, L. (ed.). Pullman, Wash.: Washington State University Press.

23. Mills, T. M. 1973. *The Sociology of Small Groups.* Englewood Cliffs, N. J.: Prentice-Hall, Inc.

24. Napier, R. W., and M. K. Gershenfeld. 1973. *Groups: Theory and Experience.* Boston: Houghton Mifflin Co.

25. Phillips, G. M. 1973. *Communication and the Small Group.* Indianapolis: Bobbs-Merrill Co., Inc.

26. Pressman, J. L. 1970. "Decision-Making and Public Policy: The Perils and Possibilities of Fragmentation," *Elements of Outdoor Recreation Planning.* Driver, B. L. (ed.). Ann Arbor, Mich.: University of Michigan Press.

27. Reinke, K. B., and B. Reinke. 1973. "Public Involvement in Resource Decisions: A National Forest Seeks Public Input For Recreation Development," *Journal of Forestry,* 71(10):656.

28. Rosenfeld, L. B. 1973. *Human Interaction in the Small Group Setting.* Columbus, Ohio: Charles E. Merrill Publishing Co.

29. Shaw, M. E. 1976. *Group Dynamics: The Psychology of Small Group Behavior.* New York: McGraw-Hill Book Co.

30. Stankey, G. H. 1972. "The Use of Content Analysis in Resource Decision Making." *Journal of Forestry,* 70(3):148.

31. Stankey, G. H., J. C. Hendee, and R. N. Clark. 1975. "Applied Social Research Can Improve Public Participation in Resource Decision-making," *Rural Sociology,* 40:65.

32. Sweitzer, D. L., D. M. Freeman, and R. M. Alston. 1975. "Ensuring Viable Public Land-Use Decisions—Some Problems and Suggestions," *Journal of Forestry,* 73(11):705.

33. Taylor, H. F. 1970. *Balance in Small Groups.* New York: Van Nostrand Reinhold Co.

34. U.S. Forest Service. 1974. "Guide to Public Involvement in Decision Making." Washington, D.C.

35. Young, R. C. 1970. "Establishment of Goals and Definitions of Objectives," *Elements of Outdoor Recreation Planning.* Driver, B. L. (ed.), Ann Arbor, Mich.: University of Michigan Press.

PART II

RECREATION RESOURCE MANAGEMENT

Resource management obviously means different things to different people. It is used here to mean the manipulation of resource variables (air, water, vegetation, and so forth) and people in order to maintain, or possibly reconstruct, the desirable natural resource setting for various recreational pursuits, which may range from very active, high-density recreation to dispersed types of activities.

USE VERSUS PRESERVATION

Many outdoor enthusiasts and resource managers view outdoor recreation as a conflict, or tension, between recreational use and strict preservation of the existing ecology. The preservationist wants to maintain the landscape in a pure wilderness state, unaffected by modern man; he also wants it to be unrestricted in terms of use. This is where the conflict lies. One cannot have a totally pristine environment and yet have unconfined, unrestrained use. This is an anomaly in a society such as ours which places such great demands on existing wilderness areas.

In his attempt to maintain the existing landscape, the resource manager has altered the natural ecology through fire suppression, insect control, and other preventitive programs. The result is that through an attempt to preserve the original landscape, the pristine environment was destroyed. Although the natural ecology is in dynamic equilibrium at any one time, it is constantly changing, and that the pristine environment is really one that is shaped and reshaped by natural forces. Thus, management action has unintentionally altered the very condition that it is purported to preserve.

CONSERVATION VERSUS PRESERVATION

Public desires as well as those of the recreation management should probably be classified as conservation rather than preservation, since both are actually oriented to certain land uses. No one would ever recommend putting a fence around a piece of land and allowing no use whatsoever. As stated in *Webster's New World Dictionary, conserve* means to keep from being damaged, lost, or wasted. The conflict in conservation is over the kinds of uses allowed from wilderness to high density recreation facilities. The manager must develop operational objectives and specific recreation management programs within the goals for the specific area to keep the resource from being damaged, lost, or wasted. It is hoped that, in the process of developing the resource management, we do not lose sight of the fact that we are to also conserve the recreational experiences.

This is where the real tension lies—between resource conservation and recreational experience conservation. As a manager, how does one weigh these two factors? Which should take preference? There is no dogmatic response—only rational decision making based on the merits of the individual case. Regardless, resource managers must consider all kinds of factors, including social values, in selecting resource management strategies for specific situations.

GENERAL PRINCIPLES OF RECREATION RESOURCE MANAGEMENT

As presented by Jubenville,[16] the principles of recreation resource management are as follows:

1. Recreation resource management is linked to social values; thus, the problems of management are "people problems," even in resource management.
2. Integrity of resource is important, but quality of experience is also important.
3. The site may be manipulated, but hardening the site is the last alternative.
4. There is always a limitation of site, both physically and socially, for a given recreational experience.
5. There is a limitation on the potential for recreational experiences on all sites.
6. Accessibility is recreation's best friend and worst enemy.
7. The resource does not merely offer activities; it also offers aesthetics and natural beauty.
8. There is a point of irreversibility in the maintenance of the integrity of the resource; once this is reached, it may be impossible to restore the site to its original condition.
9. The wildland setting offers unique experiences at most points of the recreation opportunity continuum; man's work may, at times, complement the opportunity, but it can never truly substitute for the setting.
10. Resource management can be no better than the attitudes, interests, and values of the user.

CHAPTER 5

Site Protection and Renovation

Site protection and renovation are necessary to maintaining the important aesthetic and environmental values associated with developed sites, including trails, backcountry campsites, and other places where concentrations of recreationists could potentially deteriorate the quality of the site. Site protection implies positive management action to reduce the effects of human use on the site. It is important to correlate future management strategy with the site planning process so that one can protect the site values either through proper design, or through well-organized management strategies that work within the limits of the design (Fig. 5–1).

Site renovation is a secondary approach that focuses on renovating a deteriorated site. It can be a fallowing process, which allows the site to recover naturally, or it can be an active process in which specific treatments are done to speed up the recovery.

CONCEPTS IN SITE MANAGEMENT

Site management is described by the following:

$$\text{Well-managed site} = f \begin{cases} \text{Site location} \\ \text{Site design} \\ \text{Recreational use patterns} \\ \text{Environmental conditions} \\ \text{Management strategies} \end{cases}$$

The well-managed site is one that is properly selected through the area planning process to enhance the recreational experience and reduce possible environmental degradation. It is designed to fit the natural lay of the land, yet provide for the normal behavioral patterns of the visitor. Management strategies developed in accordance with the variables of site location, resource qualities, and expected use patterns will protect the site after its development while complementing the normal behavioral patterns of the user; they are also contingent on uncontrollable environment conditions, which may cause the manager to periodically adjust his strategies to seasonal conditions.

Figure 5–1 The need for site protection and renovation. Note the bare ground caused by indiscriminate driving at this picnic site. (Photo by Alan Jubenville.)

There are six principles that the manager must consider in order to properly implement the site management program.

Proper Location. Proper location of site is important in reducing the recreationists' impact on the environment. The chosen site should fit the normal travel and behavioral patterns of the visitor, or it will not receive its expected levels of use. Besides conforming to user behavioral norms, the location of the site should be where soils are stable and vegetation is hardy; the overall area should be durable enough to sustain recreational use with minimum impact. Thus, location can subtly direct various recreational uses in regard to preserving the site values. Increased use could still maintain aesthetics of a durable site, while in other areas a subtle reduction in access to the site may lessen the environmental and aesthetic impact.

Amazing results can be obtained with the proper social and environmental location of a site; unfortunately, most managers "inherit" a poorly located site. This means that, to protect the site values, he may spend much of his budget on site maintenance and renovation. Perhaps, the more rational decision, in the long run, is to recognize the problem as being one of location and to relocate the site where the conditions are more suitable.

Dispersal of Use. The design of an area may cause concentrations of people at particular sites. This may cause the manager to adopt a quota system to regulate use and reduce environmental impact. Too often, use is concentrated on a few developed sites; or because of poor information systems, only a few sites are well known to the majority of users. Well-developed area plans and good information systems can help to disperse use either for an area or on a regional basis. People may then seek out those experiences that are most satisfying, and the impact on any one site will be lessened. The techniques for doing this will be discussed later. It is important, at this point. to understand the role of visitor dispersal in the overall site management program. Good dispersal may lessen the need to establish quota or permit systems, to rest and rotate the sites to allow natural recovery, or to initiate site treatments in order to hasten recovery from recreational overuse.

Concentration of Use on Sites. Concentration of recreational use on a developed site can help to control overall site deterioration by focusing use on more stable locations, on small acreages designed to sustain that level of use, and on known locations where services such as solid waste disposal, sewage treatment, and water quality control can be economically handled. In the past, areas for camping and other activities often were unrestricted. With the spiraling use, we can no longer afford the luxury of a "do anything, anywhere" philosophy; otherwise, our landscapes will be ravaged through recreational use. The site developed for specific uses offers an opportunity to manage both the recreational activity and the environment.

Cultural Treatments. One possible way of increasing the capacity of a site to sustain certain levels of recreational use is through cultural treatments such as irrigation, fertilization, and soil mixing. A thorough survey of the site conditions should indicate the presence of any limiting factors in the natural productivity of the area—e.g., lack of organic matter, low soil nutrient levels, and lack of moisture during latter part of growing season. Once the limiting factors have been isolated, specific cultural treatments can be devised to reduce these limitations.

Cultural treatments may increase the durability of a site, so that it is able to sustain extended recreational use without permanent deterioration, or they may be used to more quickly rejuvenate a worn-out site.

Capacity Limits. Even if cultural treatments are used, each site has capacity limits, which are natural limitations of the level of use it can sustain with minimal environmental impact. Capacity limits should be based on the ecological factors of soil, water, and vegetation if we are to maintain the acceptable natural conditions of the site. The previous steps may delay the need to limit use; nevertheless, the capacity of each site should be established in order to determine when to begin "rationing" the experience.

Naturalism and Aesthetics. Maintenance of even highly developed sites should emphasize natural aesthetics. This does not necessarily mean the site must be kept in a pristine condition, however, maintenance of the developed site should attempt to preserve existing soil, water, and vegetative conditions. In essence, management should strive to maintain the natural quality of the environs that had existed before site development (Fig. 5–2).

PROBLEMS ARE PEOPLE PROBLEMS

Problems in site management arise from the recreationist's use of the site. Some problems are due to deliberate abuse of the site; others are merely incidental to using the site. The strategies employed in site management should be related to the nature of the problem. There are three basic causes of site destruction: vandalism, ignorance, and overuse.

Vandalism. Vandalism is the deliberate destruction of conditions in a developed site. It may involve any act—from cutting vegetation and removing soil to driving across protected vegetation. This prevalent problem demands a great

Figure 5–2 The aesthetics of the campground have been maintained, yet the heavily used portion of the site has been hardened to sustain heavy use. (Photo by Alan Jubenville.)

deal of the outdoor recreation manager's attention; also, the costs of repairing the damage are staggering.

Curbing vandalism is a difficult problem, but it is necessary if we are to maintain the quality of existing sites. Good site design and on-site enforcement of regulations may reduce vandalism; however, it is often merely a symptom of some greater social problem that must be dealt with by some person or organization other than the managing agency.

Ignorance. Much of the "vandalism" that occurs is really done out of ignorance; this is a manageable problem. For example, a horseman may tie his horse to a tree while he fishes, thinking that this will protect the green meadow. After this happens two or three times, the mechanical injury to the root system kills the tree. A picnicker may drive his car across the sod to get closer to the picnic table. Although these acts can be destructive, the user did not have this intention; he just did not understand the consequences of his actions.

The manager must understand the normal behavior of the user and any of his activities that may have destructive effects. Once the manager identifies acts of destruction due to ignorance, he can develop appropriate programs to inform and educate the public. It is hoped that people will respond positively if they understand the consequences of their actions.

Overuse. Overuse is a broad term applied to excessive recreational use of a given site, to the point of permanent or temporary damage. Overuse is sometimes difficult to detect until rapid site deterioration has already taken place; nevertheless, most site management programs are aimed at its control. Such programs often combine cultural treatments which improve environmental conditions that have deteriorated. With visitor management we can reduce the impact during the recovery period. The remainder of the chapter will focus on management strategies related to overuse.

BASIC MANAGEMENT STRATEGIES

There are five possible basic management strategies in managing developed recreational sites.

1. *"Cut out, get out."* Much of our attention in managing public lands has been focused on resource uses other than recreation; this has created a laissez-faire approach to recreation management. We have allowed people to do almost anything, anywhere. The result has been conflict among user groups, resource deterioration, and a general decline in user satisfaction. This is similar to the "cut out, get out" policy of land management a century ago. At that time, the agency or enterprise merely harvested the renewable resources without any consideration of the future. Resources were inexhaustible — or, at least, we thought so.

In recreation management, some of these philosophies still exist. People seek outdoor recreation experiences on various sites; sometimes, through abuse and overuse, they destroy the very site (and experience) they so highly value. Their focus is seemingly on the *present* and not on the future. We seem to destroy one oasis and then move on to another.

Can we afford to maintain a laissez-faire approach today? The answer has to be *no*. In view of spiraling demands and diminishing supply, we must protect our existing resources while trying innovatively to increase the use of them. This does not mean we must rigidly control use in order to maintain the resource; nevertheless, we must take an active role in managing the site to protect the resource and the experience now — while ensuring that the site will be maintained for future generations.

2. *"Close, natural recovery."* If a site shows deterioration from recreational use, we can always consider closing the site and allowing the ground vegetation to rejuvenate itself. The recovery of most recreational sites will be slow, since recreation is usually relegated to sites that are poorer in terms of natural productivity. When these sites are in the earlier stages of deterioration, perhaps we could predict certain results and close the site at that point, allowing more rapid recovery.

This strategy is very appropriate for heavily used wilderness areas, which *must* be allowed to recover naturally. Heavily used developed sites, however, are generally car-oriented and are difficult to close without a tremendous public outcry. Thus, merely closing a site — allowing it to recover naturally — is not an advisable alternative except under specific conditions.

3. *"Close and culturally treat."* In this approach, the overused site is closed to public use, and certain cultural treatments are introduced to speed recovery. The treatments may include introduction of exotic species, soil aeration, and fertilization. This strategy may be necessary if the treatment (such as aerial irrigation) would cause undue inconvenience to the visitor, the presence of the visitor would disrupt the treatment, or the site would not fully recover while use continues.

This is an appropriate strategy, especially for heavily deteriorated sites. It gives maximum recovery while minimizing recovery time and inconvenience to the visitor. Appropriate information programs must be correlated with any site closing so that people can understand what is being done. If at all possible, alternate opportunities should also be made available to the public.

4. *"Rest and rotate."* In this program, additional sites are developed, so that sufficient facilities will still be available when some sites must be closed

for rejuvenation. This means that certain sites can be rested (to encourage recovery) and rotated on a regular schedule. Some managers have been very receptive to this strategy and have tried to implement it in their own administrative unit; however, most areas have not been planned and developed in such a way as to allow sites to be rested and rotated. Often, what is presented as a rest and rotation program is really a closure program, as described in strategies 2 and 3. This results in a large reduction in the service capacity to handle normal visitor loads.

5. *"Leave open, culturally treat."* Probably, this is the most ideal situation—to keep the sites open to public use while implementing some cultural program to reclaim the deteriorated areas. This may be possible in cases of minimum deterioration, but often the symptoms of overuse are not evident until major deterioration has occurred. The site sustains heavy use with little external change other than in the species composition of its ground vegetation until it reaches the threshold point at which rapid deterioration usually occurs. At that point, it is almost impossible to implement a "leave open and culturally treat" policy except on the most naturally productive, stable sites. It is simply not feasible to reclaim the site under those conditions. Probably, the only way to implement this policy is on a regular basis, scheduled well before the threshold of site durability is reached. This means that, to properly implement such a policy, each site should be thoroughly analyzed to determine the factors that may limit the use of the site (such as heavy soil, species composition, soil moisture, and soil nutrients) and to attempt to overcome them through specific cultural treatment programs designed for each site. If soil moisture is a limiting factor in maintaining the vigor of vegetation during the heavy use season, it may be necessary to establish an irrigation program, perhaps during low use periods early in the week. Light periodic applications under these arrangements are really preventive rather than remedial programs such as the first four strategies. Ideally, we would attempt to prevent the problems of overuse, and then, react with remedial programs if the preventive measures failed. The final decision will be based on economics. Often it is difficult to convince a superior that preventive programs are necessary when there are no external signs of deterioration, but it is easier to justify expenditures in order to reclaim a worn-out site. In the future, emphasis may swing more to preventive measures, which may be the best choice, in the long run, in terms of dollars spent, visitors accommodated, environmental protection, and efficiency of management.

POSSIBLE CULTURAL TREATMENTS

If cultural treatments are desirable, then the manager must choose the proper treatments, or combination thereof, for the particular circumstances. There are no universal recommendations because of the tremendous variation that occurs in local situations. A discussion of possible cultural treatments and their general application follows.

Soil Scarification. Soil scarification is the loosening of the topsoil in order to reduce compaction, which increases infiltration of water and exposes the maximum amount of mineral soil. This prepares a seedbed (naturally or artificially), promotes soil moisture conditions, and improves the physical properties of a compacted soil. Scarification seems mandatory for the renovation of most overused sites in which soil has become compacted, vegetation has been lost, and sheet erosion has taken place.

The degree of scarification will depend upon the problems associated with the particular site. A plant species, to be encouraged, may not need extensive exposure to mineral soil for germination and survival, so scarification may be light, using hand tools such as a rake. On the other hand, the soil may be deeply compacted—with an almost total loss of pore space for air and moisture, particularly in the upper 6 to 12 inches where most root systems are located. This may require mechanical scarification using heavy equipment, such as a tractor and disk. Even if the deteriorated portion of the site is going to be planted or sodded, it is still advisable to improve the physical properties of the soil by scarifying and leveling.

In reducing soil clumping caused by compaction, pore space—and consequently, soil aeration—is increased. Root respiration is dependent on the amount of oxygen (O_2) available in the soil. At low oxygen levels, root respiration is reduced; at high levels, respiration is increased. In turn, mineral absorption into the roots is directly associated with the level of respiration. Adequate soil aeration is "favored by a coarse-textured soil, or a fine-textured soil with open granulations. Such conditions permit rapid exchange of gases ... with the atmosphere."[35] Fine-textured soils such as clays may have more pore space initially, but may become quickly compacted under heavy recreational use, particularly during extremely high moisture conditions.

Surfacing of High Use Areas (Fig. 5–3). The extreme solution in surfacing is to *pave* the high use areas where heavy compaction occurs. This drastically alters the environs. On extremely heavy soils, where use and precipitation levels are high, paving may be a reasonable answer, particularly if other soil con-

Figure 5–3 Surfacing of high use areas may be necessary. Proper site design can encourage proper use. (Photo by Alan Jubenville.)

ditions are neither available nor suitable for development in the general area, or the recreational use cannot be diverted to more suitable sites during high moisture periods.

A more desirable solution may be to surface these areas with other materials, such as gravel or coarse sand. This would help to reduce compaction and retard erosion by encouraging water infiltration; it also tends to be more aesthetically pleasing. In the heavily used portions of a site, such as around the picnic table, a reduced amount of erosion and dust is probably the best we can hope for. Plants will simply not survive in those conditions. Thus, the problem should really be eliminated in the initial site planning, through the proper surfacing of known or suspected heavy use areas. Certainly, resurfacing on a periodic basis is necessary in order to check sheet erosion and dusty conditions; however, it is impossible to eliminate the dust problem that occurs with many of the medium- to fine-textured soils. Light watering may reduce the dust problem. Even some chemicals may help, but too much moisture while recreational use is high may cause severe compaction—the problem that surfacing was supposed to eliminate in the first place.

Irrigation. Water seems to be a major limiting factor in site renovation, as indicated by the results of Beardsley and Herrington (1970).[1] Regardless of other treatments used, irrigation seems to be mandatory for the heavily deteriorated sites. Better results seem to come from watering, fertilization, and seeding, or from watering and seeding. No other treatment or combinations of treatments gave significant results in the re-establishment of ground vegetation without adequate water.

Two types of irrigation are possible—flood and aerial. In flood irrigation, portions of the site are surface-flooded by using a ditch system to transport the water. The site must be closed during the irrigation period. This type of irrigation could be done on sites that are closed during the renovation period. Flood irrigation would be difficult to administer where there is much variation in topography; therefore, it is seldom used.

Aerial irrigation is used fairly extensively on medium to high density sites because of the ease of control, flexibility of application, and efficiency of water use. Aerial irrigation systems can be portable or can be permanently installed, such as an underground sprinkler system. It is easier to direct and control the volume of waterflow using the aerial system. A portable system allows flexibility in handling local, isolated incidents. For permanent sites in which irrigation is done on a continuous basis, an underground system is more efficient and can be regulated so that any portion of the system can work independently of the rest of the system.

There are problems associated with irrigation that are beyond the immediate concern of improving site conditions. Beardsley and Herrington[1] list these as site design, cost, engineering, and public relations. Site design is important so that irrigation can be done with minimum inconvenience during use of the site. Unfortunately, most sites are not designed this way.

One 1969 study showed the cost of irrigation to be $95 per family unit.[2] These costs may vary; certainly, they have escalated in the intervening years. Regardless, irrigation represents a significant item in already strained budgets; thus, the ultimate decision will be based on economics.

If one decides to use irrigation as a means of site maintenance or site renovation, one must also face the problem of public relations. People should be made aware of any inconveniences or of a closing before they reach the site, and an explanation should be offered so that people understand the need for an irrigation program. If a site is closed, there should be information available on an alternate site. Good public relations is a strong, positive, information program, which makes people aware of the situation and of the action being taken and which encourages public feedback so that the system can be improved.

Fertilization. Fertilization implies adding material, such as commercial fertilizers, to the soil to improve plant growth. Too often, the manager uses some standard fertilizer mix (N-P-K, plus some micronutrients), without understanding the problem or possible solutions. Proper fertilization requires some knowledge of soil chemistry. Most states have a soil-testing laboratory to test the specific chemistry of the soil and to make recommendations about correcting soil deficiencies. These deficiencies must be related to the plant species that one wishes to grow, since each species may have different requirements and levels of tolerences for specific mineral elements.

Nitrogen, phosphorus, and potassium are the primary elements utilized in the development of fertilizers; other macronutrients that are necessary for plant growth are calcium, magnesium, and sodium. Necessary micronutrients include sulfur, manganese, iron, boron, copper, zinc, and molybdenum. Symptoms of deficiencies of any of these elements may show up in the vegetation. The real problem may be shown in the pH of the soil; at a given pH, some elements are not readily available in a usable form. For example, below a pH of 4.7, tree seedlings, particularly the more fastidious, deciduous species, may suffer from a low availability of nitrogen or phosphorus, potassium, or other bases. An alkaline pH above 7.0 may decrease the availability of phosphates, iron, boron, zinc, and manganese. If we consider both the nutritional and biological needs, the desirable soil pH for coniferous species is around 5.0 (although some healthy stands may have a somewhat lower pH.) For deciduous species, the desirable range is nearer 5.7 to 6.5[35]

Vegetation. There are several decisions to be made about revegetating a worn-out site: Do you plant or seed the area? What species do you use — native or exotic? The choice depends entirely on the situation, however a wrong choice may be costly.

More research is now being done on exotic species which appear to be hearty and can sustain heavy recreational use. Even if they prove desirable, they must be adaptable to the local site conditions. Any choice of vegetation should also concern the aesthetics it creates.

Thinning. In thinning, competing overstory vegetation is removed so that the remaining vegetation is released; this is primarily for the improvement of hardiness. By exposing the ground cover to more sunlight thinning also improves its hardiness; therefore, it is an excellent tool to improve ground cover conditions under forest canopies. (Thinning will be discussed further in Chapter 6.)

MONITORING VISITOR EFFECTS ON THE SITE

There are several techniques that can be used to monitor the effects of recreational use — line transect, milacre plots, and photo file. The monitoring should always be done from a permanent point so that repeated measures can be obtained over time. The line transect method is especially useful in monitoring the change not only in per cent ground cover but also in species composition. A more detailed discussion of this technique can be found in any applied ecology text.

The milacre plot method is commonly used to measure both the change in vigor and the per cent ground cover. Permanent plots (6.6 feet square) are established in the medium-to-heavy use, light use, and zero use zones of a site and are remeasured on a regular interval. The zero use zone is usually an isolated place that is located adjacent to the site with the same vegetation type. This zone gives an estimate of the vegetative changes not directly influenced by recreational use — a form of ecological yardstick. In the medium-to-high use zone (the primary use portion of the designed site), one can determine the extent of damage and can also project possible management programs. Measurement of the light use zone should indicate the overflow effects from the main portion of the site. The number of sets of plots needed will be determined by the variability of the site vegetation and use patterns. (A set of plots is three plots — one for each zone.)

The photo file technique is merely a photo recording of vegetational changes that is taken from permanent photo points, using a standard camera mount. The technique is extremely valuable in cases where one is primarily interested in change in per cent ground cover. In all of these techniques, care must be exercised to protect the permanent points from careless destruction by the user, or there will be no comparable data.

ADAPTING STRATEGY TO LOCAL SITUATION

Adapting strategies to the local situation requires that you integrate available knowledge of soils, climate, and plant species with knowledge of site design, visitor use, and environmental effects. The objective is to produce a situation that encourages normal visitor behavior on the site but also maintains and protects the environment in which the recreation takes place. In sum,

$$\text{Well-managed local site} = f \begin{cases} \text{Normal recreational use} \\ \text{Stabilized, managed environment} \end{cases}$$

There are other experts that one should rely on, including:

Staff expertise. Too often, staff specialists are not utilized in problem analysis. Because of their special training, these people may be better able to analyze a portion of the problem and to offer solutions than the immediate manager.

University Extension. Specialized assistance can often be obtained from university extension programs offered primarily at land grant colleges.

Soil Conservation Service. The SCS offers services in soil mapping and soil development recommendations as well as technical aspects of specific conservation practices.

State Soil Testing Lab. The labs will provide soil analyses and specific recommendations to improve soil chemistry for a given type of vegetation.

State Department of Conservation. Many of these departments offer special consulting to public and private agencies.

City/County Planning Office. Coordination of management action is often done through city and county planning offices; also, they may be able to advise on legal requirements.

SELECTED READINGS

1. Beardsley, W. G., and R. B. Herrington. 1971. *Economics and Management Implications of Campground Irrigation—A Case Study.* U.S. Forest Service Research Note INT-129.
2. Beardsley, W. G., and J. A. Wagar. 1971. "Vegetation Management on a Forested Recreation Site," *Journal of Forestry* 69:728.
3. Brame, R. H., 1972. "Maintenance of Picnic and Camp Areas." Proceedings, *7th Annual Southeast Park and Recreation Training Institute.* p. 3.
4. Burden, R. F., and P. F. Randerson. 1972. "Quantitative Studies on the Effects of Human Trampling on Vegetation as an aid to the Management of Semi-Natural Areas," *Journal of Applied Ecology* 9(2):439.
5. Carey, J. B. 1965. "The Use of Soil Survey in Making Engineering Studies in Recreation Areas," *Northeast Fish and Wildlife Conference.* Harrisburg, Pa.
6. Cieslinski, T. J., and J. A. Wagar. 1970. "Predicting the Durability of Forest Recreation Sites in Northern Utah—Preliminary Results," U.S. Forest Service Research Note INT-117.
7. Cordell, H. K., and C. K. Sykes. 1969. "User Preferences for Developed-Site Camping," U.S. Forest Service Research Note SE-122.
8. Echelberger, H. E. 1971. Vegetative Changes at Adirondack Campgrounds 1964 to 1969. U.S. Forest Service Research Paper NE-142.
9. Forbes, R. D. (ed.). 1956. *Forestry Handbook.* New York: Ronald Press Co. (Chapter 12).
10. Gibbs, L. C. 1964. "Fertilizing Ornamental Shrubs and Small Trees," *Park Practice Guidelines Maintenance* 12:50.
11. Harper, J. C., II. 1963. "Growing Turf Under Shaded Conditions." Pennsylvania State University, Agricultural Extension Special Circular 149. State College, Pa.
12. Helgath, S. F. 1975. "Trail Deterioration in the Selway-Bitterroot Wilderness," U.S. Forest Service Research Note INT-193.
13. Herrington, R. B., and W. G. Beardsley. 1970. *Improvement and Maintenance of Campground Vegetation in Central Idaho.* U.S. Forest Service Research Paper INT-87.
14. Howard, G. S. 1972. "Plants for Problem Areas of Western United States," *Yearbook of Agriculture;* p. 154–167. Washington, D.C.: U.S. Government Printing Office.
15. Jemison, G. M. 1967. "Impacts of Recreation on the Ecology of Temperate North American Forests," Proceedings, Tenth Technical Meeting, International Union for the Conservation of Nature, (Lucerne, 1966) 7(1):185.
16. Jubenville, A. 1971. "Principles of Recreation Resource Management" (unpublished manuscript), Laramie, Wyo.: University of Wyoming.
17. LaPage, W. F. 1967. *Some Observations On Campground Trampling and Ground Cover Response.* U.S. Forest Service Research Paper NE-68.
18. Lyon, T. L., H. O. Buckman, and N. C. Brady. 1952. *The Nature and Property of Soils.* New York: Macmillan Co.
19. Mackie, D. K. 1966. "Site Planning to Reduce Deterioration," *Proceedings, Society of American Foresters,* p. 33.
20. Magill, A. W. 1970. *Five California Campgrounds . . . Conditions Improve After Five Years" Recreational Use.* U.S. Forest Service Research Paper PSW-62.
21. Magill, A. W., and R. H. Twiss. 1965. "A Guide for Recording Esthetic And Biological Changes With Photographs," U.S. Forest Service Research Note PSW-77.
22. McCall, W. W. 1969. "Learn to Interpret Your Soil Test Results," University of Hawaii, Cooperative Extension Service Circular 432. Honolulu, Hawaii.
23. McCall, W. W. 1970. "What's in the Fertilizer Bag," University of Hawaii, Cooperative Extension Service Circular 441. Honolulu, Hawaii.
24. McEwen, D., and S. R. Tocher. 1976. "Zone Management: Key to Controlling Recreational Impact in Developed Campsites," *Journal of Forestry* 74(2):90.
25. Orr, H. 1971. "Design and Layout of Recreation Facilities," *Recreation Symposium Proceedings* U.S. Forest Service, Northeast Forest Experiment Station. p. 23.
26. Partain, L. E. 1966. "The Use of Soil Knowledge in Recreation Area Planning," Virginia Polytechnic Institute, Agricultural Extension Bulletin 301, p. 180.
27. Reckman, R. W., J. Letey, and L. H. Stolzy. 1966. "Compact Subsoil Can Be Harmful to Plant Growth," *Parks and Recreation.* 43(2):334.
28. Ripley, T. H. 1962. "Tree and Shrub Response To Recreational Use," U.S. Forest Service Research Note SE-171.
29. Rudolph, P. O. 1967. "Silviculture for Recreation Area Management," *Journal of Forestry* 65:385.
30. Spurr, S. H. 1964. *Forest Ecology.* New York: Ronald Press Co.
31. Stevens, M. E. 1966. "Soil Surveys As Applied to Recreation Site Planning," *Journal of Forestry* 64:314.
32. Tesdale, S. L. 1956. *Soil Fertility and Fertilizers.* New York: Macmillan Co.
33. Tocher, S. R., J. A. Wagar, and J. D. Hunt. 1965. "Sound Management Prevents Worn Out Recreation Sites," *Journal of Forestry* 63(3):151.
34. Walker, L. C. 1964. "Fertilizing Shade and Forest Trees in Parks," *Park Practice Guidelines, Maintenance* 11:45.
35. Wilde, S. A. 1958. *Forest Soils.* New York: Ronald Press Co.

Chapter 6

Vegetation Management

The primary emphasis of this chapter is on the silviculture manipulation of the overstory vegetation—before, during, and after site development. Specific vegetation management practices will be discussed, as well as related visitor management practices. The chapter also presents possibilities for site redevelopment—i.e., when vegetation reaches the point of biological maturity, and the decision must be made to either abandon the site or regenerate the stand. The last section discusses insect and disease problems and management strategies. Related topics that will be discussed elsewhere include ground vegetation on a site (Chapter 5), turf management (Chapter 7), vegetation management through natural agents (Chapter 8), and managing the natural aesthetics of the landscape (Chapter 9).

SILVICULTURAL PRACTICES PRIOR TO DEVELOPMENT

The three primary silvicultural treatments are thinning, sanitation cutting, and rights-of-way.

Thinning. (Fig. 6–1). This practice requires coordination with long range planning. The intent of thinning is to prepare the site for development and to improve the condition of the vegetation prior to recreational use. Site preparation may precede site development by 2 to 10 years, depending on how the vegetation responds, and it may be done at regular intervals until development.

Thinning opens up the stand of trees in order to increase light to the site, thereby increasing the quantity and hardiness of both the ground cover, or visitor's carpet, and the remaining overstory vegetation. This improves aesthetics, reduces dust, increases natural screening, and promotes desirable shading conditions. The trees should be cut off at ground level where the stumps do not readily decay; this may require a small trench around the base of the tree so that the chain saw operator can manipulate the saw (Fig. 6–2). In thinning, some of the dominant and codominant trees and all the intermediate and suppressed trees are removed, thus improving both crown size and general vigor of the remaining trees. In addition, it can be used, much as an improvement cut, to favor certain species that are more durable on the potential new site. In the process, the light reaching the ground should improve species composition and vigor of the existing ground vegetation to sustain its recreational use; thus, specific recommendations must be based on the silvical character-

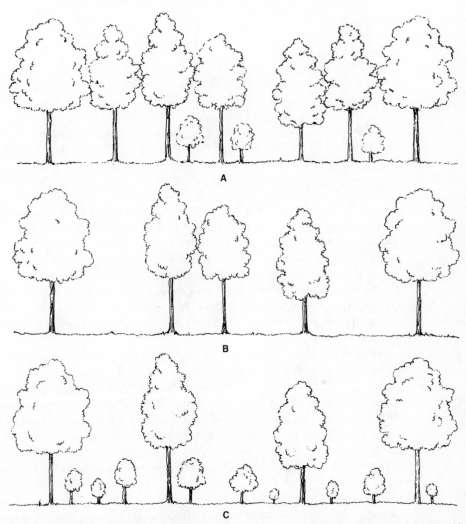

Figure 6–1 Graphic illustration of the effects of thinning. *A*, Nearly 100 per cent overstory stocking with little understory; *B*, thinning of overstory to improve growing conditions and ground cover; *C*, five years after thinning, the trees have bigger, more healthy crowns and well-established ground vegetation.

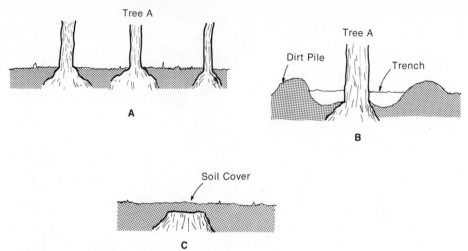

Figure 6–2 Cutting trees at ground level. *A*, Removal of Tree A; *B*, the trench around the tree measures approximately 3 feet across and 18 inches deep; *C*, after removal of Tree A, the area is covered with 6 to 10 inches of soil.

istics of the species. Appendix A lists general habitat and requirements of various tree species and the general soil requirements in terms of natural habitat. Thus, one may more easily determine which species to favor. Thinning guidelines can be developed based on wind firmness (the less windfirm the trees, the smaller the spaces between trees, and the greater the need for more than one thinning prior to development) and on competitive ability (the less competitive species tend to grow in even-aged stands). Since certain species are generally predominant in a given region, these guidelines could be developed regionally.

For wind-firm, even-aged stands of trees, one thinning is usually needed three to five years prior to development and is done by removing approximately one-third of the crown density. For truly uneven-aged stands, which have a mixture of size and age classes, there should be no thinning prior to development, since theoretically the desired conditions already exist. However, typically one will find only two or three size and age classes, which appear in clusters or in multi-story canopies. If the size classes are in clusters, each of these should be carefully thinned to improve conditions for that portion of the site.

Multi-story stands are generally in some stages of successional change—i.e., the less competitive (intolerant) species has been invaded by the more competitive (shade tolerant) species. There are several ways this could be handled, depending on the species and the type of recreation use. If the understory species is more desirable in terms of aesthetics and durability to recreational use, the overstory species could be removed; thinning would then be delayed until time of development. The new overstory should be well stocked (50 per cent or more), thrifty in external appearance, and at least 25 feet high prior to site development. This height will provide well-established trees that have good canopy size, yet adequate room below the canopy for normal movement of people and vehicles. If the overstory is desirable, the understory is removed, and then the overstory is thinned.

If the species are not wind firm, the pre-development thinning should be done in two stages, starting 6 to 10 years prior to development. The first thinning should remove approximately 20 to 25 per cent of the crown canopy, and the second phase should open the canopy to the desired level.

For additional treatments to improve the hardiness of the ground vegetation, refer to the section on site treatments in Chapter 5.

Sanitation Cutting. Sanitation cutting is the removal of trees that have been affected by disease or insect attacks or have sustained mechanical injuries that would make them highly susceptible to such attacks. These cuttings are made prior to development in order to improve the general health of the stand and to reduce possible loss of live trees during the life of the development. If the insect or disease problem involves removing a significant number of trees, relocation should be considered.

The stand should be given a complete inventory to determine the degree of infestation; then, each tree to be removed should be individually marked. If the disease can be transmitted through root grafts, the adjacent trees may also have to be removed, in that case, it would be advisable to burn each removed tree.

Rights-of-Way. Rights-of-way for major road development should be staked out to determine the types of vegetation and microclimate the road will pass through. No pre-development cutting may be necessary if the microclimatic conditions are favorable, the species composition is reasonably uniform, and the species are wind firm. In areas where the species is susceptible to wind throw because of a shallow root system, partial completion of the right-of-way may be more desirable than total completion, which would occur at the time of development. This will also allow minimum access prior to development of the site.

SILVICULTURAL TREATMENTS DURING DEVELOPMENT

The cuttings made during the development phase are similar to those of the predevelopment phase. Sanitation cuttings are made to remove any insectning) is done at time of site development; up to 50 per cent of the crown cover is removed to allow sunlight into the site. This removal may be uniform or variable, depending on the objectives for specific portions of the site in terms of sun/shade requirements. The campground unit may require an average amount of shade, whereas the comfort station and water point should have more than average sunlight.

The final right-of-way for the access road, including the shoulders of the road bed, is accomplished at time of development. If there is a dense stand of trees, the edge of the right-of-way may be feathered to improve aesthetics and to reduce shading along the shoulder in case grasses are to be established.

The remaining trees should be pruned along the bole from 12 to 16 feet high after all other development cuttings have been made. It is an expensive procedure that requires close attention to detail in order to minimize mechanical damage to the tree; timing and technique are also important. Pruning is often criticized because it opens the tree to insect and disease attacks. Again timing is important in reducing this problem. On the other hand, pruning

removes dead limbs and those that may receive mechanical injury from the recreationists. Pruning should be done in the spring so that the tree has an opportunity to form callous tissue over the wound immediately. If it is done in late
summer after growth has ceased, or during the fall, the tree will be more susceptible to insect attack through the open wounds. Insects may deposit their
eggs in the wounds for overwintering.

Proper technique for removal of tree limbs is to undercut the limb with a
pruning saw at the bole of the tree (Fig. 6–3) and then to cut the limb off at a
spot located above the undercut and even with the bole. The undercut will
keep the limb from tearing the bark below. Limbs up to 2 inches in diameter
should heal naturally without being sealed artificially; those over 2 inches
should be sealed immediately. To encourage rapid healing of the larger
wounds, light scarification (with the saw) around the wound may help (Fig. 6–
4). Where healing will be slow because of the size of the wound, immediate
sealing of the wound may be necessary. Trees under which recreation is to take
place should be pruned to approximately 12 feet in height. One should always
leave at least 50 per cent of the bole area in live crown.

The last treatment during the development phase is the mini-development, which involves preparation of such areas as open-play space at a group
picnic area or a guard station at a campground. A small clear cutting is made
where the mini-development is to be located, and all trees are removed. Those
trees that may interfere with the development site are also removed, and consideration is given toward the effects of root systems that may cause great damage to foundations and sewer systems.

POST-DEVELOPMENT TREATMENTS

Periodic surveys should be scheduled, using data collection forms, to
assess the condition of the overstory vegetation. This fulfills the legal as well as
professional obligation to minimize hazards yet maintain desirable, natural aesthetics. The survey should focus on the following:

1. Disease- and insect-infected trees.
2. Mechanical injury to tops from ice or wind.
3. Mechanical injury from recreational use, primarily from cutting on the
   bole and from trampling on the root collar.
4. Stagheading (die-back of tree top), which may indicate severe soil compaction or biological overmaturity of species.
5. General vigor and coloration of the crowns.

Not all trees with negative signs need to be removed immediately. These

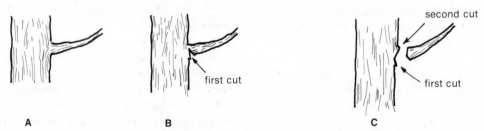

Figure 6–3 Pruning of large limbs. *A*, Original limb; *B*, initial cut; *C*, removal of limb.

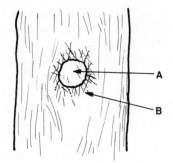

Figure 6-4 Stimulating scar tissue growth. *A*, Wound from limb removal; *B*, light scratch from saw to stimulate scar tissue growth.

trees should be classified as either *cut* or *watch* trees. The *cut* ones are removed because they are a hazard to visitors or to the general health of the other trees. The *watch* trees are flagged and observed during subsequent surveys to determine whether or not their condition is stable. If individual trees are important in the landscape design of the site, specific treatment such as tree surgery may be recommended by an arboriculturist. The individual employed in seasonal site maintenance should receive instructions on making and reporting casual observations while working on any site. This will provide some random observations in between surveys.

Thus, post-development cuttings are designed to maintain the general health of the stand of trees and to remove public hazards, through the use of sanitation cutting and hazard tree cutting, and possibly, some thinning — although, generally, thinning is not necessary except on the better sites. Usually, recreational use reduces the pre-development tree vigor. Since the crowns grow at a rate proportionate to the root system, they cannot expand very fast if the system becomes restricted by compacted soil.

One post-development treatment that has not been given sufficient attention is the expansion of the site. If the site had been chosen to allow for future expansion, the cycle of treatments is repeated, starting with pre-development on each new area; however, these treatments must be coordinated with the existing site, since the area is simply an expansion of that site. In sum, this means that vegetation management strategies must be included in the initial site planning so that all management activities can be coordinated.

SITE REGENERATION

Ultimately, the manager must concern himself with regenerating the overstory vegetation in order to redevelop the site. After trees have reached their biological maturity, they begin to deteriorate. At some point, the decision must be made to regenerate the site or to abandon it. Not much consideration has been given to the problem because most developed sites are relatively new, and the trees have not yet reached the point of massive deterioration. Also , little research is available on the techniques for regenerating vegetation on recreational sites. A theoretical discussion of some possibilities for regenerating the overstory vegetation follows.

Option 1: Relocate. If there is a minimum investment involved and if several potential sites are available, relocation seems to be the most logical choice. There is less inconvenience to the user; it is possibly less expensive to develop; and it offers an opportunity to update the design of the site.

Option 2: Close and Regenerate. Probably the least desirable alternative is to close the site so that the overstory can be regenerated. This is inconvenient for the user, since the site would be closed for a number of years. Other sites would have to handle the user demand for the 7 to 10 years required for the vegetation to reach a sufficient height (at least 20 to 25 feet). Vegetation less than this in height tends to be damaged by indiscriminate behavior and even through normal use. If there are several similar sites in the area, only one new site may be needed so that regeneration of sites can be done by rotation. For example, in Figure 6–5, A_5 is the newly developed site; it replaces A_1 during the regeneration period. A_1 then replaces A_2 during the next regeneration; A_2 replaces A_3, and so on.

The regeneration method should be compatible with the silvical requirements of the forest types being regenerated and with the site conditions. Natural regeneration would probably take too long to re-establish; therefore, planting is the most logical choice. Possibly, a two-cut shelter wood would be desirable although it would appear as a three-cut shelter wood. The operation would be as follows:

1. In one cut, remove all competing and undesirable understory along with approximately 50 to 60 per cent of the overstory.
2. Plant older nursery stock, possibly 2-1 or 2-2 stock.* The root system would be larger and therefore better able to survive and grow quickly; the remaining overstory would provide protection to the seedlings during the re-establishment period (about 3 years).
3. After establishment, the remaining overstory would be removed. In another 4 to 10 years, the seedling will have grown to sapling size – the minimum size desired prior to reopening the site. Possibly fertilization and irrigation can reduce the re-establishment time.

Option 3: Redesign and Re-establish. By this alternative, the entire site is not closed, however, individual units (such as those in a forest campground) are permanently closed, and intermediate areas are then opened (Fig. 6–6). The steps would be as follows:

1. The vegetation on the proposed new units would be re-established in a sufficient amount of time to have the newly established vegetation grow to a minimum height of 20 to 25 feet prior to designing, developing, and opening new units. This would require a great distance in between existing units.
2. The old units are regenerated – perhaps similarly to the discussion in option 2.

---

*2-1 refers to two years in the seed bed and one year in the transplant bed at the nursery.

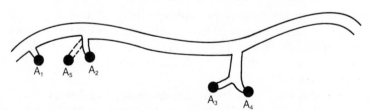

Figure 6–5 Rotation of similar types of sites during regeneration. A_5 is the new site that is being used to replace A_1 while it is being regenerated, and so on. This is possible only in cases where age and site variability will allow rotation over an extended number of years, possibly decades.

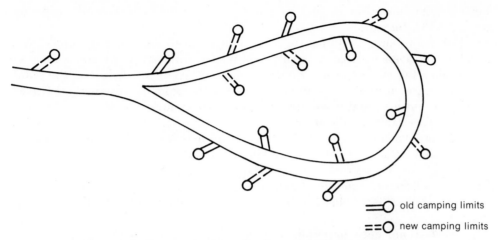

=○ old camping limits

==○ new camping limits

Figure 6-6   Diagram showing option to re-establish or redesign site.

The arguments against this option are strong. People would question why the units had not been developed, since demand generally outstrips the supply in most recreational opportunities. The public would probably decry the destruction of portions of the site. Also, the situation would dictate that smaller units (openings) be regenerated at one time rather than the entire site. Small openings may not meet the biological requirements for adequate regeneration. Finally, this would only be possible on low density occupancy sites in which individual units are adequately separated, so that they can be relocated in the intermediate zones.

METHODS OF REGENERATING

There are three methods of regenerating trees: natural, artificial seeding, and planting. Natural regeneration, even when associated with cultural treatments, is generally not as desirable as the other two methods for the intensive use sites. Natural regeneration is probably the only viable choice on the dispersed use areas because of both the cost and the basic management philosophy of maintaining the "wild" character of the landscape. On a number of the smaller, heavily used locations some cultural treatment to encourage rapid regeneration may be advisable; also during that time it is not difficult to shift use patterns. The exact natural regeneration requirements can be obtained from the United States Department of Agriculture's *Woody Seed Manual*,[16] the U.S. Forest Service publications on silvical characteristics for each species,[17] the state conservation department, or the local county agriculture agent.

Machine planting is generally not a viable alternative since the area to be planted is usually small. If the need arises, one can usually contract a local operator to do the work.

Seeding can be done either by broadcasting over large openings or by spot seeding; but again, this has limitations where recreation use occurs. It takes longer to regenerate the trees, and there is always the possibility of failure because of unusual environmental conditions. The exact seeding requirements can be determined by using the sources that were suggested in the preceding section on natural regeneration.

For natural areas, one has no other choice but to regenerate naturally. If a species has been extirpated locally within a natural area and one wishes to reintroduce the same species, the seeds should be collected close to the point of introduction and on sites similar to those of the point of introduction. This is expensive but essential if we are to maintain maximum genetic integrity—just any local seed source will not do.

Of more concern to the outdoor recreation manager is an artifical means of regenerating trees. The selection of species should be based not only on the site conditions but also on the intended use; i.e., the site may require shade trees, wind-firm trees, wildlife food, and so forth. The manager then selects the species that has those characteristics yet is also adaptable to local site conditions.

The last and most important regeneration method is hand planting. The selection and handling of planting stock are important to the success of your planting program; therefore, the stock should be obtained from a local, nursery-grown, certified seed source. The seed source should be a location with environmental conditions similar to those of the planting site. It is often advisable to buy transplant stock (transplanted from the seed bed) because it has a larger root system and thus more resistance to the shock caused by planting on a new site.

Once the seedlings have been obtained, they should be heeled-in until ready for planting. This requires digging a V-shaped trench in a shaded moist location. The sides of the trench should be approximately 3 to 4 inches longer than the root systems. Each bundle of seedlings is opened and then spread out along one side of the ditch. The loose soil, with some additional organic matter, is placed back into the ditch and watered heavily. Finally, the seedlings are tamped with the foot. Care should be exercised to minimize damage to roots.

When it is time to plant, the seedlings are then lifted out and placed in an open container filled with sufficient water to cover the roots. The soil opening for the seedling should be large enough to accommodate the root system without bending or changing the natural root formation. Depth is extremely important; ideally, the seedling should be planted approximately one-half inch below the depth at which it grew in the nursery: Too deep or too shallow planting will cause excessive vegetation mortality.

There are two types of planting tools—the dibble (or planting bar) and the mattock (Fig. 6–7). Either method is satisfactory; however, mattock planting is necessary on hard, heavy soils, and also, when using transplant stock with large roots.

INTRODUCTION OF EXOTICS

Exotic simply refers to a species that does not ordinarily grow on a particular site. Up to this point, the rule of thumb has been to avoid exotics. Often, this is not possible; in addition, some exotics have very desirable characteristics, and we may wish to take advantage of such species. Careful review of species within the region, discussion with local experts, and trial plantings may

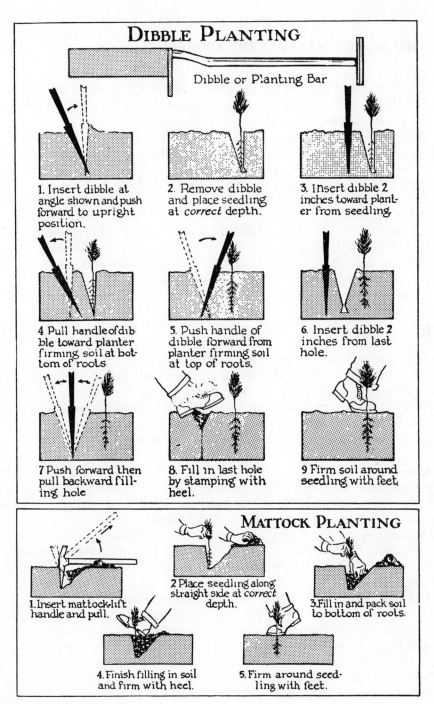

DIBBLE PLANTING

Dibble or Planting Bar

1. Insert dibble at angle shown and push forward to upright position.

2. Remove dibble and place seedling at *correct* depth.

3. Insert dibble 2 inches toward planter from seedling.

4 Pull handle of dibble toward planter firming soil at bottom of roots

5. Push handle of dibble forward from planter firming soil at top of roots.

6. Insert dibble 2 inches from last hole.

7 Push forward then pull backward filling hole

8. Fill in last hole by stamping with heel.

9 Firm soil around seedling with feet.

MATTOCK PLANTING

1. Insert mattock·lift handle and pull.

2 Place seedling along straight side at *correct* depth.

3. Fill in and pack soil to bottom of roots.

4. Finish filling in soil and firm with heel.

5. Firm around seedling with feet.

Figure 6–7 Planting methods. (From *Forestry Handbook,* edited by Reginald D. Forbes. Copyright © 1955 by The Ronald Press Company, New York.)

help to identify the best exotics for your planting program. A list of exotics that are adaptable to specific regions is shown in Table 6–1 and Figure 6–8.

RELATED VISITOR MANAGEMENT PROGRAMS

Management of overstory vegetation is not complete until it has been integrated with the visitor management program. There are several programs to coordinate, beginning with the area and site planning.

Area and Site Planning. With proper area planning, the potential site will be located where it will facilitate use but not encourage overuse, and where the environment is durable enough to sustain the use. This would involve determining the ability of the overstory vegetation on that site to sustain use without undergoing rapid or unreasonable deterioration. Site planning includes making a detailed study to determine the suitability of all facets of the site, including vegetation. This would allow adjustments to be made at specific locations on the site. If the findings of the study show the proposed development to be infeasible, the potential site can be either relocated (requiring new feasibility studies) or dropped completely from consideration.

Dispersal of Use. Adequate dispersal of use should reduce environmental impact on a given site, as is discussed in Chapter 11. Because of the lack of information on certain site developments; or the "oversell" of a particularly desirable site development, people tend to concentrate on sites that are well known to the general user population. This causes severe environment degradation, including vegetation damage. A good regional and area information program can help to voluntarily disperse use and to reduce the average impact. Dispersal of use is probably more desirable than other programs because it tends to be less inconvenient to the user and less costly. It also generates better public reaction than does either immediate rationing or hardening of the site.

Hardening of Site. Hardening of the site, using gravel or other porous surfaces, reduces soil compaction, maintains soil aeration—and improves water infiltration—thus maintaining a reasonable soil environment for root growth, nutrient absorption, and water uptake, The extreme of site hardening is paving, which may change the natural aesthetics but even then, it can be done tastefully. In some circumstances, paving may be a very desirable alternative for controlling the effects of recreational use, but it eliminates the potential for growing vegetation.

Physical Barriers. Physical barriers may be established to subtly direct use and to minimize damage to the vegetation. Barriers, which are usually native material or vegetation, can be used to direct use away from sensitive vegetation or heavy soils—all of which could ultimately affect the vigor of the overstory vegetation if use were allowed to continue without restrictions.

Interpretation. Much visitor damage is done out of ignorance because the visitor did not understand the consequences of his action (such as cutting bushes for hot dog sticks). A good interpretive program could reduce this type of damage by explaining the natural processes and showing the effects of careless acts on these processes.

TABLE 6–1   TREES SUITABLE FOR AN URBAN ENVIRONMENT*

SPECIES			GROWTH RATE	GROWING CONDITIONS	HARDINESS ZONES
PIN OAK *QUERCUS PALUSTRIS* 20 TO 25 METERS			MODERATE TO FAST	FULL SUN. RICH, LOAMY, WELL-DRAINED, SLIGHTLY ACIDIC SOIL.	4–8
WILLOW OAK *QUERCUS PHELLOS* TO 18 METERS			MODERATE TO FAST	FULL SUN. RICH, WELL-DRAINED, ACID SOIL	5–8
UPRIGHT GINKGO *GINKGO BILOBA* "FASTIGIATA" TO 18 METERS			SLOW	HIGHLY TOLERANT OF URBAN CONDITIONS.	4–8, INCLUDING CALIFORNIA
GREEN ASH, *FRAXINUS PENNSYLVANICA* "MARSHALL'S SEEDLESS" TO 20 METERS			FAST	FULL SUN. LOAMY, WELL-DRAINED, NEARLY NEUTRAL SOIL.	3–8, INCLUDING CALIFORNIA AND PACIFIC NORTHWEST
MODESTO ASH *FRAXINUS VELUTINA* VAR. *GLABRA* TO 20 METERS			FAST	TOLERANT OF DRY, ALKALINE SOIL.	5–8, PARTICULARLY CALIFORNIA AND SOUTHWESTERN DESERT AREAS
NORWAY MAPLE *ACER PLATANOIDES* 12 to 30 METERS			MODERATE TO FAST	FULL SUN. TOLERANT OF POOR SOIL.	3–10, EXCEPT SOUTHERN CALIFORNIA AND SOUTHWESTERN DESERT AREAS
JAPANESE PAGODA *SOPHORA JAPONICA* "REGENT" TO 20 METERS			SLOW TO MODERATE	TOLERANT OF POOR SOIL. DOES BEST IN NEARLY NEUTRAL, WELL-DRAINED SOIL.	4–7
THORNLESS HONEY LOCUST *GLEDITSIA TRIACANTHOS* VAR. *INERMIS* "SHADEMASTER" TO 25 METERS			FAST	FULL SUN OR PARTIAL SHADE. TOLERATES DROUGHT AND RANGE OF SOIL CONDITIONS.	4–10
SERVICEBERRY *AMELANCHIER CANADENSIS* OR *A. LAEVIS* 7 TO 12 METERS			MODERATELY FAST	PARTIAL SUN. MOIST SOIL.	4–8
GRECIAN LAUREL *LAURUS NOBILIS* TO 10 METERS			SLOW	FULL SUN. WELL-DRAINED ACID OR ALKALINE SOIL.	7–8, INCLUDING PACIFIC NORTHWEST, NORTHERN CALIFORNIA AND SOUTHERN STATES

*From "Urban Trees," by Thomas S. Elias and Howard S. Irwin. Copyright © 1976 by Scientific American, Inc. All rights reserved.

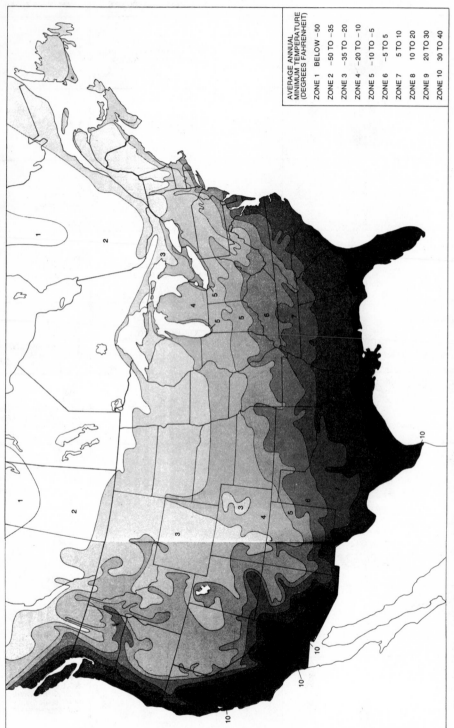

Figure 6–8 Hardiness zones of the United States and part of Canada reflect differences in the average annual minimum temperature and thus differences in the species of trees that can be expected to flourish in each zone. The map is based on a compilation and prepared at the Arnold Arboretum of Harvard University. Table shows the range of minimum temperatures. (From "Urban Trees," by Thomas S. Elias and Howard S. Irwin. Copyright © 1976 by Scientific American, Inc. All rights reserved.)

AVERAGE ANNUAL
MINIMUM TEMPERATURE
(DEGREES FAHRENHEIT)

ZONE 1 BELOW −50
ZONE 2 −50 TO −35
ZONE 3 −35 TO −20
ZONE 4 −20 TO −10
ZONE 5 −10 TO −5
ZONE 6 −5 TO 5
ZONE 7 5 TO 10
ZONE 8 10 TO 20
ZONE 9 20 TO 30
ZONE 10 30 TO 40

INSECT AND DISEASES—A CONTINUED PROBLEM

Insects and diseases are endemic in most areas, but rarely do they reach epidemic proportions. The best preventive measure is to keep trees healthy, with reasonable growth rate and minimum mechanical damage. Obviously, the trees will not be as healthy as they would be if no recreation use had occurred on the site; however, the strategies outlined in Chapters 5 and 6 should help to promote healthy trees. Some individual trees may be valuable enough to receive individual treatment, e.g., using fertilizers and water to keep them healthy, removing infected limbs, or spraying the infected area.

There should be some control measures instituted when certain insects or diseases are detected; however, unless there is a potential outbreak of a disease or the individual may die, it would probably be better and more economical to merely watch the area to ensure that a major problem does not arise. Unfortunately, since the tree is not in its best growing environment on a recreational site, it may rapidly deteriorate and die with any insect or disease attack. The other consideration is that the insect or disease problem, if not checked, may spread to other areas outside the immediate site.

In sum, the best approach is to maintain healthy trees. Periodically inspect for any insect or disease problem. If a major problem emerges, use the specific, recommended control and warn other residents and agencies of the potential problem. Ripley,[11] through a synthesis of his considerable research, recommends the eastern species of trees that are shown in Table 6–2 for developed recreation sites. A complete list of recommended western species is shown in Appendix B, and a list of insects, diseases, types of injury, and specific prevention/control measures is shown in Table 6–3.

TABLE 6–2 LIST OF CONIFERS AND HARDWOODS

Hardwoods		Conifers
1. Hickories	12. Red maple	1. Shortleaf pine
2. Persimmon	13. American holly	2. Hemlocks
3. Sycamore	14. Sourwood	3. White pine
4. White ash	15. Black birch	4. Pitch pine
5. Beech	16. White oaks	5. Virginia pine
6. Sassafras	17. Black walnut	
7. Buckeye	18. Red oaks	
8. Yellow-poplar	19. Black locust	
9. Dogwood	20. Magnolia	
10. Blackgum	21. Black cherry	
11. Yellow birch	22. Blue beech	

Note: The above conifers and hardwoods are listed in order of decreasing ability to withstand the impacts of recreation use, as gauged by disease infection, insect infestation, and decline. (From Ripley, T. H. 1962. "Tree and Shrub Response to Recreational Use." U.S. Forest Service Note SE-171. p. 2.)

TABLE 6–3. LIST OF DAMAGING INSECTS AND DISEASES*

SOME DAMAGING FOREST INSECTS

Name of Insect	Species and Size or Type of Tree Affected	Parts of Tree Affected and Evidence of Insect's Presence	Nature of Injury	Prevention and Control
Aphid, balsam woolly—*Adelges* (*Dreyfusia*) *piceaa* Ratz.	Balsam fir. Trees of any size	Trunk and branches. Small sap-sucking insect can be seen on bark	Insect withdraws sap from trees, thus weakening and eventually killing some trees	No practical direct control known. Favor spruces (white, red, and black) by cutting balsam fir to low diameter. Oil emulsions or nicotine sulphate sprays are effective
Beetle, Black Hills—*Dendroctonus ponderosae* Hopk.	Ponderosa pine, chiefly the weaker trees over 12″ d.b.h. except during epidemics, when any type of tree may be attacked	Inner bark. Small (¼″ or somewhat larger in diameter) accumulations of pitch on bark of trunk of tree	Insect tunnels in inner bark, in severe cases girdling tree, which leads to death. Young fast-growing trees usually drown insects by large exudation of pitch and thus survive	Remove weak, slow-growing and old trees from stand. Maintain rapid growth of young trees by regular cuttings. Prevent spread by felling infested trees, removing bark, and burning it
Beetle, eastern spruce bark—*Dendroctonus piceoperda* Hopk.	White, red, and black spruce	Inner bark. Similar to Black Hills beetle	See Black Hills beetle	See Black Hills beetle
Beetle, engraver or Ips—*Ips* spp.	All pines, chiefly under 12″ d.b.h. Severity of attack varies with species and locality	Inner bark. Small accumulations of pitch on bark of trunk of small trees or branches of large trees	Similar to western pine beetle	Continuous cutting leads insects to infest slash rather than living trees. If cutting is discontinued, green slash should be burned. Pulling tops away from clumps of young trees reduces hazard
Beetle, hickory bark—*Scolytus quadrispinosus* Say.	All hickories. Weakened trees of the larger sizes most susceptible	Inner bark. Small holes in trunk and small accumulation of fine sawdust at base of tree	Insect tunnels in inner bark, thus girdling tree in severe attacks and killing some trees	Unknown

*From Westveld, R. H. 1958. *Forestry in Farm Management*. New York: John Wiley & Sons, Inc. pp. 297–307.

Some Damaging Forest Insects (*Continued*)

Name of Insect	Species and Size or Type of Tree Affected	Parts of Tree Affected and Evidence of Insect's Presence	Nature of Injury	Prevention and Control
Beetle, June— *Phyllophaga* spp.	Chiefly the oaks, but occasionally other hardwoods of any size	Leaves. Large hardshelled beetle feeding on leaves	Trees will be partially or completely defoliated. A single defoliation has little effect other than possibly reducing tree's growth. Repeated defoliations cause marked reduction in growth, and death of the weaker trees	Do not allow a grass sod to develop in or adjacent to woodland. Maintain cultivated crops in fields adjacent to farm forest composed largely of oaks, if possible
Beetle, mountain pine—*Dendroctonus monticolae* Hopk.	Chiefly lodgepole, sugar, and western white pine, but sometimes ponderosa pine. Chiefly the less vigorous mature trees, but in epidemics lodgepole pines of any type are attacked	Inner bark. Pitch accumulations on trunk of tree	Same as western pine beetle	Keep stand in a vigorous, rapid-growing condition. Infested trees, other than western white pine, may be treated as for western pine beetle. For the latter insert into the sap stream in late summer or early fall, not more than 90 days after infestation, a copper sulphate solution
Beetle, southern pine—*Dendroctonus frontalis* Zimm.	Longleaf, slash, shortleaf, and loblolly pine, especially the last two species. Chiefly weak trees, especially mature ones.	Inner bark. Pitch accumulations on trunk of tree	Similar to western pine beetle	Same as western pine beetle
Beetle, southwestern pine—*Dendroctonus barberi* Hopk.	Ponderosa pine. Chiefly unthrifty mature trees	See western pine beetle		

SOME DAMAGING FOREST INSECTS (*Continued*)

Name of Insect	Species and Size or Type of Tree Affected	Parts of Tree Affected and Evidence of Insect's Presence	Nature of Injury	Prevention and Control
Beetle, western pine—*Dendroctonus brevicomis* Lec.	Ponderosa pine. Chiefly the less thrifty mature and overmature trees. Worst during drought periods	Inner bark. Small accumulations of resin on bark of tree	Insect tunnels in cambium layer. Extensive tunneling girdles the tree, which causes tree's death. Young, fast-growing trees usually drown insects by large exudation of pitch, and thus survive	Remove weak, slow-growing and old trees from stands, and leave maximum number of thrifty large-crowned trees. Maintain rapid growth in young stands by regular cuttings. Prevent spread by felling infested trees, removing bark from them, and burning it
Borer, bronze birch—*Agrilus anxius* Gory.	Chiefly yellow and paper birch trees in pole and later stages that are growing in open stands or that have been weakened by overexposure or adverse change in environment	Foliage, bark, and wood. Adult feeds on foliage. Larvae tunnel into inner bark and into wood. Defoliation and small entrance holes in bark	Tree is badly weakened and thus easy prey for other destructive agents. Various pests combined often kill trees	Maintain stand dense enough for trees to give each other mutual protection. No practical control to save infested trees
Borer, locust—*Cyllene robiniae* Forst.	Black locust. Slow-growing and unthrifty trees under 6″ d.b.h. in open stands most susceptible	Trunk. Entrance holes in bark	Tree is girdled; often so severely weakened mechanically that it breaks off	Plant trees preferably on sites on which they will grow rapidly. Growing other species in mixture. On sites where growth of black locust is slow, cut trees after a few years' growth, thus allowing faster-growing sprouts to develop. Thin systematically to maintain rapid growth. No practical control to save infested trees

SOME DAMAGING FOREST INSECTS (*Continued*)

Name of Insect	Species and Size or Type of Tree Affected	Parts of Tree Affected and Evidence'of Insect's Presence	Nature of Injury	Prevention and Control
Budworm, spruce—*Cacoecia fumiferana* Clem.	Spruces and firs; most severe on the latter. All sizes and types of trees affected. Jack pine, open-grown, large-crowned trees	Foliage, new growth attacked first. Caterpillars feeding on foliage	Trees will be partially or completely defoliated. Reduction in growth results from a single year's damage, but death generally ensues after repeated attacks	No practical direct control. Favor spruces by cutting firs to a low diameter in spruce-fir stands. Cut large-crowned jack pines and develop young jack pine stands that will have a closed canopy in 10 to 15 years
Cankerworm, spring—*Polaecrita vernata* Peck.	Numerous hardwoods, especially sugar maple, elms, and yellow birch. Trees of any size affected	Foliage. Caterpillars feeding on foliage	Partial or complete defoliation. Weaker trees often killed by more than one defoliation; stronger trees survive but their rate of growth is reduced	No control other than spraying with arsenate of lead or banding trees with tanglefoot
Caterpillar, forest tent—*Molacosoma disstria* Hubn.	Quaking aspen, ashes, birches, sweetgum, black tupelo, oaks, sugar maple	Foliage. Caterpillars feeding on foliage	Partial or complete defoliation. If repeated for several years many trees die, but, when occurring for only a year or two, the damage is chiefly in form of reduced growth	Same as spring cankerworm
Moth, European pine shoot—*Rhyacionia buoliana* (Schiff.)	Red pine. Chiefly trees under 30′ tall	Terminal bud. Hole where insect entered terminal bud, and later the turning brown of the terminal needles	Terminal buds are killed, together with some of the terminal needles	Where damage is severe do not plant red pine. Elsewhere cut and burn infested tips annually until infestation is controlled

SOME DAMAGING FOREST INSECTS (*Continued*)

Name of Insect	Species and Size or Type of Tree Affected	Parts of Tree Affected and Evidence of Insect's Presence	Nature of Injury	Prevention and Control
Moth, gypsy— *Porthetria dispar* L.	Oaks, alder, gray and river birch, basswood, willows, copper, boxelder, and hawthorn are most susceptible, followed by paper birch and tamarack. Eastern hemlock and northern white pine attacked by large caterpillars. Size or condition of tree not important	Foliage. Caterpillars feeding on foliage	Partial or complete defoliation. A single defoliation causes little damage to hardwoods, but is usually fatal to pine and hemlock. Repeated defoliations weaken tree so that other pests, together with the gypsy moth, kill many hardwoods	Do not allow the most susceptible species to constitute 50% of a stand
Sawfly, jack pine— *Neodiprion banksianae* Roh.	Jack pine. Size and condition of tree not important	Foliage, chiefly the old growth. Caterpillars feeding on foliage	Partial or complete defoliation, especially the latter when working in conjunction with the spruce budworm. Reduced growth of tree results	Spray with arsenate of lead
Sawfly, larch— *Lygaeonematus erichsonii* (Hartig)	Tamarack of any size	Same as above	Same as above. In Lake States severe defoliation once eliminated, at least temporarily, most of the tamarack	Spray with arsenate of lead
Sawfly, LeConte's —*Colaspis brunnea* (Fab.)	Longleaf, slash, shortleaf, and loblolly pine. Chiefly trees of reproduction size	Same as above	Same as above	Spray with arsenate of lead
Scale, golden oak— *Asterolecanium variolosum* (Ratz.)	Chestnut oak. Worst on trees of seedling and sapling size on poor sites. Sprouts suffer more than seedlings	Bark. Small scale insects cover bark	Severely infested parts, sometimes involving whole crown, are killed	No practical method

SOME DAMAGING FOREST INSECTS (*Continued*)

Name of Insect	Species and Size or Type of Tree Affected	Parts of Tree Affected and Evidence of Insect's Presence	Nature of Injury	Prevention and Control
Scale, oyster shell—*Lepidosaphes ulmi* (L.)	Chiefly the ashes of any size or condition	Bark. Small scale insects in large numbers almost covering the bark completely	Same as above	Combination of summer oil and nicotine
Sphinx, catalpa—*Ceratomia catalpae* Bois.	Hardy catalpa of any size or condition	Foliage. Caterpillars feeding on foliage	Partial or complete defoliation, leading to reduction in growth and, if recurrent attacks occur, some trees may die	Spray with arsenate of lead or Paris green
Tipmoth, jack pine—*Rhyacionia* spp.	Jack pine, particularly the smaller trees	Terminal bud and stem of current year's growth. Browning of terminal needles	New growth of stem is killed, causing deformity and loss of height growth. If working with other pests, some trees are killed	Cut and burn infested tips
Tipmoth, Nantucket—*Rhyacionia frustrana* (Comst.)	Shortleaf and loblolly pine seedlings under 6' to 8' tall	Same as above	Same as above	Maintain fully stocked stands, if possible, with some hardwoods in mixture. On poor sites especially, avoid planting large areas of the species affected at one time
Weevil, Pales or Snout—*Hylobius pales* Boh.	Chiefly northern white pine, but sometimes attacking several of the conifers associated with this species. Seedlings under 3' tall	Bark and cambium layer. Grubs feeding on bark	Trees are killed by girdling, which follows destruction of bark and cambium layer	When planting do not set trees out until third season after cutting of white pine in or adjacent to the area to be planted. If natural reproduction is to be relied upon, get dense reproduction as far in advance of cutting as possible

Some Damaging Forest Insects (*Continued*)

Name of Insect	Species and Size or Type of Tree Affected	Parts of Tree Affected and Evidence of Insect's Presence	Nature of Injury	Prevention and Control
Weevil, white pine—*Pissodes strobi* Boh.	Chiefly northern white pine under 25 to 30 years old. A few other conifers, notably Norway spruce, have been damaged, but less severely	Current year's terminal shoot. Pitch accumulation at point where insect entered, and browning of foliage of terminal shoot in early summer	Terminal shoot is killed, leading to forking or crookedness of bole, as well as causing a loss of height growth	When planting, plant 1,200 to 1,500 trees per acre (1,800 where infestation is severe). If site will support hardwoods, mix some of them (up to 50%) in with the white pine; otherwise, mixing in other conifers will reduce the insect hazard. Infested trees can be improved by cutting infested tips at the whorl of branches just below the lowest evidence of any larval activity, and burning them each year that infestation is evident

Some Damaging Diseases of Trees

Name of Disease	Species and Size or Type of Tree Affected	Parts of Tree Affected and Evidence of Disease's Presence	Nature of Injury	Prevention and Control
Blight, brown-spot needle—*Septoria acicola* (Thum.) Sacc.	Chiefly longleaf pine. Most damaging to seedlings under 18″ tall, but infects trees through sapling stage. Other southern pines affected to a limited degree	Foliage. In early stage of infection, scattered small brown spots appear on needles. Eventually entire needle becomes brown and dies	Infected foliage is killed, thus greatly reducing crown area. Severe infection kills some trees, but chief damage is greatly reduced height growth	Carefully controlled burning during winter at intervals of 3 years until the seedlings reach a height of 18″
Blight, chestnut—*Endothia parasitica* (Murr.) A. & A.	Chestnut only. Size or condition of tree unimportant	Bark and cambium layer on trunk and branches. The cankerous growth is generally yellowish brown. The fruiting body is yellow or orange	The tree is gradually girdled as the infection encircles the main stem. Death ensues	Since the infection spreads very rapidly from tree to tree there is no practical means of control. Already practically all chestnut has been infected, and few trees with more than a few years of life remain

SOME DAMAGING DISEASES OF TREES (*Continued*)

Name of Disease	Species and Size or Type of Tree Affected	Parts of Tree Affected and Evidence of Disease's Presence	Nature of Injury	Prevention and Control
Canker, nectria—*Nectria* spp.	All hardwoods. Infection begins during sapling stage. Thrifty trees apparently are as susceptible as unthrifty trees	The lower part of the trunk, chiefly below 20' above ground. Attacks the cambium layer and wood through dead branch stubs. A cankerous open wound with decay showing in exposed wood in advanced stage. In early stage, depression and cracking of bark from which callous tissue shows	Some trees that are completely girdled are killed. Chief damage is deterioration of wood, which reduces the merchantability of the most valuable part of the tree	Select infected trees for cutting in all cultural operations, which should begin during sapling stage. Pruning of dead limbs from healthy trees may reduce the danger of infection
Canker, tympanis—*Tympanis* spp.	Red pine. Northern white pine attacked but not damaged. Infection begins during sapling stage. Worst on poor sites and south of optimal range of red pine in East	Cambium layer and wood on trunk. A cankerous wound. Accompanied by heavy exudation of resin and some decay in wood	Chiefly disfigurement and decay of trunk, thus reducing the tree's merchantability. Trees killed occasionally by girdling	Grow red pine on sites of average or better-than-average quality for the species within its range. Plant other species in mixture and space 8' by 8'. Prune and thin young stands
Disease, Dutch elm—*Ceratostomella ulmi* (Schwarz) Buisman	All species of elms. Weakened or unhealthy trees are most susceptible	Trunk and branches, working in the wood, into which it gains entrance by spores being carried by the dark elm bark beetle and possibly other insects. Discoloration and withering of foliage are first symptoms	Infected trees are generally killed	Cut and burn diseased trees. Peel bark from stumps and treat exposed wood with creosote. Remove weak and unthrifty trees from forest
Disease, little-leaf (causal agent unknown)	Shortleaf pine chiefly in Piedmont plateau. Occasionally loblolly pine	Needles are shorter than normal and chlorotic	Affected trees die in 5 to 7 years after first symptoms of infection	Unknown. Salvage dying trees

SOME DAMAGING DISEASES OF TREES (*Continued*)

Name of Disease	Species and Size or Type of Tree Affected	Parts of Tree Affected and Evidence of Disease's Presence	Nature of Injury	Prevention and Control
Disease, strumella— *Strumella coryneoidea* Sacc. and Wint.	All northern species of oak. Infection begins during sapling stage. Thrifty trees apparently are as susceptible as unthrifty trees	Same as nectria canker, except that cankers seldom occur more than 8' above ground	Same as nectria canker	Same as nectria canker
Mistletoe, dwarf (several species)— *Arceuthobium* (*Razoumofskya*) spp.	Many of the western conifers, but most common on ponderosa pine. Trees of any size or condition. Occurs to a limited extent on some eastern conifers, notably black spruce	Limbs and trunk. The plant itself is the best evidence. Witches' brooms form in crown. Swellings form on infected stems	Causes reduction in growth and sometimes kills the tree, especially the younger ones. When present on the trunk the quality of the wood is lowered locally owing to high resin content of wood	Effective control appears almost impossible. Cut most severely infected trees during each cutting operation
Rots. (Many different kinds of rot attack different parts of the tree and various species. Those that attack the trunk are of greatest significance. Tree species differ widely in their susceptibility and in the damage they suffer)	All species. Sprouts are more susceptible than seedlings during early life. Susceptibility increases with increase in age. Injuries that break the bark, thus exposing the wood, increase rot hazard	Branches, trunk, and roots. Evidence varies with type and location of rot. The following are good clues: fruiting bodies on branches or trunk or on the ground underneath the tree (these originate in the roots); decayed wood showing through abrasions in the bark; decayed branch stubs or partially decayed live limbs; large wounds on trunk that are completely healed over; the exudation of sap or ill-smelling liquid from cracks or crotches. Rot in the trunk of old trees often cannot be detected because the wounds through which the rot entered at an early age have healed over so completely that they are no longer in evidence	Decay of wood, increasing annually. In severe cases, decay of wood will equal or exceed growth of new wood. Reduction of growth is sometimes associated with rot. Mechanical weakening of roots of trunk may cause windfall or windbreakage. Lowered vitality of tree may make it more susceptible to other destructive agents, especially insects	Protect trees from injurious agents such as fire, livestock, and other animals, wind, etc. Use care in logging to avoid mechanical injury to trees. Remove trees that are badly injured in storms, or in logging. Cut severely decayed trees to reduce sources of infection

SOME DAMAGING DISEASES OF TREES (*Continued*)

Name of Disease	Species and Size or Type of Tree Affected	Parts of Tree, Affected and Evidence of Disease's Presence	Nature of Injury	Prevention and Control
Rust, eastern gall—*Cronartium quercuum* (Berk.) Miyabe (*C. cerebrum*)	Slash and loblolly pine most susceptible. Shortleaf and longleaf pine have low susceptibility. Infection occurs early in life, usually during sapling stage. Infection can occur only where an alternate host—various oaks, especially the black oaks, or post oak—is near by	Branches and trunk. An elongated cankerous wound on the pines, evidenced by swelling at the edges, and exposure of wood in center. In spring, orange fruiting bodies cover the canker for a short period. Short (⅛″) brownish threadlike fruiting bodies on under surface of oak leaves reveal sources of infection	Tree is deformed at point of infection. Merchantability of trees is reduced if trunk is affected. Complete girdling kills some small trees	Be sure to secure planting stock from nurseries which have no infection, as verified by the state nursery inspector. Favor longleaf or shortleaf pines in planting or cutting on sites to which these species are well suited, if oaks are present
Rust, southern fusiform—*Cronartium fusiforme* (Pk.) Hedgc. & Hunt	Same as eastern gall rust (above)			
Rust, western gall—*Cronartium harknessii* (Moore) Meinecke	Ponderosa and lodgepole pine chiefly, but occurring also on any of the hard pines of the West	Similar to eastern gall rust	Similar to eastern gall rust	Remove badly infected trees in cuttings
Rust, white pine blister—*Cronartium ribicola* Fisch.	All five-needled pines, of which the most important are eastern white, western white, and sugar. Trees of any size or condition. Infection can occur only where an alternate host, species of the genus *Ribes* (currant and gooseberries) is within 900′	Branches and trunk. Bark at point of infection becomes yellow or orange at first. Later blisters develop, the bark cracks, and resin exudes copiously	Tree is slowly girdled. For large trees this may require 20 to 25 years, thus eventually killing the host	Eradicate all currant and gooseberry bushes within 900′ of pines. Inspection and, if necessary, re-eradication of alternate host every several years after initial eradication. Cut infected pines
Wilt, oak—*Chalara quercina* Henry	Probably all oaks. Develops most rapidly on black oaks	Leaves wilt; first symptoms begin in top of crown	Affected trees die in a few to several weeks	Practical means unknown. Salvage dying trees

SELECTED READINGS

1. Arno, S. F. 1965. "Silviculture in Western National Parks" (Unpublished manuscript), Missoula, Mont.: University of Montana.
2. Barratt, J. W. 1962. *Regional Silviculture of the United States.* New York: The Ronald Press Co.
3. Boyce, J. S. 1961. *Forest Pathology.* New York: Mc-Graw-Hill Book Co.
4. Elias, T. S., and H. S. Irwin, 1976. "Urban Trees," *Scientific American* 235(5):111.
5. Forbes, R. D. 1956. *Forestry Handbook.* New York: The Ronald Press Co.
6. Graham, S. A., and F. E. Knight. 1965. *Principles of Forest Entomology.* New York: McGraw-Hill Book Co.
7. Haller, J. 1957. *Tree Care.* New York: Macmillan Publishing Co.
8. Howard, C. S. 1972. "Plants for Problem Areas of the Western States," *Yearbook of Agriculture,* p. 154.
9. Neeley, D. and E. B. Himeleck. 1962. "Fertilizing and Watering Trees," Circular 52. Urbana, Ill. Natural History Survey, University of Illinois.
10. Neff, P. E. 1965. "Applied Silviculture in Managing Outdoor Recreation Sites," *Proceedings of Society of American Foresters,* p. 34.
11. Ripley, T. H. 1962. "Tree and Shrub Response to Recreational Use," U.S. Forest Service Research Note SE 171.
12. Rudolph, P. O. 1967. "Silviculture for Recreation Area Management," *Journal of Forestry* 65:385.
13. Settergren, C. D., and D. M. Cole 1970. "Recreation Effects on Soil and Vegetation in the Missouri Ozarks," *Journal of Forestry* 68:231.
14. Smith, D. M. 1962. *The Practice of Silviculture.* New York: John Wiley & Sons, Inc.
15. Spurr, S. H. 1964. *Forest Ecology.* New York: The Ronald Press Co.
16. U.S. Department of Agriculture, 1948. *Woody Plant Seed Manual.* Misc. Publ. 654.
17. U.S. Forest Service. 1965. *Silvics of Forest Trees of the United States.* Agriculture Handbook 271.
18. Wagar, J. A. 1965. "Cultural Treatment of Vegetation on Recreation Sites," *Proceedings of Society of American Foresters,* p. 37.
19. Westveld, R. H. 1958. *Forestry in Farm Management.* New York: John Wiley & Son, Inc.

CHAPTER 7

Turf Management

Too often, we may overlook turf management because we feel it is applicable only in special situations. In reality, we all are involved in some form of turf management—whether in stabilizing cuts and fills or in hardening a site for recreational use. We should recognize this and attempt to adopt strategies for the particular management problem. The objectives of a turf management program may vary according to the park or recreation area (Fig. 7–1), but the success depends on both the analysis of local conditions and the development of strategies to meet these conditions (Fig. 7–2).

The basic systems that affect turf development are soils and climate. Soils are the media in which grass seeds can germinate, establish a root system, and grow through absorption of water and minerals. The physical properties (depth, texture, structure, organic matter) and chemical properties (exchange capacity, available nutrients, pH) of the soil determine the natural productivity of the site

Figure 7–1 Turf management at developed recreation sites. (Photo by Alan Jubenville.)

Figure 7–2 The development and maintenance of turf at high elevation—Jackson Lake Lodge. (Photo by Alan Jubenville.)

and thus its potential and limitation for development. It may be possible to adjust some of these factors to increase the productivity in terms of the development and maintenance of sod on the site.

Climate also affects the potential for turf development. Temperature and precipitation will directly influence the level of turf development, the adaptability of species to the edaphic conditions, and the relative hardiness of the site to recreation use. Thus, management recommendations for specific regions should be based on species adaptability and growth patterns. For example, if two grasses having different growth patterns are adaptable to a particular site, the one that ceases growth early might be more desirable, since grasses are more susceptible to damage from trampling during their succulent period of growth.

Soil conditions, species composition, and even cultural treatments can alter site conditions to produce the desired sod. However, we must ask ourselves the following questions: Is this what we really want to do? Is it economically feasible? What are the probabilities that the program will succeed (how predictable is the outcome)?

REGIONAL REQUIREMENTS

There are some regional recommendations for turf grass that can help in the selection of appropriate species. Different turf grass regions are shown in Figure 7–3. General recommendations are given in Table 7–1, and the associated natural soil conditions are described in Table 7–2. We will be discussing the general species recommendations for cool and warm regions.

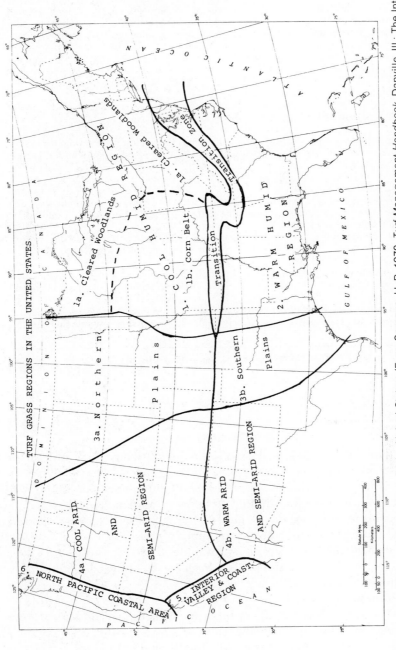

Figure 7-3 Major turf grass zones in the United States. (From Sprague, H. B. 1970. *Turf Management Handbook.* Danville, Ill.: The Interstate, p. 13.)

TABLE 7–1 TURF GRASS REGIONS IN THE UNITED STATES*

---

1. Cool Humid Region

   Suited to cool-season grasses such as bluegrass, fescue and bentgrasses. Soils generally acid, and often low in fertility. Sprinkler irrigation desired to supplement rainfall.

   1a. Transition Zone

   A difficult zone, where either cool-season or warm-season grasses may be grown; but summers are too hot for desired growth of cool-season grasses, and winters are too long and cold for desired growth of warm-season grasses. Supplemental irrigation must be used carefully to favor the type of grass desired. Soils are generally acid and low in native fertility.

2. Warm Humid Region

   Suited to warm-season grasses, such as bermudagrass and St. Augustinegrass. Soils generally strongly acid, and may be relatively infertile. Sprinkler irrigation needed to supplement rainfall.

3. Plains Regions

   3a. Northern Plains

   Suited to cool-season grasses, but artificial watering is essential for good lawns. Soils are not naturally acid, and may be well supplied with mineral nutrients.

   3b. Southern Plains

   Suited to warm-season grasses, and sprinkler irrigation is indispensable to strong turf to supplement uncertain rainfall. Soils are not naturally acid, but are less likely to be fertile than Northern Plains soils.

4. Arid and Semi-arid Regions

   4a. Cool Arid and Semi-arid Regions

   Suited to cool-season grasses, but sprinkler irrigation must be provided throughout the growing season. Soils are not acid, and are generally well supplied with mineral nutrients.

   4b. Warm Arid and Semi-arid Regions

   Suited to warm-season grasses, but sprinkler irrigation is imperative throughout the growing season. Soils are not acid, but are somewhat less fertile than regions to the North.

5. California Coast and Interior Valleys

   Suited to warm-season grasses, but sprinkler irrigation is imperative during the warm, dry, growing season. Soils generally are not acid, and have moderate amounts of mineral nutrients.

6. North Pacific Coastal Areas

   Suited to cool-season grasses. Rainfall generally adequate except in midsummer when sprinkler irrigation is required. Soils are usually moderately acid, and have fair-to-low mineral nutrient content.

---

*From Sprague, H.B. 1970. *Turf Management Handbook.* Danville, Ill.: The Interstate, p. 4–5.

COOL REGIONS

The turf grasses best suited to the cooler regions are the bluegrasses, bentgrasses, fescues, and ryegrasses. Each species has its own particular characteristics, which the manager should attempt to match to those of the site. The following discussion is limited to a few important species, since new varieties are constantly being developed that are genetically superior for specific turf uses. Thus, there are usually new types of grasses to use in solving the current site management problems. For example, there are turf grasses for golf courses that require less watering; this conserves the limited amount of water that is available for that function.

Bluegrasses *(Poa)*

Kentucky bluegrass *(Poa pratensis).* This type of bluegrass grows well during cool weather but becomes less vigorous during warm periods. It is not shade tolerant, and it requires a soil with medium to high fertility, nearly neutral pH, and good water-holding capacity. It is not hardy enough to sustain medium to heavy recreational use without deterioration.

Roughstalk bluegrass *(Poa trivialis).* This species has characteristics similar to those of Kentucky bluegrass but differs in its adaptability to moderate shade, particularly under warmer conditions.

TABLE 7-2 NATURAL SOIL CONDITIONS IN THE PRINCIPAL TURF GRASS REGIONS*

Region	Average Rainfall	Natural Vegetative Cover	Natural Soil Characteristics	
			Topsoil	Subsoil
	(in. yearly)		(general conditions)	(general conditions)
1. *Cool Humid Region*				
A. Cleared woodlands	30 to 50	Mostly forest	Thin, grayish-brown, acid	Yellowish or light gray, heavy textured, strongly acid
B. Corn Belt	30 to 40	Tall grasses	Dark brown, high in humus, slightly to strongly acid	Lighter brown, lower in humus, slightly to moderately acid
2. *Warm Humid Region*	30 to 50	Mostly forest	Thin, grayish to yellow, strongly acid	Strongly red or yellow, heavier textured, strongly acid
3. *Great Plains*				
A. Northern	12 to 30	Short to tall grasses	Brown to dark brown, humus stronger near surface, neutral to alkaline	Brown or lighter colored, little humus, lime nodules present
B. Southern	15 to 30	Short to tall grasses	Reddish brown (except Texas Black-lands), neutral to alkaline	Light reddish brown, heavier textured, lime nodules present
4. *Semi-arid and Arid*				
A. Cool, northern	3 to 12	Sparse grass and shrubs	Light grayish, alkaline	Light grayish, hardpan common, calcareous
B. Warm, southern	3 to 15	Sparse grass and shrubs	Light reddish brown, alkaline	Reddish brown, friable, highly calcareous
5. *California Coast and Interior Valleys*	10 to 20	Grass and shrubs	Dark reddish brown, neutral to alkaline	Reddish brown, some lime present
6. *North Pacific Coastal Area*	30 to 50	Mostly forest	Generally gray or grayish brown, thin, acid	Yellowish or light gray, heavier textured, strongly acid

Special soil conditions:
A. *Alluvial soils:* Found on the flood plains of rivers and lesser water courses. Formed from sediment deposited periodically by water. Often relatively rich in organic matter (if dark colored) and nutrients. Highly variable in texture.
B. *Excessively sandy soils:* Widely distributed. All sands are low in water-supplying power and subject to wind erosion. Generally low in nutrients, and easily leached by rainfall.
C. *Alkali and salty soils:* Occur locally throughout drier regions, wherever internal soil drainage is imperfect. Salty soils mostly occur on coastal plains, where sea or brackish water penetrates.

*From Sprague, H. B. 1970. *Turf Management Handbook.* Danville, Ill.: The Interstate, p. 15.

Canada bluegrass *(Poa compressa)*. Although not aesthetically pleasing because of its coarse appearance, this sod is drought-resistant and therefore is generally used where there are poor soil and moisture conditions.

Annual bluegrass *(Poa annua)*. This annual is shade tolerant. Owing to its adaptation and profuse seed development, it can germinate and survive on compacted soils as long as the soil surface is not dry. However, since it tends to die-back during the summer, it is usually used only as a temporary site stabilizer or in a mixture with other grasses.

Fescues *(Festuca)*

Chewing fescue *(Festuca rubra commutata)*. This improved strain of red fescue adds bright green color to the turf grass mixture and improves wearability of the mixture under recreational use. Also, it does well under a variety of environmental conditions.

Reed fescue *(Festuca elatior arundinacea)*. This tall grass is adaptable to a variety of soil moisture and temperature conditions. It is suitable for sites maintained in a rough rather than manicured condition. The cuttings should be no less than 4 inches in height and then only at infrequent intervals. Fertilizing is necessary to maintain high productivity.

Meadow fescue *(Festuca elatior)*. This fast growing yet persistent species can be valuable in a turf mixture used to establish new sod.

Bentgrasses *(Agrostis)*

Creeping bentgrass *(Agrostis palustris)*. This species can grow under a variety of environmental conditions except shade. It is suitable for golf greens and other closely manicured sites that have regular topdressings; therefore, it is not generally suitable for lawns.

Colonial bentgrass *(Agrostis tenuis)*. This makes a suitable lawn grass when mixed with bluegrass and fescue.

Velvet bentgrass *(Agrostis canina)*. This species has the important characteristics of shade tolerance, drought resistance, and ability to survive under varying temperature conditions.

Ryegrass *(Lolium)*

Perennial ryegrass *(Lolium perenne)*. Of the ryegrasses, this is probably the most widely used; in a seed mixture, it rapidly establishes a temporary sod until other grasses eventually establish the permanent sod.

WARM REGIONS

Most warm region grasses are established by sprigging; only common bermudagrass and carpetgrass may be established using seeds. Consequently, although a monoculture may tend to be less attractive and less disease resistant, a single species is generally used rather than a mixture of species. Since most of the warm region species will survive in any warm zone area, it is imperative to select the one that is most suited to the specific edaphic conditions and recreational use.

Common carpetgrass *(Axonopus affinis)*. This is a common turf grass that is restricted to the sandy, low fertility soils and high moisture conditions of the southeast coastal plains. Carpetgrass requires little care after initial establishment.

Common bermudagrass *(Cynodon dactylon)*. This species grows well throughout warmer regions where moisture is not limited. It spreads quickly and lives long on any site having fertile, reasonably well-drained soil. As stated by Sprague[10] there are four weaknesses of common bermudagrass: it is not shade tolerant; it will turn brown with the first light frost; it has a high fertility requirement and thus may be invaded by other species if not properly fertilized; and it is not very green. Although it has only a moderate tolerance to drought, it is probably the most drought resistant of all the warm region grasses.

Hybrid bermudagrass. Several bermudagrass hybrids have been developed that are superior to the common species as a turf grass. They are usually more vibrant in color, more vigorous in growth, with less fertility requirements, and more disease resistant.

St. Augustinegrass *(Stenotaphrum secundatum)*. This shade tolerant grass is adaptable to a variety of soil conditions. It requires frequent fertilization and mowing to maintain vigorous growth. If soils are acidic, liming should be done to raise the pH closer to neutral.

Centipedegrass *(Eremochloa ophiuroides)*. It has characteristics similar to those of carpetgrass. Centipedegrass responds well to fertilization, and can be used in regenerating worn-out sites.

SPECIAL USES FOR COOL REGION GRASSES

Reed fescue. This can be used for large sites that are not extensively managed (such as open-play areas) in the warm regions outside the coastal plain area.

Kentucky bluegrass. In warm regions, this species does well in the partially shaded areas of fertile sites. Cool region grasses that may be adaptable to specific warm region situations should be tested before any primary application is made. There are many other cool region grasses that could be discussed here, but we have omitted those tending to have limited distribution or application. For a more complete list, refer to the monographs under the Selected Readings.

DEVELOPMENT OF TURF

There are two ways of establishing turf—seeding and vegetative planting. The choice of method will depend on the grass selected for use.

SEEDING

Seeding is usually done in early spring or in early fall when temperature and moisture conditions are good. In cool regions, early fall seeding allows reasonable establishment before dormancy. In warm regions, it is usually done in early spring, but if moisture is not limited, it can be done at any time.

Seed mixtures are usually planted in the cooler regions. The exact seed mixture depends on the site conditions and the specific recreational use, but it usually includes perennial ryegrass, which will quickly occupy the site until the permanent grasses establish a sod.

Seed quality is important and is therefore ensured through federal and state laws. Species, purity, and percentage of germination must be shown on the label along with percentage of weed seeds.

After the seed has been obtained, the seedbed must be prepared before planting begins. It is less expensive to install structures such as drain tiles or water bars at this time than it would be after planting. If major reshaping is to be done to the landscape prior to planting, the topsoil should first be carefully removed. It can then be replaced after the reshaping operation. Liming, fertilizing, and any adding of organic matter to improve soil conditions should also take place prior to planting. These additives are then rotatilled into the soil to a depth of about 6 inches. The organic matter not only can improve soil fertility but also can increase its water-holding capacity—for example, if sandy soils are a problem, clay can be added to improve water-holding capacity and the cation exchange capacity. Since lime and fertilizer are translocated downward, not laterally, the surface application of these materials should be uniform prior to rotatilling.

Seeding is done immediately after seedbed preparation. Seeding rates, expressed in pounds per acre or pounds per 1000 square feet, are based on species mixture, purity, and per cent germination. The seeds are broadcast evenly over the surface. The seeding technique recommended by Sprague[10] is to divide the seeds into two equal portions. One-half is broadcast in one direction; the other half is broadcast in a line perpendicular to the first half. The seeds are lightly raked into the seedbed, and the surface is then rolled. Finally, the seedbed is lightly but evenly mulched with straw.

VEGETATIVE PLANTINGS

Vegetative plantings can be done by sprigging, spot sodding, or complete sodding. All these methods require the same ground preparation as seeding. Each has a perferred use, depending on the circumstances, costs, and management objectives.

Complete sodding has often been overlooked because of a supposedly high cost of implementation. We might take a closer look at this method. Recent cost analyses by a local park district indicated that on an area that is 2.5 acres or less, complete sodding is cheaper than other methods.* This study took into account the following local circumstances at high altitudes: high probability of at least partial failure of seeding; man-hours spent in maintaining constant attention prior to sod establishment; and the short growing season.

Site stabilization on steeper slopes and the need to harden heavy-use portions of sites may dictate that complete sodding be done. Often management concerns will dictate the primary choice, if there are sufficient monies to support the program.

In the sprigging method, the grass plant is separated into sprigs or runners (pieces of stolons) that are planted to generate new sod. The sprigs are spread evenly over the area by means of a preplanned grid system; they are then pushed into the soil until it approximately reaches the root collar. A notched dibble can be used to push the sprigs into the soil. This minimizes damage to the sprig yet still maintains planting efficiency. Finally, soil is pressed down firmly with the heel of the boot.

Vegetative planting can also be accomplished by the spot sodding method, which is the planting of small pieces of sod at regular intervals over the entire

---

*Personal communication with Mr. Ralph Holen, Laramie Parks and Recreation Department, Laramie, Wyoming.

area. The sod is lifted from the nursery and cut into 3- to 4-inch squares, which are planted 6 to 12 inches apart. A hole is made for each piece of sod, which is then planted about one-half inch below surface level and is secured by stamping down with the shoe. As the plant takes hold, it will send out runners. Usually, this method and sprigging take a considerable time to grow into a dense sod.

Watering and possibly mowing must be done carefully in order to enhance turf growth and establishment, after which, regular turf management should be practiced.

MANAGEMENT OF TURF

Regular maintenance is essential for most grasses and, particularly, for those located in an area of active recreational use. We will be discussing two important aspects of turf maintenance: soil chemical treatments and cultural treatments of the sod.

SOIL CHEMICAL TREATMENTS

Soil acidity problems generally occur in areas where there is excessive precipitation or artificial watering. Although some grasses may survive under these conditions, all grasses will grow better at a more neutral pH. One possible treatment to improve soil fertility is *liming*. The exact liming schedule should be determined by soil analysis. For general recommendations on liming, consulting a person who is knowledgeable about local conditions (such as the County Agent or Soil Conservationist) may suffice. In high precipitation areas, 1 to 2 tons of crushed limestone per acre should be sufficient to promote good sod development. However, a soil analysis made at a competent laboratory is the most accurate guideline, since the relative acidity of soil can also vary according to texture.

After development of the sod, one should continue the liming program periodically to maintain a nearly neutral pH; this will maximize available plant nutrients. High soil acidity reduces the decay of dead roots, thus reducing humus breakdown. This interferes with normal root development and with percolation of water into the soil. Furthermore, highly acidic soils usually contain large amounts of certain elements; soluble aluminum and manganese, which are toxic in large quantities, and unusable forms of nitrogen. This is a result of acid-forming fertilizers, which cause the replacement and leaching of calcium and magnesium from the upper soil layer. It can be corrected by the application of crushed limestone.

Fertilizing is the other chemical treatment for improving soil fertility; however, it may create acidic soil conditions that must be corrected with lime if the added nutrients are to be available for plant use. This should be done only after a complete soil analysis has been made.

Fertilizers are usually labeled according to the percentage by weight of available nitrogen (N_2), phosphate (P_2O_5), and potash (K_2O). These three primary nutrients are necessary for vigorous plant growth. Thus, 100 pounds of a 10-5-5 fertilizer has 10 pounds of usable nitrogen, 5 pounds of phosphate, and 5 pounds of potash. As a general rule, an application of 25 to 30 pounds of a

10-5-5 fertilizer per 1000 square feet of area is advisable for seedbed preparation. About two-thirds of the fertilizer is mixed throughout the soil, and the remaining one-third is mixed into the upper inch. During the establishment of sod, one should also check the color of the young plants; for example, if the young leaves are pale green, additional nitrogen may be necessary.

The fertilizing of established sod should be done with a 10-5-5 fertilizer, which is applied at a rate of 15 pounds per 100 feet at least twice a year.[10] A light watering will aid in moving the fertilizer into the top inch of the soil.

In the cool regions, the fertilizer applications should be done in the spring and fall. The fall applications should be done to accelerate the spring growth of the sod, particularly if the growing season is short. In the warmer regions, the applications are normally made in the spring and midsummer because of the lengthy growing season.

CULTURAL TREATMENTS OF THE SOD

The manager should be familiar with the following cultural treatments: cleaning, topdressing, aeration, mowing, watering, scarifying, and weeding.

Cleaning. This is the removal of tree leaves to maximize the amount of light reaching the ground cover. Cleaning promotes healthy growth of the sod from spring through the early fall. It also reduces undesirable surface moisture and heating; these can be detrimental to grass blades and can also promote the conditions for disease of the grass.

Topdressing. Topdressing—i.e., spreading a thin layer (one-fourth inch or so) of fertile topsoil over the sod and lightly working it in—can improve soil conditions on poor sites. It can also be used to level minor rough spots in the sod. A specific application of topdressing is in the maintenance of golf greens. This is done by first scarifying the area to remove matted bentgrass, and then top-dressing it to improve the fertility of the site and the vigor of the grass.

Scarifying. This is the mechanical disturbance of the sod cover and adjacent soils that is achieved by slicing into them. The slicing removes dead grass accumulation and may, with the right equipment, penetrate into deeper soil depth to improve water percolation into the soil.

Aeration. This is the mechanical removal of sod-soil cores to improve soil aeration, to increase percolation and penetration of fertilizers, and to reduce root competition (Fig. 7–4). Some of these additional benefits could be obtained through other treatments; but improved soil aeration can be only obtained by the removal of small cores. Slicing or similar scarifying techniques that penetrate the sod do not remove any soil or sod. Consequently, the point of penetration is closed quickly.

Mowing. This procedure can cause great damage to the mature grasses if not done properly. Where recreation use is anticipated or adverse environmental conditions already exist (such as shading), the grass should be mowed at greater heights than normal, up to 2 inches, and possibly at less frequent intervals. The longer grass has greater photosynthetic area and consequently would be more hardy. The "rougher" appearance may be a more desirable outcome than dead spots on the turf. Remember that the objective is to stimulate growth; if mowing is done to too short a height or too frequently, the result may weaken rather than improve the vigor of the grass. However, in recreation sites, there are other considerations, such as aesthetics and playing conditions (Fig. 7–5).

Watering. This is done to supplement the natural water regimen. In high moisture areas, this may be necessary only during severe droughts. In dry

Figure 7–4 Aeration of the soil is an important cultural treatment. (Photo by Jack D. Butler, Colorado State University.)

Figure 7–5 Gangmower used for large mowing operations. (Photo by Jack D. Butler, Colorado State University.)

areas, watering and the irrigation systems can be very extensive. Artificial watering to maintain turf growth should be done for extended periods of time at frequent intervals to get good penetration. Otherwise, frequent intervals of light watering may encourage weeds to germinate and grow in the sod.

Weeding. Weeding is important if we are to maintain a dense sod. This means we should do all the chemical and cultural treatments properly to foster good sod vigor after establishment. Any treatment not done properly can promote the growth of weeds, which should be checked. Once these weeds have been established, selective herbicides are needed to remove them. The use of the herbicides will depend on local conditions and should be only undertaken by someone who is knowledgeable about the chemicals and their proper use.

If there has been an apparent lack of proper turf maintenance, renovation of the sod may become necessary. The manager must assess the problem and realign his maintenance program to improve the condition of the turf. He may be faced with the decision either to revamp the program or start over with new turf! This renovation should be carefully integrated with visitor dispersal programs to protect the site (see Chapter 11).

SEASONAL MANAGEMENT SCHEDULES

Some authors have offered specific schedules which they feel must be adhered to in order to properly maintain the turf. I would suggest that there is sufficient variation in the recreational use, environmental conditions, and species composition that the local manager should develop his own seasonal schedule. This may mean separate schedules for each park or even for portions of a specific park where there are different management programs.

This chapter only gives an overview of turf management and the main variables and management techniques used by the outdoor recreation manager. More detailed information can be found in additional reading or obtained through local agencies, such as the Agricultural Extension Service, the Soil Conservation Service, and other specifically related state organizations.

SELECTED READINGS

1. Augustine, M. F. 1966. "Vegetation to Stabilize Critical Areas in Building," *Soil Conservation* 32 (4): 78.
2. Barkley, D. B., R. R. Blaser, and R. E. Schmidt. 1965. "Effect of Mulches on Microclimate and Turf Establishment," *Agronomy Journal* 57: 189.
3. Blaser, R. E. 1963. "Principles of Making Turf Mixtures for Roadside Seeding," *Highway Research Records, No. 23*. National Research Council. p. 79.
4. Curry, R. J., L. E. Foote, O. N. Andrews, Jr., and J. A. Jackobs. 1964. "Lime and Fertilizer Requirements as Related to Turf Establishment along the Roadside," *Highway Research Records, No. 53*. National Research Council. p. 26.
5. Hanson, A. A. 1965. *Grass Varieties in the United States*. Agricultural Handbook No. 170. Agricultural Research Service, U. S. Department of Agriculture.
6. Hanson, A. A., and F. V. Juska (eds.). 1969. *Turfgrass Science*. Agronomy No. 14. Madison, Wisc.: American Society of Agronomy, Inc.
7. Hood, R. 1964. "Turfgrass Management Stretches Dollars," *Ohio Public Works* 95 (7):76.
8. Musser, H. Burton. 1962. *Turf Management*. U.S. Gold Association.
9. Proceedings of Scotts Turfgrass Research Conferences, 1970–75. Vols. 1–6.
10. Sprague, H. B. 1970. *Turf Management Handbook*. Danville, Ill.: The Interstate.
11. Triplett, G. B., Jr., and R. R. Davis. 1966. "Spot Treatment for Perennial Grass Weeds," *Research Summary*, Ohio Argriculture Research and Development Center, p. 9.
12. Venegris, J. 1973. *Lawns: Basic Factors, Construction and Maintenance of Fine Turf Areas*. Indianapolis: Thomson Publications.

CHAPTER 8

Fire History and Management

This chapter will focus on the historical role of fire and the primary decisions that a resource manager must make concerning fire, in order to maintain the natural ecosystem. The role of fire will certainly depend upon the recreation manager's objectives for the particular area. In this respect, it is not as important to determine whether a fire is good or bad as it is to examine the effects of fire in regard to management objectives.

If the objective is to be the absolute protection of high-value timber, crops, or recreational development, then any fire may be destructive—to the point of being potentially devastating. Under these circumstances, all wildfires would immediately be suppressed. On the other hand, the manager's objective may be to maintain fire as a primary natural force—to be used in shaping the ecosystem.

Discussion of the biological, physical, and chemical aspects of fire will be general. In this chapter, sufficient detail is given to indicate the need for specific management strategies concerning fire. The emphasis will be on the planning, timing, and implementation of these strategies.

HISTORY OF FIRE MANAGEMENT

A knowledge of the historical role of fire in a given situation is important if we are to properly use fire in the management of natural areas. Fire has always been a primary force in shaping vegetation patterns. This has subsequently affected the total ecosystem, including flora, fauna, soil, and water. During early times, fires were caused by weather cycles, particularly in places where natural fuels had built up during the intervening years between fires. If not intense enough to kill, these fires usually caused some reshaping of vegetation structure, opening it to insect and disease attacks. A fire could completely destroy a stand of trees or could create a die-back that resulted in a large fuel buildup, leading to an even more destructive wildfire (Fig. 8–1).*

---

*Wildfires are started naturally and allowed to burn a normal course without outside interference.

Figure 8–1 A natural wildfire above Jackson Lake, Grand Teton National Park. (Photo by the National Park Service.)

Indians used fire as part of their culture. They may have started fires that destroyed forests and plains, but most of these were done accidentally. Fire was typically used for cooking, heating, and signaling, and occasionally, for driving game or waging war against an enemy tribe. The Indians' use of fire, plus the accidental starting of wildfires (usually from campfires), did have an effect on the ecology; however, as stated by Brown and Davis:

> . . . firsthand testimony of old Indians of Western tribes indicates that they had great fear of conflagrations and a high respect for fire's destructiveness. . . . It is at least a fair assumption that no habitual or systematic burning was carried out by the Indians.[4]

During the nineteenth century, white men began to invade and settle the Midwest, the Upper Plains, the Northern Rockies, and the West Coast. The use of fire changed drastically—abuse would be a more correct term. The forest and prairie vegetation became an obstacle to westward expansion and settlement. The native vegetation had to be cleared for farming and community development, and later for industrial development. The easiest and cheapest means of clearing a forest was to start a fire and allow it to burn until a change in weather would extinguish it. Also, settler-caused fires were thought to be an encouraging sign of progress. People felt that the forest was inexhaustible and that agriculture was part of a "manifest destiny." Fires were regarded with indifference unless they threatened personal property or the accessible "firewood" stands.

In the late nineteenth century, the size, intensity, and frequency of fires greatly increased with the rise of settlements and logging. Many of the great fires in American history occurred during this time.

The placing of land in public ownership and the creation of agencies to administer the lands and resources caused a change in the official policy on forest fires. Experts agreed that forest fires destroyed valuable timber and should therefore be eliminated. Action was initiated by many states and also received presidential support.

> Even so, only the strong emotional zeal for conservation awakened by Pinchot and others and given vigorous implementation by Theodore Roosevelt as President made it possible to reverse the trend and initiate a positive policy of protection of forest resources.[4]

As the benefits of increased timber production were realized, a basic fire protection philosophy became accepted as the proper means for maximizing timber production and for developing other resource values, including recreation. This policy continues today. Also, since fires are generally considered destructive, the policy has been to immediately suppress them. The beginning programs were primarily educational for the purpose of reducing the number of fires. Man used hand tools in limited suppression programs. Later, power equipment, even heavy vehicle equipment, was used to suppress all fires, regardless of origin or potential effects. There was no other objective for the use of fire other than immediate elimination. Thus, for more than three-quarters of a century, the policy on forest fires excluded fire as a natural force in the formation of ecosystems. By eliminating one of the primary forces of change, we created unnatural conditions in the wildlands of the United States. However, we felt this to be necessary in the overall management of land and valuable resources, even in so-called natural areas.

Public educational programs were instituted in the 1940's to promote a fire prevention policy. Today, we are still feeling the effects of such concerted antifire campaigns as "Smokey the Bear." The public perceived only the need to prevent and suppress fires. In 1963, a select committee headed by A. Starker Leopold reviewed the ecosystems management programs of the National Parks and concluded that the elimination of fire had drastically altered the natural park ecosystem.[19] The dynamic succession of vegetation had been disrupted. Fire climax communities were eliminated, and the vegetation succession was allowed to reach a climax. There was little recycling of nutrients, dynamic recycling of successional stages, and maintenance of diverse age/species structure. We were attempting to stabilize the natural structure through fire prevention and suppression rather than allowing the normal dynamics to take place. The committees primary recommendation was to return the ecosystem to "prewhiteman" conditions.

This does not mean that a fire prevention policy is absolutely wrong, but it is not valid in every situation, particularly in natural areas.

Some professionals do recognize the positive role of fire in the natural ecosystem but also find that higher administrations and the public do not accept this philosophy. Thus, we are reluctant to take a forward look in our approach toward the role of fire. Although we recognize this need, we have been ineffective so far in implementing fire management plans in the managing of natural areas. At the other extreme, some overzealous managers have attempted to implement a policy of fire management in the ecosystem without any knowledge of the historical role of fire in that particular ecosystem. This may be just as devastating as no fire management in places where fire has historically played only a very minor role.

Over the past three-quarters of a century, fire prevention and suppression have reduced the diversity of life forms, particularly in the wilderness where, theoretically, we have been dedicated to maintaining the diversity and dynam-

Figure 8–2   Uniform canopy, or lack of age/species diversity.

ics of the natural ecosystem (Fig. 8–2). Technological advancements have now made it easier to reach isolated fires and suppress them. Several years ago, from my campsite in the Bob Marshall Wilderness, I witnessed a fire suppression operation on Cardinal Mountain. Two large helicopters of equipment and men were flown in. Small, motorized equipment was used to secure a fire line. The crew mopped up inside the line and the fire was quickly suppressed.

Ironically, the fire, which had been burning for two days, covered less than 50 acres. Even if allowed to burn, the fire would probably have covered only 100 to 150 acres before it reached natural boundaries, which would have contained it. A walk through the burned area a few days after the suppression operation revealed that the deterioration of the site by men and equipment far surpassed the damage by fire—and all this was done in an area "dedicated to the maintenance of the natural ecosystem."

Can we afford that type of fire management? Do our management strategies concerning fire fit the objectives for the area? Do we really understand the long term effects of our management policies? Should we attempt to zone for fire management based on specific objectives? How do we properly "reintroduce" fire into the ecosystem? These questions, and perhaps others, are the ones to which we should be seeking responses if we are to maintain fire as a primary force in the shaping of our natural ecosystems.

THE EFFECTS OF FIRE

This section will focus on the effects of fire so that we may have a better understanding of the natural role. Predicting the behavior of wildfires is difficult because of the tremendous variation in the conditions under which they can take place. Fire behavior on the same site may differ from day to day because of changing environmental conditions. Consequently, even the fire researcher has difficulty in evaluating field data because many of the significant factors do not remain constant.

> Fires respond to fuels, weather, and topography, with so many variables operating that it is nearly impossible to exactly duplicate fires in outdoor test plots, even where measured samples give assurance of reasonably uniform fuels and weather conditions and topography are carefully selected.[4]

Nevertheless, the manager should understand the potential effects of fire, if he is to manage that fire.

EFFECTS ON OVERSTORY VEGETATION

The effects of fire on overstory vegetation are significant to our discussion because the overstory tends to have a pronounced influence on the microclimate. In addition, we will emphasize the relative resistance of certain species to fires of less than lethal temperatures (lethal fires cause a *complete* loss of vegetation and a change in microclimate). Fires that cause extensive damage through "partial kill" are more important to the manager because they are more common than lethal fires, and they cause the typical ecological changes associated with wildfires.

Susceptibility to Fire Damage

1. Initial temperature of the vegetation. Foliage temperatures of over 100°F may occur naturally, and 70 to 80°F is common. The higher the initial temperature, the less additional heat is necessary to bring about lethal temperatures and the more quickly they can develop. This point is of importance in prescribed use of fire, since initial temperatures can be controlled by selecting the time of burning.

2. The size of the critical tree portion exposed and its morphology. Young trees, leaves, and small branches are easily killed because they can quickly be heated to a lethal temperature. Buds are particularly important, and their resistance to heat damage is directly related to size.

3. The thickness and character of the bark. Of all the protective mechanisms of the tree, the bark is the most important. This is especially true near the ground surface where most fires occur. Bark is an excellent insulating material; "bark structure, in general, is a natural design for insulation board." The insulating capacity of the bark layer depends on its structure, composition, density, moisture content, and thickness. It is known that these things vary widely by species, growth habitat, and possibly by seasons to some degree, but complete information is not available.

4. Branching and growth habit. Other things being equal, trees that self-prune readily and develop high and open crowns are more successful in escaping fire damage because they are less susceptible to crown fires and they accumulate less litter close to the stem.

5. Rooting habit. Roots have thin cortical covering and, if near the surface, are easily damaged by fire. Shallow-rooted species, like the spruces and most of the true firs, are frequently damaged by ground fires through root injury, even though the stem and crown are not affected.

6. Organic material covering the mineral soil. The depth and character of the organic mantle on the ground may largely control damage by surface fires to the roots, especially of the more shallow-rooted trees. If the mantle is fairly thick and the lower part does not burn, its high insulating ability will

protect roots from damage. If, however, the organic mantle burns, it becomes a source of heat rather than of protection, and damaging soil temperatures are likely to result.

7. Flammability of foliage. Evergreens as a group, and conifers especially, are more flammable than deciduous hardwoods. There are significant differences between conifer species, though these are not of critical importance in damage susceptibility. There are wider differences within hardwoods, particularly as between deciduous and evergreen species. The differences are least in times of severe drought, and at such times some species of both groups, mostly occurring in scrub or brush types, will burn furiously. In general, however, green hardwood foliage will not carry a forest fire except when abnormally dry.

8. Stand habit. Because of their greater liability to crown fires, coniferous trees that grow in dense stands or are commonly associated with abundant subordinate vegetation are more subject to fire damage than those occurring in sparsely canopied open stands with scanty subordinate ground cover. Canopy density is of little importance in hardwoods because the foliage is relatively nonflammable. Damage is controlled mostly by the flammability of subordinate vegetation and surface fuels. The volume and vertical distribution of available fuels, affecting crown-fire incidence, and the duration and intensity of the fire are closely related to stand habit.

9. Season and growth cycle. The seasonal stage of growth affects net damage in three ways. First, it greatly affects the total moisture content of the crown, which in turn affects its flammability. Second, succulent growth is much more susceptible to fire damage. So growing tips and cambium are more easily damaged during the active growing stage than during the dormant state. Third, the ability of the tree to recover is affected by the food reserves in the roots, which fluctuate with the season. Fortunately, the rapid growing stage, when food reserves are low, is also the period of lowest susceptibility to crown fires.*

Natural Fire Resistance. The relative resistance of tree species is determined by basal bark thickness of mature trees, character of the individual tree crown and of the forest stand, and rooting pattern (Tables 8–1 and 8–2). Typically, the less intense fires are ground fires that may cause damage to the lower bole. Mature trees, which have thick bark on the lower bole, are more resistant to fire injury than younger trees, which have thinner bark and more succulent tissue.

The character of the individual tree crown is important since the low, dense crowns are more susceptible to crown fires than the higher, less dense ones. Similarly, stands of trees that grow in a very dense pattern, such as spruce or fir, are more prone to devastating crown fires than ones that grow in open stands, such as Ponderosa pine. Rooting pattern (deep versus shallow) will obviously determine the susceptibility of the roots to injury.

Physical Damage. A fire that caused partial damage to an area will usually leave, on the standing trees, some basal injury that heals over, forming a scar (Fig. 8–3). Since this indicates previous fire damage, one can determine the history of fire in the existing stand (both frequency and intensity) from the older, living trees. These scars also make the tree more susceptible to insect and disease attacks because of the increased ease of entry and the decreased vigor of the tree.

Effects on Microclimate. The microclimate is the sum of local site factors that create a unique climate for that specific site and distinguish it from ad-

---

*From Brown, A. A. and K. P. Davis. 1973. *Forest Fire: Control & Use.* (2nd ed.) New York: McGraw Hill Co. p. 48.

TABLE 8-1 RELATIVE FIRE RESISTANCE OF SELECTED CONIFERS OF THE WESTERN UNITED STATES (AFTER STARKER (1934) AND FLINT (1925))*

Species	Basal Bark Thickness of Mature Trees	Character of Tree Crown	Character of Stands	Rooting Habit	Associated Lichen Growth
Extremely resistant (old trees only):					
Redwood (*Sequoia sempervirens*)	Extremely thick	High and moderately open	Dense	Deep	Not a factor
Western larch (*Larix occidentalis*)	Very thick	High and very open	Moderately open	Deep	Medium
Highly resistant:					
Ponderosa pine (*Pinus ponderosa*)	Very thick	Moderately high and open	Open	Deep	Light
Douglas-fir (*Pseudotsuga menziesii*)	Very thick	Moderately high and dense	Dense	Deep	Heavy
Moderately resistant:					
White and grand fir (*Abies concolor* and *grandis*)	Thick	Low and dense	Dense	Moderately shallow	Heavy
White pine and sugar pine (*Pinus monticola* and *lambertiana*)	Medium	Moderately high and dense	Dense	Medium	Medium
Lodgepole pine (*Pinus contorta*)	Very thin	Moderately high and open	Open	Deep	Medium
Low resistance:					
Western red cedar (*Thuja plicata*)	Thin	Low and dense	Dense	Shallow	Moderate to heavy
Western hemlock (*Tsuga heterophylla*)	Medium	Low and dense	Dense	Shallow	Heavy
Engelmann spruce (*Picea engelmannii*)	Thin	Low and dense	Dense	Shallow	Heavy
Sitka spruce (*Picea sitchensis*)	Thin	Moderately high and dense	Dense	Shallow	Heavy
Very low resistance:					
Alpine fir (*Abies lasiocarpa*)	Very thin	Very low and dense	Dense	Shallow	Heavy

*From Brown, A. A. and K. P. Davis. 1973. *Forest Fire: Control and Use.* New York: McGraw-Hill Book Company, pp. 52–53.

TABLE 8–2 RELATIVE FIRE RESISTANCE OF SELECTED TREE SPECIES OF THE EASTERN UNITED STATES (AFTER STARKER (1934) AND OTHERS)*

Species and Resistance Group	Basal Bark Thickness of Mature Trees	Character of Tree Crown**	Character of Stands	Rooting Habit
Highly resistant:				
Longleaf pine (*Pinus palustris*)	Thick	High and open	Open	Very deep
Resistant:				
Pitch pine (*Pinus rigida*)	Medium	Moderately high and open	Moderately open	Medium deep
Pond pine (*Pinus serotina*)	Medium	Moderately high and open	Moderately open	Medium
Red pine (*Pinus resinosa*)	Medium	Moderately high and dense	Moderately open	Deep
Slash pine (*Pinus elliottii*)	Medium	Moderately high and open	Moderately open	Medium deep
Shortleaf pine (*Pinus echinata*)	Medium	Moderately high and open	Moderately open	Medium deep
Loblolly pine (*Pinus taeda*)	Medium	Medium height and density	Moderately dense	Medium
Moderately resistant:				
Chestnut oak (*Quercus montana*)	Thick		Moderately dense	Medium
Yellow poplar (*Liriodendron tulipifera*)	Medium		Moderately dense	Medium
Black and post oak (*Quercus velutina, stellata*)	Medium		Moderately open	Medium
Eastern white pine (*Pinus strobus*)	Medium	Medium height and density	Medium dense	Medium
Jack pine (*Pinus banksiana*)	Medium	Medium height and density	Moderately open	Medium
Of intermediate resistance:				
Red oak (*Quercus rubra*)	Medium		Medium	Medium
Hickory (*Carya* spp.)	Medium		Moderately dense	Medium
Sweetgum (*Liquidambar styraciflua*)	Moderately thin		Moderately dense	Medium
White oak (*Quercus alba*)	Moderately thin		Moderately dense	Medium
Of low resistance:				
Sugar maple (*Acer saccharum*)	Moderately thin		Dense	Medium
Scarlet oak (*Quercus coccinea*)			Dense	Medium
Yellow birch (*Betula lutea*)	Moderately thin		Dense	Medium
Black cherry (*Prunus serotina*)	Moderately thin		Dense	Medium
Spruces (*Picea* spp.)	Thin	Low and dense	Dense	Shallow
Aspens (*Populus tremuloides* and *grandidentata*)	Thin	High and open	Medium	Medium
Cedars (*Thuja* and *Juniperus* spp.)	Thin	Medium height and density	Dense	Shallow
Firs (*Abies* spp.)	Very thin	Low and dense	Dense	Shallow

*From Brown, A. A. and K. P. Davis, 1973. *Forest Fire: Control and Use.* New York: McGraw-Hill Book Company.
**Not considered significant for hardwoods since fires seldom burn in crowns.

Figure 8–3 Butt scars caused by ground fires.

callous tissue formed

old fire scar

jacent sites by factors such as soil, water, vegetation, and solar radiation. These interact to produce the local air temperatures, relative humidity, soil moisture regimen, and air movement. Probably the greatest single factor in maintaining the existing microclimate is the overstory vegetation. If it is destroyed, temperatures rise, moisture is lost, humidity decreases, and air movement increases, accelerating the drying effect. The degree of change in microclimate will determine the plant succession on the site. If the change is too drastic, plant succession will be extremely slow, with potentially dramatic effects on soil, air, and water conditions.[4] Other effects may be temporary loss of wildlife and bird habitat, change in water flow and chemistry of nearby streams, and so forth. The microclimate is a complex and dynamic system that can affect large areas outside the fire's perimeter. This requires monitoring the effects of a fire on all aspects of the microclimate as well as on the surrounding influence areas.

Effects on Soil. The effects of fire on soil include loss of unincorporated organic material, change in physical conditions through erosion and possibly through aggregation of soil particles, change in soil chemistry, and loss of soil organisms by heating. Unincorporated organic material forms a layer over the mineral soil and, as it breaks down, becomes soil nutrients. It protects the soil from heating and allows water infiltration without compaction of the soil surface.

The physical conditions of the soil are changed by compaction and erosion of the exposed mineral soil. The compaction of the heavier soils is due to the force of raindrops hitting the soil. Fire seals the surface of the soil, causing runoff and subsequent erosion, or it bakes the soil particles to form larger aggregates, reducing pore space, aeration, and nutrient exchange. Fire also produces charcoal, which is black, durable, and high in heat-absorptive capacity.[4] This creates higher-than-normal surface-soil temperatures that may have a lethal effect on the establishment of natural reproduction of ground cover. Some increased surface temperature will be caused by the loss of the protective overstory vegetation.

Fire produces chemical changes in the soil through combustion of organic material. The immediate effect of this process is the release of mineral elements into the soil, increasing available plant nutrients. The surge of nutrients may stimulate revegetation of the site unless the soil is very sandy — in which case, the nutrients would be completely leached out of the soil, away from the root zone. In heavier soils, the increased nutrient supply can last several years.[4] The leaching effect may affect the total ecosystem. For example, preliminary research data by Michael Parker[28] indicate that fire and subsequent leaching play an important role in the maintenance of the natural productivity of lakes.

After a fire, the pH of the soil becomes more basic in the primary root zone area. This decrease in acidity may cause an increase in nitrification by the immediate invasion of light-seeded, nitrogen-fixing organisms that are more adaptable to the higher pH levels. Even small changes in pH can cause significant changes in the growth of vegetation.[33]

The significant biological effects of a fire are often equated only with the changes occurring in the flora and fauna. Other, less apparent biological effects may occur in the soil. Fires that destroy the protective humus layer often reduce the number of beneficial soil organisms. In non-lethal fires, either the increased soil temperatures or a change in the soil chemistry may stimulate the productivity of soil organisms.[4]

A BASIC APPROACH TO FIRE MANAGEMENT

There are several steps that the manager must follow in sequence in order to develop a management plan that will maintain fire as a primary natural force shaping the ecosystem:

Reconstruction of fire history. The first and most important step is to reconstruct a fire history, and in the process, indicate successional trends in the primary vegetation types. It is not sufficient to reconstruct a fire history without a knowledge of the general effects on the ecology as measured by changes in vegetation.[38] A contemporary fire history may also be misleading because of modern man's intervention in the natural role of fire. The manager must first correlate this history to the cyclical history of fire since the last glacial period.[38]

Inventory of existing conditions. An inventory of existing soil and vegetative conditions is necessary in order to determine the effects that modern man has had on ecological succession. This is done by comparing present conditions to those derived from extrapolating the fire history from the last glacial period to the present era. These theoretical conditions should not include the effects of modern man, whose primary ecological effects have been caused by fire prevention and suppression.

An inventory of existing conditions can also be used as baseline data for determining changes that may be brought about by future fires, either naturally or artificially introduced.

Establishment of policy. After the above comparison is made, a policy must be established on the desirability of moving the existing situation toward the conditions represented by the theoretical model. This is commonly called the "burn or no burn" decision. The accepted policy is that all natural fires, especially those caused by lightning, are allowed to burn and all man-made fires are suppressed. This places a great emphasis on prevention programs to reduce the number of man-made fires. The public should be made aware of the difference between man-made and natural fires and the policies associated with each of these.

Additional policy on "burn or no burn" decisions must be made if there are conflicts of goals. When these arise, a goal-priority system must be established to determine which decision will take priority. In areas where priorities such as intensive developments (housing, recreation sites, and so forth) exist, the policy must be *no burn.* However, if the decision is *to burn,* then another decision must be made on which method to use—to let natural fires burn or to "control burn" by introducing fires artificially in order to achieve the same objectives. These are all priority decisions that must be made before implementing any natural fire management plan. If the policies are not established, the manager will be under pressure from the public, other agencies, or higher headquarters when a major fire erupts. He may choose a less desirable alternative, or he may switch to such a course of action while caught up in the emotion of managing a particular fire.

Coordination with other agencies. Because of legal and tactical considerations, coordination is essential for the management of fire. The state, through one of its agencies, may have a legal role or at least a role with statewide, coordinating responsibilities. The agency should coordinate strategies with adjacent agencies in order to minimize conflict in policy and maximize efficiency in implementation of the policy.

Interpretation of the natural role of fire. This is also essential to the success of any fire management plan. The public must understand the natural role of fire, the objectives for the natural area, and the means to achieve these objectives. Interpretation is the best practical approach to informing and educating the public about the management of fire in a natural area. This does not necessarily mean everyone will accept the plan, but it should offer better criteria for judging the policy and its implementation.

Reconstruct Fire History. Reconstruction of fire history utilizes fire dating, historic records, and interviews. Fire dating is done by examining fire scars on living vegetation or by carbon dating. Standing trees can be a living testimony of a natural catastrophe, such as a wildfire. Fire scars on living trees can be dated by counting tree rings (Fig. 8–4). However, using fire scars to date fire history has its limitations. Logging, mining, and other biologically disruptive land uses have eliminated most of the older, virgin trees that could have given the manager a chronological fire record over several hundred years. Without these older trees, it would be difficult to reconstruct the natural cycle of fire, since recent fire history has been directly affected by fire suppression. Except for isolated tracts of old timber, only wilderness areas and dedicated natural areas are good chronographs of fire history. However, even these areas have been included under the universal policy of modern fire suppression. Also, destructive fires may have eliminated the older trees for fire dating. This means the manager may have to search harder for the remaining clusters of trees that escaped the destructive fires. Even then, the geographic boundaries

Figure 8–4   Fire-dating using old fire scars. (From Heinselman, M. L. 1969. "Diary of the Canoe Country's Landscape," *Naturalist* 20(1):13.)

of the individual fires may be difficult to determine if only clusters of older trees are left instead of the original, expansive forests.

The history of fire for a particular area should be limited to geographic boundaries so that the fire management plan can focus on when and where fire has been a major force in the ecology of the particular area. Also, the procedure for reintroducing a fire artificially should be based on the specific geographic boundaries and cycle of the previous fire history.

Too often, a more modern policy that reintroduces fire is universally applied without concern to geographic boundaries or to fire cycles within those boundaries. (Interestingly, researchers are finding many areas in which fire has played only an insignificant ecological role.)

Carbon dating can also help in compiling a fire history, and if large enough pieces of charcoal are located, the species involved in the fire can be determined. A more sophisticated technique is to first make a pollen analysis of lake sediments in order to determine the dynamic successional changes and to then date each layer of sediment, using carbon dating. This type of research is still relatively new, but it offers an interesting approach to the reconstruction of fire history. As stated by Cushing:

> In this core, then, is a year-by-year record of events in and around the lake—much like the record of tree rings in a stump, but reaching back much farther in time. When we prepare and examine a layer with the microscope, we can identify and count the pollen grains that blew into the lake during that year's accumulation of mud. With enough patience, we might hope to find year-to-year variations in the amount and kinds of pollen that could tell us something about the annual fluctuations in climate far in the past. Of greater interest at present, however, is the possibility of tracing the effects of forest fires through several generations of trees.

Our study is aided by the presence of fragments of charcoal in the layers. These microscopic bits of charred wood and leaves must have been blown and washed into the lake just as the pollen was, and from changes in their abundance in the layers we expect to determine the frequency of forest fires in the vicinity. When we add to this information data on the pollen frequency in the same layers, we can reconstruct the history of the vegetation, drawing on what we know of the effects of recent fires.[5]

Historical records, from newspaper clippings to trappers' diaries, are useful in dating fires for a particular locale. They can help in verifying tree ring counts on old, fire-scarred trees as well as in establishing a fire history for a particular locale in which there is no living vegetation to serve as evidence. In that case, one should search for other written accounts, such as paintings, hospital records, and other local, historical accounts, to verify the date and location of the fire. If the fires occurred within the last 75 years, personal interviews with early residents of the area could assist in the reconstruction of a detailed fire history.

Inventory of Present Conditions. Since the ecosystem is shaped by fire, all components should be sampled to determine the present condition of the vegetation (overstory and ground cover), fauna (vertebrate and nonvertebrate), water (open bodies and ground water), and soil (soil profile and chemistry). If possible, permanent sampling units should be established for each major ecosystem component, where the fire management zones are very large. These could be updated every 10 to 50 years, depending on the expected frequency of fire and the normal dynamic changes brought about by weather and other agents.

The updating policy may appear to be too idealistic; but without updated baseline data, we cannot determine the specific effects of a given fire. Possibly a small drainage that appears to represent the typical conditions of the area can be singled out for intensive sampling.

The exact sampling and analysis techniques should correspond to those specifically recommended for each component, such as soil profile, soil chemistry, composition and condition of overstory vegetation and so forth. Since these are specific and detailed, they are too extensive and complex to be treated in a general discussion of fire management policy. The manager must recognize the need to sample and analyze each component. (Some of the techniques for these procedures are discussed elsewhere in the text. However, specific sampling techniques should be pursued in texts specifically designed for the ecosystem component being studied.)

Establish Policy for Specific Locale. Policy regarding the use of fire in maintaining the natural ecosystem must be accompanied by an appropriate information and education program so that people will know what is being done and why. You cannot hide a wildfire; people are immediately aware of it. They usually respond negatively when a fire is allowed to burn or, worse yet, when a fire is introduced.

A "burn or no burn" decision must be made as part of the management plan. As stated earlier, man-made fires are disruptive to the normal fire cycle and tend to occur around points of high-density recreational use. Thus, the basic policy for these fires is to suppress them. If the first-order decision is one that allows natural fires to burn, the second-order decision must involve the value of a fire in the context of a particular locale. Higher values are generally those associated with the protection of life and property; these include physical developments as well as renewable natural resources, such as timber or agricultural crops. Obviously, the protection of developments and renewable natural resources is not important within the natural area; however, it is important to have protection along the border of the area—where there may be conflicting values or private holdings. Thus, the ideal boundaries for natural areas in which fire is a primary ecological force should be located on easily identifiable topographic features that serve as natural firebreaks. If there are no good firebreaks, the decision may be to not allow natural fires to burn because of the possible destruction of property.

In areas where the external boundary of the property joins another agency's or private land, maximum coordination must be adopted as a strategy to protect these lands.

The actual method used to introduce fire may be "natural fire" or "control burn." Policy regarding natural fire has already been discussed. Control burn refers to fire introduced artificially for the purpose of creating ecological changes. It can be accomplished on days when fuel, moisture, and weather conditions will allow a desirable burn yet easily confined to a specific area. Also, a larger area can be divided into zones having well-defined, natural firebreaks, and fire can then be introduced into each zone on a scheduled basis, rather than allowing a major catastrophic fire to occur over the entire area. This may be easier to do in the larger areas that are already bisected by road networks and trail systems, or in places where periodic ground fires already reduced fuel buildup that, in turn, has reduced the potential of the introduced fire to reach the crown and destroy the overstory (as in the giant sequoia).[31] Many smaller, natural areas or those divided into zones by roads or trails may require the use of control burns if fire is to approach its true ecological role.

In sum, the best we can hope for in fire management is to maintain a mosaic of areas where fire can be maintained or reintroduced as a primary ecological force. We must realize that, in modern America, the maintenance of the complete natural role of fire—even within dedicated natural areas such as our national parks—is becoming nearly impossible because of conflicting land use goals.

SELECTED READINGS

1. Agree, J. K. 1974. "Fire Management in the National Parks," *Western Wildlands* 1(3):27.
2. Aldrich, D. F., and R. W. Mutch. 1972. *Wilderness Fires Allowed to Burn More Naturally.* U.S. Forest Service Fire Control Note 33(1): Washington, D.C.: U.S. Government Printing Office.
3. Aldrich, D. F., and P. W. Mutch. 1975. *Fire Management Prescription: A Model Plan for Wilderness Ecosystems.* U.S. Forest Service Research Paper InT (in progress).
4. Brown, A. A., and K. P. Davis. 1973. *Forest Fire: Control and Use.* New York: McGraw-Hill Book Co.
5. Cushing, E. J. 1969. "The Changing Landscape: Clues from the Canoe Country's Lakes," *Naturalist* 20(1):18.
6. DeSilvia, E. R. 1965. "Prescribed Burning in the Northern Rocky Mountain Area," *Tall Timbers Fire Ecology Conference, Proceedings, No. 5.* Tall Timbers Research.
7. Douglas, G. W., and T. M. Ballard. 1971. "Effects of Fire on Alpine Plant Communities in the North Cascades, Washington," *Ecology* 52:1058.
8. Gill, A. M. 1974. "Towards an Understanding of Fire Scar Formation: Field Observation and Laboratory Simulation, *Forest Science* 20: 198.
9. Hartesveldt, R. J. 1964. "Fire Ecology of the Giant Sequoias," *Natural History* 73(10):12.
10. Heinselman, M. L. 1966. "Vegetation in Wilderness Areas," *Trends* 3(1):23.
11. Heinselman, M. L. 1969. "Diary of the Canoe Country's Landscape," *Naturalist* 20(1):2.
12. Hendrickson, W. H. 1962. "Fire in the National Park Symposium," *Tall Timbers Fire Ecology Conference, Proceedings, No. 2.* Tall Timbers Research.

13. Holbrook, S. H. 1943. *Burning an Empire*. New York: Macmillan Co.
14. Houston, D. B. 1973. "Wildfire in Northern Yellowstone National Park," *Ecology* 54(5):1111.
15. Howe, G. E. 1975. "The Evolutionary Role of Wildfire in the Northern Rockies and Implications for Resource Managers," *Tall Timbers Fire Ecology Conference, Proceedings, Volume 14*. Tall Timbers Research.
16. Kelgore, B. M. 1975. "Restoring Fire to National Park Wilderness," *American Forests* 81(3):16, 57.
17. Kluskas, R. W. 1972. "Control Burn Activities in Everglades National Park," *Tall Timbers Fire Ecology Conference, Proceedings, Volume 12*. Tall Timbers Research.
18. Komarek, E. V., Sr. 1966. "The Use of Fire: A Historical Background," *Tall Timbers Fire Ecology Conference, Proceedings, Volume 6*. Tall Timbers Research.
19. Leopold, A. S., S. A. Cain, I. N. Gabrielson, C. M. Cotlam, and T. L. Kimball. 1963. "Wildlife Management in the National Parks," *The Living Wilderness* 83:11.
20. Loope, L. L., and R. P. Wood. 1975. "Fire Management in Grand Teton National Park," *Tall Timbers Fire Ecology Conference, Proceedings, Volume 14*. Tall Timbers Research.
21. Lunan, J. S., and Habeck, J. R. 1973. "The Effects of Fire Exclusion on Ponderosa Pine Communities in Glacier National Park, Montana," *Canadian Journal of Forest Research* 3:574.
22. McLaughlin, J. S. 1972. "Restoring Fire to the Environment of the National Parks," *Tall Timbers Fire Ecology Conference, Proceedings, Volume 12*. Tall Timbers Research.
23. Mutch, R. W. 1970. "Wildland Fires and Ecosystems—A Hypothesis," *Ecology* 51(6):1046.
24. Mutch, R. W., and D. F. Aldrich. 1973. *Wilderness Fire Management: Planning Guidelines and Inventory Procedures*. U.S. Forest Service, Region 1, Missoula, Montana.
25. National Park Service. 1975. *The Natural Role of Fire: A Fire Management Plan*. Yellowstone National Park, Wyoming.
26. National Park Service. 1975. *Final Environmental Assessment: Natural Fire Management Plan for Yellowstone National Park*.
27. Pack, C. L. 1922. "The Greatest Enemy of the Forest—Fire," *The School Book of Forestry*. The American Tree Association. p. 53.
28. Parker, M. 1975. "Preliminary Results of the Study: Mineral Cycling on Natural Productivity of Lakes." University of Wyoming.
29. Perala, D. A. 1972. "Repeated Prescribed Burning in Aspen." U.S. Forest Service Research Note NC-171.
30. Phillips, C. B. 1973. "Fire in Wildland Management," *Journal of Forestry* 71(10)624.
31. Rundel, R. W. 1973. "The Relationship between Basal Fire Scars and Crown Damage in Giant Sequoia," *Ecology* 54:210.
32. Sellers, R. E., and D. G. Despain. 1974. "Fire Management in Yellowstone National Park," *Tall Timbers Fire Ecology Conference, Proceedings, Volume 14*. Tall Timbers Research.
33. Spurr, S. H. 1964. *Forest Ecology*. New York: Ronald Press Co.
34. Sweeney, James R. 1967. "Ecology of Some Fire Type Vegetation in Northern California," *Tall Timbers Fire Ecology Conference, Proceedings, Volume 7*. Tall Timbers Research.
35. Taylor, D. L. 1973. "Some Ecological Implications of Forest Fire Control in Yellowstone National Park, Wyoming." *Ecology* 54(6):1394.
36. Thompson, G. A. 1964. "Fires in Wilderness Areas," *Tall Timbers Fire Ecology Conference, Proceedings, Volume 14*. Tall Timbers Research.
37. Wilde, S. A. 1958. *Forest Soils*. New York: Ronald Press Co.
38. Wright, H. E., Jr. 1969. "Forest History of the BWCA since the Last Glacial Period," *Naturalist* 20(1):14.
39. Wright, H. E., Jr., and M. L. Heinselman (eds). 1973. "The Ecological Role of Fire in Natural Conifer Forests of Western and Northern America," *Quaternary Research* 3:317.

Chapter 9

Visual Resource Management*

Plan in full awareness of nature's forces, forms,
and features—the sweep of the sun, the air currents,
the peaks and hollows of the earth, rock and soil
strata, vegetation, lakes and streams, watersheds
and natural drainage ways—and this awareness
should obviously entail planning in harmony with
the elements of nature. If we disregard them we
will engender countless unnecessary frictions and
preclude those experiences of fitness and
compatibility that can bring so much pleasure and
satisfaction to our lives.[16]

Approximately 87 per cent of man's perception of the landscape is based
on sight. If man is to enjoy the aesthetic beauty of the landscape, we must protect the important visual elements (Figure 9–1). Where possible, we can also
manipulate the observer in terms of viewing distance, lighting, and vertical
position, so that his enjoyment of the observed landscape is enhanced. Too often,
planners interpret this approach in the context of the superlative landscape and
forget the typical landscape. If we agreed with this interpretation, we would be
remiss in our jobs as recreation managers because there are very few superlative landscapes. Most people participate in recreational activities on typical,
regional landscapes. Furthermore, we are already protecting the superlative
landscapes and have been for decades, but we are rapidly losing the typical
landscape to incompatible and destructive uses. This in turn lowers the quality
and desirability of the landscape as a place for living as well as for enjoying
recreational activities. This does not mean that all incompatible land uses must
cease. However, to protect the treasured beauty of our surrounding landscapes,
we must alter many of the existing land use practices. This may mean, in some
instances, renovating the landscape to produce an acceptable visual environment.

In most cases, there are no simple answers. Innovative approaches are necessary because of the conflict in public interest, ranging from aesthetic to economic, over land use and the potentially high cost of maintaining or renovating
landscapes. With a minimal investment, a midwest city was able to turn
"eyesores" (i.e., old gravel pits) into beautifully landscaped, open space areas

---

*Parts of this chapter have been adapted from U.S. Forest Service. 1973. *National Forest Land-
scape Management*, Vol. I, and (1974) "The Visual Management System," *National Forest Landscape Management*, Vol. II. Washington, D.C.: U.S. Department of Agriculture.

Figure 9–1 Varied landscape showing the Alpine Zone, Snowy Range, Wyoming. (Photo by Alan Jubenville.)

for water-based recreational activities. The municipal government even bought up gravel reserves outside its jurisdiction so that, as the city expands, the water-based parks can be an integral part of the new neighborhood—at *zero* cost.

Visual resource management is a new term that refers to the way in which the visual qualities of a landscape are handled in order to produce the maximum aesthetic response. This is achieved by minimizing the visual impact of manmade developments and manipulating the natural landscape to enhance the visual experience where desirable, such as areas in which visual monotony exists (Fig. 9–2).

MODEL OF AESTHETIC RESPONSE

There are several models that attempt to describe how people respond to the landscape.[4, 6, 8, 10, 13, 15, 17.] Many of these focus on the landscape elements and simply disregard the observer.[5, 12, 17] Other models are based on personal biases without any theoretical reasoning as to relationships or predictability. Some researchers have translated peoples' responses to the landscape into quantitative terms.[10, 13, 15] However, the basic model of aesthetic response is more than a function of a static, unchanging landscape; it is a response to many variables.

$$VP = f (B.O., E.C., C.O., O.L.R.),$$
$$VP = \text{the aesthetic response of the observer,}$$
$$B.O. = \text{the background of the observer,}$$

Figure 9–2 Monotonous landscape showing the plains above Medicine Bow, Wyoming. (Photo by Alan Jubenville.)

E.C.   = the environmental conditions under which the observation takes place;
C.O.   = the character of the object being observed; and
O.L.R. = the observer/landscape relationships.

How people will respond to the visual parts of the landscape depends on the background of the individual, i.e., the previous learning experiences to which the individual has been exposed. These experiences will shape the attitudes of the user toward certain environmental manipulations. For example, people who live in high density areas may perceive gateway towns to national parks as desirable settings in which to accommodate their needs; whereas someone who wants to experience the aesthetic enjoyment of the unmodified landscape may perceive these towns as manmade disasters.

The environmental conditions under which observation takes place can vary considerably, often during the course of a day. The character of the landscape is determined by size, shape, color, relief, color pattern, vegetation, and water; it can be relatively uniform (a plateau covered with lodgepole pine) or varied (a rock gulley in the subalpine zone).

The observer/landscape relations are further discussed by Litton.[7] The relationship of observer to observed is important and can affect the objectives of visual resource management. Litton et al.[8] offer a theoretical model to describe how people react to the aesthetics of a landscape (Fig. 9–3).

The thesis in formulating an aesthetic response model is that the landscape is more than a state of mind[10]; it is an array of environmental stimuli bombarding the individual to which he reacts according to his state of mind and the conditions under which the observation takes place. Thus, to be effec-

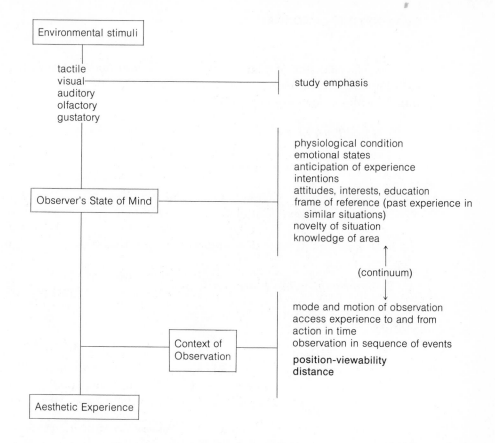

Figure 9–3 Aesthetic response model. (From Litton, R. B., Jr., R. J. Tetlow, J. Sorenson, and R. A. Beatty. 1974. *Water and Landscape.* Port Washington, N.Y.: Water Information Center, Inc. p. 12.)

tive in management prescription, the manager must be able to describe the landscape—both the physical aspects and the observer's response—in tangible terms. This should provide a firmer grasp of the effects of landscape manipulation on the aesthetic experience of the user. If the response is predictably negative, the project should be redesigned, relocated, or eliminated in order to maintain the natural appeal of the existing landscape. Possibly, the manager will complete the original projects, but with the realization that it may have negative effects. Sometimes environmental manipulations will enhance the asesthetic appeal of the landscape, depending on the existing condition (from past land uses) and on the state of mind of the observer. Removing offensive sights (e.g., junkyards) and removing vegetation (e.g., to create natural-appearing openings in a forest landscape) are examples of enhancing the aesthetics of the existing landscape.

CLASSIFYING LANDSCAPES

The classification of a landscape is based on properly describing the physical elements in terms of their visual effects. One of the methods used—the building-block process—is as follows:

1. *Flow Pattern*

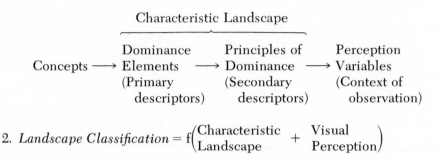

2. *Landscape Classification* $= f\begin{pmatrix} \text{Characteristic} & + & \text{Visual} \\ \text{Landscape} & & \text{Perception} \end{pmatrix}$

CONCEPTS

Several different concepts have been used to describe the landscape and man's reaction to it.[5, 8, 12] However, the approach most aligned to the objectives of visual resource management uses the following concepts.[*]

Characteristic Landscape (Fig. 9–4). Each landscape, regardless of size or

---

[*]As discussed in: U.S. Forest Service. 1973. *National Forest Landscape Management*, Vol. I. Washington, D.C.: U.S. Department of Agriculture.

Figure 9–4 Characteristic landscape of the Alpine Zone, Snowy Range, Wyoming. (Photo by Alan Jubenville.)

segment being viewed, has an identifiable character that is created by its unique combination of visible features, such as land, vegetation, water, and structures.

Variety. Variety in the landscape is a desirable visual quality. Monotonous landscapes are not pleasing to the user and discourage the observer, creating a lackadaisical perceptual response to the existing environmental stimuli. The problem is, How much variety is enough? For a given area, the variety can be increased from zero (low appeal) an acceptable level. Beyond this level, the usual appeal may decrease until it again reaches zero. Planting trees on an open hillside may increase variety and visual appeal; but at some point, adding more trees may, in fact, reduce both these qualities of the landscape. Planting could continue until the hillside is entirely covered with trees, creating a new monotonous landscape.

Deviation. Deviation refers to the manmade alterations in the characteristic landscape. The majority of land has been subjected to use development. Thus, deviation, (including those created by recreational developments) have been made and will continue to be made on the landscape. Deviations that emulate the elements of the natural landscape or create a desirable variety can be made acceptable to the observer. Unfortunately, decisions about these matters are usually based on economics, with little consideration toward landscape aesthetics. Nevertheless, more people are becoming aware of the appeal of the landscape. Although they realize some modification is necessary to provide the needed goods and services for our modern society, they still feel the deviations should be made with consideration toward the visual environment. Everyone would like to live in an aesthetically pleasing neighborhood, yet many of us don't. In most cases, too little attention was given to visually disruptive land use, so that unacceptable deviations occurred. Given proper concern, deviations can be made acceptable, even enjoyable, to the user.

DOMINANCE ELEMENTS

The four elements that compete for dominance in any landscape are form, line, color, and texture. It is important to analyze their relative strengths in the visual dominance of the existing landscape and the possible effects the proposed development may have on these elements. Developments should generally complement, or at least not detract from, the more dominant elements. If they detract from the dominant elements or supplant them, they may destroy the natural harmonious appeal of the landscape, or worse, create a landscape that people will react to negatively.

Form. Form is the mass of an object or of a combination of objects that appears unified. When seen in two dimensions, it is referred to as shape (Fig. 9–5).

Line. Line is the intersection of two planes. In nature, it occurs in shorelines, timberlines, meadow edges, avalanche paths, vegetation boundaries, ridgelines, and tree trunks. In Figure 9–6, line is readily visible where the lake and the mountain meet. Another example is the line of a major river, that appears in an area or regional landscape.

Color. Color patterns of landscapes are important in differentiating objects. The perception of color often depends greatly on the observer's position; distant colors appear muted while foreground colors seem stronger and more

Figure 9–5 Form. The dominant conical form of Sugarloaf Mountain, Wyoming, accented by the horizontal plane of Lewis Lake. (Photo by Alan Jubenville.)

Figure 9–6 Line. Snake River drainage, Wyoming, as viewed from Rendezvous Mountain. (Photo by Alan Jubenville.)

Figure 9–7 Texture. Note the different texture in the oblique photo of Lodgepole Pine type and the adjacent meadows. (Photo by Alan Jubenville.)

dominant. This is especially true when the same color is being viewed from varying distances. Contrast is created by this element. Color can be expressed in terms of *hue* (the quality such as blue and green) and *value* (the tonal quality between light and dark). Value tends to dominate hue, except in very close viewing; however, a detectable variation in hue will give greater clarity to the elements of the landscape, for example, the golden yellow of a dandelion meadow in contrast with the brilliant blue of a mountain lake.

Texture (Fig. 9–7). The dominant texture, or grain, of the landscape varies with distance. From short distances, individual trees or leaf patterns may dominate. From greater distances, stands of trees may form the dominant texture. From extreme distances, the texture of the entire viewing area may appear homogeneous.

PRINCIPLES OF DOMINANCE

Six principles affect the visual dominance of form, line, color, and texture in a landscape:

Contrast. Contrast is important in the discrimination of form. In an area dominated by heavy texture, with little variation, any change in the landscape will produce sharp contrasts and will be quickly recognized by the observer. In the varied landscape manmade openings should appear natural so that they conform with dominant forms caused by natural variation.

Sequence. There are two aspects to sequence: sequential landscapes and sequential experiences. Sequential landscapes are those in which the dominant elements of form, line, color, and texture are repeated in the specific area. Potential developments or activities for the area should thus be evaluated in terms of visual effect on the continuity of these elements. Any development or activity imposed on a specific area should complement its landscape sequence. Otherwise, the development will most likely be perceived as being incongruous, or out-of-sequence.

Sequential experiences are also important: "A well-planned sequence of visual experiences can enrich the viewer appreciation."[20] Since most people travel by developed transportation systems, such as roads or trails, we might try to maximize the enjoyment of hiking or driving experiences by utilizing sequence. Perhaps the focus of a trail is St. Mary's Peak. Exposing the peak to the hiker at certain distances should heighten his anticipation for the next exposure as well as increase his appreciation of this dominant feature. With constant exposure to the peak, however, the change may be so continuous and gradual that it is difficult to really appreciate.

Axis.   Axis is the main line of focus created by converging lines toward some central point. Secondary attention is then focused on the approach to the focal point. Axis can be natural (such as a river, an elongated ridge, or a narrow valley) or manmade (such as a road, a fence line, or a bridge). It can be used intentionally to focus attention on natural or manmade objects of interest. The tunnels on the road through Mt. Rushmore National Memorial Park form the axes which focus attention on Mt. Rushmore. In identifying axes and focal points for the visitor, the manager should try to maintain the continuity of the axis, the immediate landscape around the axis, and the background of the particular landscape. If the continuity is disrupted, attention may be directed away from the primary object, lowering the visual experience of the visitor.

Convergence.   In convergence, several axes meet at a single focal point. The area around the convergence point is a dominant part of the landscape; thus, any development in this area should blend with the character of the landscape. Even then, the development should involve an area on which the manager wishes to focus the visitor's attention, such as a visitor center.

Multi-dominance.   Multi-dominance is created by two or more similar focal points in a landscape view. This may occur naturally in the form of border fields or rock outcroppings, but usually occurs with manmade activities such a timber harvesting or mining exploration. If the series of objects are competing for landscape dominance, they can distract the viewer and create an inferior view.

Enframement.   Enframement is caused by vertical axes (such as rock walls or timber edges) intercepting a flat plane (such as a valley, road or lake). It often reinforces the other dominance principles.

VARIABLE FACTORS

There are eight environmental factors that influence the way in which dominance elements are perceived. These can often be controlled indirectly by manipulation of the observer. "In analyzing the influence of variable factors on visual perception, it is most important to choose the [environmental] conditions which give the [land use] activity the greatest contrast with the characteristic landscape.[10] (*Note:* bracketed words have been added for clarification.). Although these factors may vary considerably, their occurrence and influence can generally be predicted. The motion of water plummeting over a waterfall is breathtaking in early summer; by fall, this motion may be reduced to a trickle of water. When the motion of water is high, the visual experience is more intense. This type of information gives the manager a level of predictability that can be incorporated into his management planning. This applies to other variables as well.

Motion. Motion can be an influential force in capturing the visual interest of the observer. Water is probably the most important source of motion in the natural landscape, other sources are wind, rain, snow, and avalanches. Motion can attract and hold the attention of the observer in this way; it may be used to draw attention to or away from various land use activities. In some places, it may be difficult to control the negative effects of land use or to screen these effects using intervening topography or vegetation. Possibly, the natural motion in the existing landscape could be used to divert attention away from the negative scene.

Light. All objects reflect sunlight to some degree. Natural light varies daily and seasonally, producing contrast, which affects the visitor's visual perception of the landscape. We know that variety is important in producing an aesthetic response in the individual; we also need to understand how light can enhance this response by emphasizing or masking the landscape elements.

For a scenic road corridor, we may choose light conditions that maximize contrast in the landscape and produce better visual perception of forms, lines, colors, and textures. We could also choose to reduce light intensity and reflection; this subdues the elements of the landscape so that negative land uses are less apparent along the road corridor.

The direction of the light is also important. It is determined by the time of day, the season of the year, and the position of the observer relative to the source of light. Backlighting—i.e., facing into the light—obscures details so that only the general outline is discernible. Frontlighting—facing away from the light—tends to produce less contrast and, consequently, less interest in the scene. Shadows tend to be shorter, they fall away from the observer, and more surface tends to be in direct sunlight.

Sidelighting generally produces the greatest contrast; thus, it is usually the best lighting in which to evaluate scenes for visual acuity or for manmade activity (visitor center, road layout, and so forth). This information can aid us in selecting observer locations (overlook, trail location) that will maximize the visual experience. Consideration should be given to the time of day at which the observation would normally take place. It is also important to remember that the angle of the sun and the intensity of the light vary with each season.

Atmospheric conditions. These determine the way in which the dominance elements are seen. The visual impact of a scene is reduced by cloud cover, fog, or precipitation, the landscape should not be evaluated under those conditions. However, some atmospheric phenomena can accent the landscape elements of form, line, color, texture. Water on the opposite side of a mountain peak may effect the creation of a fog or a cloud bank that can serve as a backdrop, accenting particular elements. An impressive scene that is usually obscured by fog or clouds may become even more dramatic to the observer when seen in the abrupt contrast of gleaming brilliantly in the sunlight. Mount McKinley is an example of this type of response. Although I have personally visited Mount McKinley National Park, my only glimpse of the peak has been from a commercial jetliner at 27,000 feet. As the clouds abruptly parted, the peak was exposed. Then, just as quickly, the clouds again covered the mountain. I remember it as being one of the greatest visual experiences I have ever had, yet it lasted only a moment.

Distance. Color value affects the visual qualities of the landscape.

Figure 9–8   Photo showing distance-viewing zones.

As distance increases, the color value decreases because of the scattering of light rays. At great distances, the landscape is reduced to uniformity of both color value (usually blues or grays) and relief (less perceived vertical change). The distance at which an object can no longer be identified depends on two factors: the size of the object and the degree of contrast with its surroundings. Viewing zones were established with criteria that included an overlap of distances (Fig. 9–8). The zones and their characteristics are shown in Table 9–1.

Observer position.   Observer position is the vertical location of the individual in relation to the object being observed. The three positions are normal (at the same level as the object observed), inferior (below the object observed), and superior (above the object observed). The superior and inferior positions are only important in areas having reasonable topographic relief. The superior position offers opportunities for maximum viewing and orientation to the total landscape. Also, more surface area of a given object is exposed than in the normal position. The least surface area is exposed in the inferior position, and that is easily screened by intervening vegetation. An interpretive center may be placed in a superior position so that one can see whole plant communities and interpret the total ecosystem; yet this position would allow maximum screening to those people along the road below.

Scale.   Scale is the proportion used to measure the relative size of an object. Viewing distance affects scale relationships. Objects viewed closely are often measured in proportion to the human figure. In the intermediate and distant viewing zones, an object is seen in proportion to the total scene. When a person is looking at a pipeline corridor from a one-quarter mile distance, the irregular feathered edge may be visually acceptable to him. But when the same scene is viewed from several miles away, the corridor becomes lost within the general texture of the landscape, a monotonous view is presented.

Time.   This refers to the length of time in which an observer views a point of interest. The longer the time, the more detail he sees. "Seeing takes

TABLE 9-1 VIEWING ZONES*

Foreground Characteristics	Middleground Characteristics	Background Characteristics
• Presence—the observer is in it. • Maximum discernment of detail—in proportion to time and speed. • Scale—observer can feel a size relationship with the elements. • Discernment of color—intensity and value seen in maximum contrasts. • Discernment of other sensory experiences—sound, smell, and touch are most acute here. • Discernment of wind motion. • Aerial perspective absent.	• Linkage between foreground and background parts of the landscape. • Emergence of overall shapes and patterns. • Visual simplification of vegetative surfaces into textures. • Presence of aerial perspective—softens color contrasts. • Discernment of relation between landscape units.	• Simplification—outline shapes, little texture or detail apparent, objects viewed mostly as patterns of light and dark. • Strong discernment of aerial perspective—reduces color distinction, replaces them with values of blue and gray. • Discernment of entire landscape units—drainage patterns, vegetative patterns, landforms. • Individual visual impacts least apparent.

	Foreground	Middleground	Background
Distance	0-¼-½ mile	¼-½—3-5 miles	3-5 miles—infinity
Sight capacity	detail	detail & general	general—no detail
Object viewed	rock point	entire ridge	system of ridges
Visual characteristics	individual plants & species	textures (conifers & hardwoods)	patterns (light & dark)

*From U.S. Forest Service. 1973. *National Landscape Management,* Vol. I. Washington, D.C.: U.S. Department of Agriculture, p. 57.

time—up to three-tenths of a second is needed for the eye to fixate".[20] This means that the auto driver, as he increases in speed, will concentrate his vision on fewer objects at greater distances. The time factor primarily pertains to the visitor who is in his automobile. When out of the automobile, the visitor generally concentrates on the landscape, thus increasing his perception of detail. The visual cones and minimum fixation distances are shown in Figure 9-9.

Seasons. Season of use is important because the contrasts that strengthen landscapes vary considerably throughout the seasons. In the summer when the leaves are fully developed, the landscape may have little variety, with the heavy texture of the trees dominating the landscape. The colors of the newly emerging leaves in the spring or the frost-colored leaves of the fall may break up the monotony of a landscape; they can also decrease the visual impact of a development causing the line, color, form, and texture of the manmade structures to appear to blend more naturally with the surrounding area.

Snow tends to strengthen form and line through maximum contrast; thus, winter is often the best time for evaluating potential visual impacts.

SUMMARY OF LANDSCAPE CLASSIFICATION

The following examples are used to summarize the analysis of the landscape character. This gives the reader an opportunity to apply the information on landscape classification.

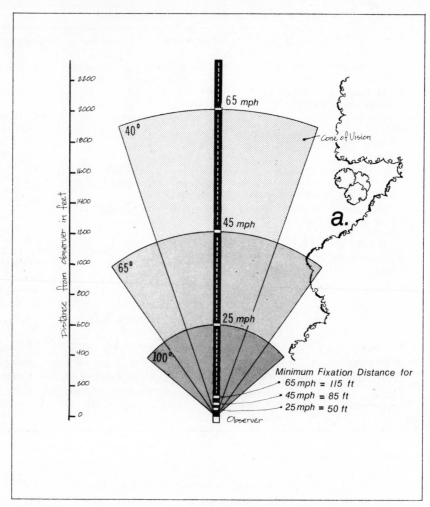

Figure 9–9 Visual cones and minimum fixation distances. (From U.S. Forest Service. 1973. *National Forest Landscape Management.* Vol. I. Washington, D.C.: U.S. Government Printing Office, p. 63.)

Figure 9–10 is a landscape characteristic of the alpine zone as viewed from the foreground and middleground zones. It has tremendous visual variation, which makes it attractive to the observer. This land has strong form in the granite outcropping, strong line in the ridges and shoreline of the lake, and excellent textural variation in vegetation, snow, and rock outcropping.

Any management practice should recognize the strong line, texture, and form. Trails should be located so as not to detract from the ridgeline on the horizon or along the lake. Any primitive campsite development should complement the texture and form and should avoid disrupting the strong lines around the lake. All activity should be avoided in the focal point at the upper reach of the lake.

Figure 9–11 is an enclosed landscape dominated in the foreground by the line of the lake, the interface of the forest and meadow, and the variation in texture. Management practices should consider the strong lines and the strong attraction of the water. The lake should be made visually accessible for the enjoyment of the casual user; any kind of intensive use or development would be

Figure 9–10 Landscape character of the Alpine Zone. (Photo by Alan Jubenville.)

too distracting. Intensive developments such as roads, trails, and campgrounds should be screened within the spruce-fir forest. There are also ecological factors to consider in reaching these types of decisions.

The landscape in Figure 9–12 is completely in the foreground and is dominated by the shoreline and the texture of the streamside vegetation. Any management action should preserve the existing line and texture if the visual integrity is to be preserved for those using the river. Campgrounds and picnic stops should be located away from the streamside; one should even consider the requirement of having the canoeist remove his craft from the water at these stops to minimize visual intrusion.

This Wyoming landscape (Fig. 9–13) is dominated by foreground texture and by background lines at the horizon and the spur ridges, plus the dominant form of the mountain peaks in the background. One other dominant feature is the line of vegetation at the interface of foreground and background. Very little middleground is visually accessible.

Any intensive land-use development is better located in the middleground where it can be screened and blended with vegetation. Any development in the foreground should blend with the texture and not be disruptive to

Figure 9–11 Arrowhead Lake, Medicine Bow National Forest. (Photo by Alan Jubenville.)

Figure 9–12 Enclosed landscape along a river bottom. (Photo by Tom Buchanan.)

Figure 9–13   Snow–capped Teton Range, Grand Teton National Park. (Photo by Alan Jubenville.)

the dominance of the mountain range in the background. Note the Chapel of Transfiguration in the right foreground.

APPLICATION OF THE VISUAL RESOURCE MANAGEMENT

This discussion will include the scale of application, the visual resource management model, and mapping techniques.

SCALE OF APPLICATION

In visual resource planning, the scale of application is divided into three major levels—regional, area, and site.

Regional Landscape.   The regional landscape is delimited by the physiographic provinces. For example, the major physiographic provinces in southeastern Wyoming—(from east to west) the eastern plains, Laramie Mountains, Laramie Basin, Medicine Bow Mountains, Platte River Basin, and the Sierra Madres—describe the characteristic, regional landscapes. Major developments such as transportation and utility systems should be evaluated in terms of the general effect on the regional landscape. Properly locating the development will ensure minimal visual impact at the regional level.

Area Landscape.   The area landscape is delimited by the visual corridor, or the envelope of space enclosed by land forms.[8] The detailed visual resource management is usually handled on an area basis. At this level, judgments are made about the specific effects of a given development on the visual experiences of the visitor. Most recreational use occurs along roads, trails, water courses, or at specific sites. The manager should give priority to any portion of the landscape that is readily seen by the visitor, but this should not be interpreted as a "green light" to exploit the remaining areas.

Site Landscape. Site landscape refers to the landscape unit on which a recreational development is placed. It is important to maintain a visually pleasing environment throughout the site. This is generally accomplished during the site planning phase. The visual effects of the site development in terms of the casual observer passing through the area, should also be considered under area landscape management.

LANDSCAPE MANAGEMENT MODEL

The basic visual resource management model is illustrated in Figure 9–14. The visual resource is inventoried according to character, variety, and sensitivity (e.g., its visual acuity, how it affects people) of the landscape. Ultimately, the resource's ability to absorb the development must be coordinated with the sensitivity of the observer to fit some visual quality objective. These objectives determine what type and level of development should be allowed in the area. (We must realize that any activity by man will detract, to some degree, from the natural aesthetics of the overall landscape).

Landscape Character. First, the character type and the subtypes of the resource must be identified. The Laramie Mountains in southeast Wyoming is one example of character type. Subtypes are areas of significant size and with visual differences to distinguish them from other subtypes.

Next, the variety classes of each subtype should be established. There are three variety classes: distinctive—those landscapes having outstanding visual qualities (such as a mountain peak, a deep gorge, or a glacial field); common—those having a variety of basic landscape elements but no outstanding features;

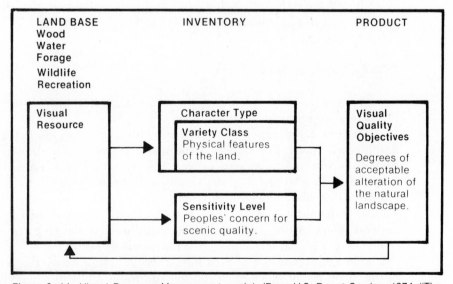

Figure 9–14 Visual Resource Management model. (From U.S. Forest Service. 1974. "The Visual Management System." *National Forest Landscape Management.* Vol. II. Washington, D.C.: U.S. Government Printing Office, p. 9.)

TABLE 9-2 CHART OF LANDSCAPE FEATURES OF RESOURCE AREA—WESTERN CASCADES CHARACTER TYPE, STEEP MOUNTAIN SLOPE SUBTYPE*

	CLASS A DISTINCTIVE	CLASS B COMMON	CLASS C MINIMAL
Landform	Over 60 percent slopes which are dissected, uneven, sharp exposed ridges or large dominant features.	30-60 percent slopes which are moderately dissected or rolling.	0-30 percent slopes which have little variety. No dissection and no dominant features.
Rock Form	Features stand out on landform. Unusual or outstanding, avalanche chutes, talus slopes, outcrops, etc., in size, shape, and location.	Features obvious but do not stand out. Common but not outstanding avalanche chutes, talus slopes, boulders and rock outcrops.	Small to nonexistent features. No avalanche chutes, talus slopes, boulders and rock outcrops.
Vegetation	High degree of patterns in vegetation. Large old-growth timber. Unusual or outstanding diversity in plant species.	Continuous vegetative cover with interspersed patterns. Mature but not outstanding old-growth. Common diversity in plant species.	Continuous vegetative cover with little or no pattern. No understory, overstory or ground cover.
Water Forms, Lakes	50 acres or larger. Those smaller than 50 acres with one or more of the following: (1) Unusual or outstanding shoreline configuration, (2) reflects major features, (3) islands, (4) Class A shoreline vegetation or rock forms.	5 to 50 acres. Some shoreline irregularity. Minor reflections only. Class B shoreline vegetation.	Less than 5 acres. No irregularity or reflection.
Water Forms, Streams	Drainage with numerous or unusual changing flow characteristics, falls, rapids, pools and meanders or large volume.	Drainage, with common meandering and flow characteristics.	Intermittent streams or small perennial streams with little or no fluctuation in flow or falls, rapids, or meandering.

*From U.S. Forest Service. 1974. "The Visual Management System," *National Forest Landscape Management*, Vol. II. Washington, D.C.: U.S. Department of Agriculture, p. 13.

and minimal—those having little variety in the basic elements (such as an unbroken canopy of lodgepole pine or a grain field).

Finally, a chart should be drawn up that classifies the basic resource features of the subtype into distinctive, common, or minimal. To illustrate this discussion, an example of a variety class chart is shown in Table 9-2, using Western Cascades as the landscape type and steep mountain lands as the subtype.

Vertical aerial photos can be used in conjunction with the criteria established variety class chart to delineate the variety classes A (distinctive), B (common), and C (minimal). The information can then be transferred to a base topographic map (Fig. 9-15).

To obtain necessary detail needed at the subtype level, the manager may be forced to establish a priority system, phasing in the visual resource management program over several years. Typically, the distinctive landscapes have been managed to protect the visual aesthetics. This is as it should be; however, we should also devote more attention to the common landscape, which is where most people participate in their recreational activities. Most landscapes are in the common category; therefore, we should give more attention to managing the

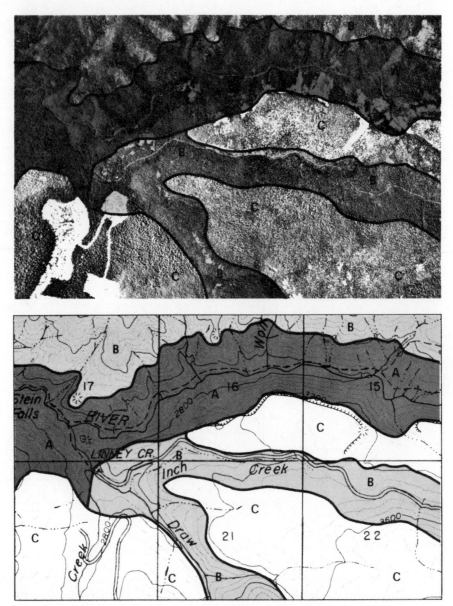

Figure 9–15 Mapping landscape variety classes A, B, and C. *Top,* Vertical photos, particularly in stereo pairs, are an excellent tool in judging the broad variety classes. *Bottom,* Prepare a detailed base map at the same scale as those currently being used for Multiple Use planning units. Prepare an overlay as shown to illustrate the variety class determination. Information on the base map will be used for all aspects of the Visual Management System process and should include but not be limited to: Topographic data (best available); landownership boundaries; existing and proposed (within 10 years) travel routes, and bodies of water. (This would include but not be limited to roads, trails, low-level commercial air routes, passenger rail routes, etc.) Information can be obtained from local, state and national route studies and transportation plans. (From U.S. Forest Service. 1974. "The Visual Management System" *National Forest Landscape Management,* Vol. II. Washington, D. C.: U.S. Government Printing Office, p. 9.)

common landscape if we are to provide adequately for recreational needs. The minimal landscape may absorb intensive developments if it has overstory vegetation for screening. Some prairie and desert lands, classified as minimal, cannot absorb any development without maximum disruption of the landscape elements.

Viewer Sensitivity. Viewer sensitivity is a composite of attitudes and viewer distance. Ideally, the mapping of attitudes of those who use the specific management area should be evaluated to determine their level of sensitivity. In the absence of such information, Table 9–3 can be used as a guideline. This is then combined with viewer distance — foreground (FG), middleground (MG), and background (BG), as shown in Table 9–1 — in order to determine the overall level of viewer sensitivity. For mapping viewer sensitivity, an overlay of all viewable areas should be prepared for all travel routes, use areas, and bodies of water. This can be done with a large scale topographic map, since all that is needed is a distance and elevation from the potential viewing point. The foreground, middleground, and background and the viewer sensitivity (in terms of attitudes) is plotted for each road, trail, recreational development, and body of water (including streams). In the past, only roads have been given consideration in relation to viewer sensitivity; however, travel on water and trail is increasing and should therefore be given equal consideration. It would seem obvious that we must also manage the quality of the landscape that is immediately adjacent to the recreational development. At level 3, it is not necessary to divide into foreground, middleground, and background because of the low sensitivity level. Overlays should then be superimposed to produce a composite overlay (Fig. 9–16).

TABLE 9–3 SUMMARY OF SENSITIVITY LEVELS[*]

Summary Table for all Sensitivity Levels:			
	Sensitivity Level		
Use	1	2	3
Primary Travel Routes, Use Areas, and Water Bodies	At least ¼ of users have MAJOR concern for scenic qualities	Less than ¼ of users have MAJOR concern for scenic qualities	
Secondary Travel Routes, Use Areas, and Water Bodies	At least ¾ of users have MAJOR concern for scenic qualities	At least ¼ and not more than ¾ of users have MAJOR concern for scenic qualities	Less than ¼ of users have MAJOR concern for scenic qualities

Level 1 — Highest Sensitivity
Level 2 — Average Sensitivity
Level 3 — Lowest Sensitivity

[*]From U.S. Forest Service. 1974. "The Visual Management System," *National Forest Landscape Management,* Vol. II. Washington, D.C.: U.S. Department of Agriculture, p. 21.

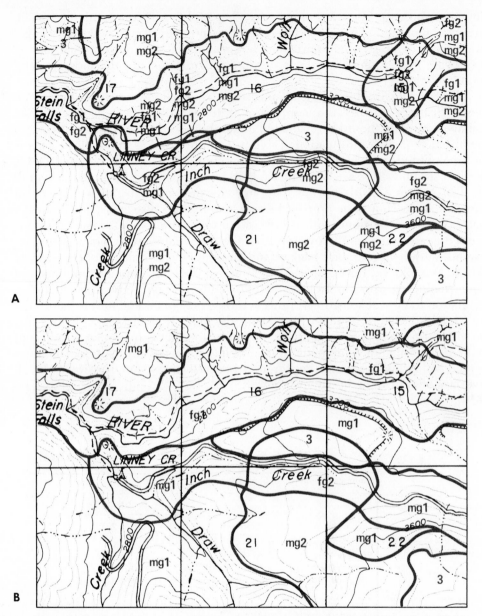

Figure 9–16 Composite overlay of Viewer Sensitivity based on general visitor attitudes (Table 9–2) and Viewing Distance Zones (Table 9–1). *A*, A composite overlay before adjustments have been made; *B*, the final overlay, showing the most restrictive sensitivity levels as shown in Table 9–4.

Note that there are multiple classifications for most zones since many are viewable from more than one distance zone or viewer sensitivity level (Table 9–3). For zones in which multiple classifications occur, the more restrictive sensitivity classification should always be used. To determine which classification is most sensitive, refer to the matrix shown in Table 9–4.

Visual Quality Objectives. Viewer sensitivity and landscape variety must be integrated into visual quality objectives. This is done using the matrix in Ta-

TABLE 9-4 CHART FOR DETERMINING MOST RESTRICTIVE
SENSITIVITY LEVEL*

	fg1	mg1	bg1	fg2	mg2	bg2
bg2	fg1	mg1	bg1	fg2	mg2	bg2
mg2	fg1	mg1	mg2	fg2	mg2	
fg2	fg1	mg1	fg2	fg2		
bg1	fg1	mg1	bg1			
mg1	fg1	mg1				
fg1	fg1					

fg 1 – Foreground Level 1
mg 1 – Middleground Level 1
bg 1 – Background Level 1

*From U.S. Forest Service. 1974. "The Visual Management System," *National Forest Landscape Management*, Vol. II. Washington, D.C.: U.S. Department of Agriculture, p. 25.

TABLE 9-5 VISUAL QUALITY MATRIX**

		Sensitivity Level						
		fg1	mg1	bg1	fg2	mg2	bg2	3
Variety Class	class A	R	R	R	PR	PR	PR	PR
	class B	R	PR	PR	PR	M	M	M* / MM
	class C	PR	PR	M	M	M	MM	MM

SYMBOL	OBJECTIVE
R	Retention
PR	Partial Retention
M	Modification
MM	Maximum Modification

*If a *3B* area is adjacent to a *Retention* or *Partial Retention* visual quality objective, select the *Modification* visual quality objective. If adjacent to *Modification* or *Maximum Modification* objective areas, select *Maximum Modification*.

**From U.S. Forest Service. 1974. "The Visual Management System," *National Forest Landscape Management*, Vol. II. Washington, D.C.: U.S. Department of Agriculture, p. 43.

ble 9–5; the result is shown in Figure 9–17. The visual quality objectives are as follows:

Preservation (P). The intent is that the only changes allowed are the natural, ecological ones, realizing that some local impact from recreational use may occur. These are roadless areas where the main development is the trail system, plus possibly some primitive campgrounds; all of which should be designed to blend with the visual resource.

Retention (R). Retention refers to planning developments so that they are not evident to the casual observer. They should maintain the existing landscape elements of form, line, color, and texture, as viewed from the same point(s) where the majority of the casual observation takes place.

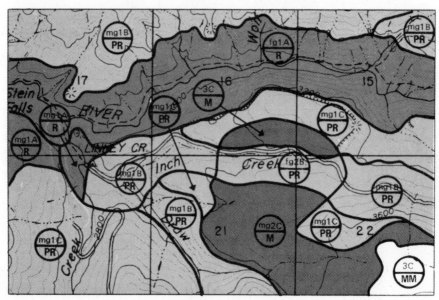

Objective Map

Symbol	Objective	Code
R	RETENTION	
PR	PARTIAL RETENTION	
M	MODIFICATION	
MM	MAXIMUM MODIFICATION	

Preservation does not appear on the
chart but is indicated by:

P   PRESERVATION

Assign Preservation Objective to all
existing and proposed (within 10 years)
Special Classified Areas.

Figure 9–17 The application of visual quality objectives, integrating landscape variety and viewer sensitivity. Note those areas in need of either rehabilitation or enhancement by the appropriate symbol beside the quality objective, *e* for enhancement and *reh* for rehabilitation. Rehabilitation should be noted when management activities in a particular area do not conform to an agreed upon quality objective. Enhancement notation should come from a detailed landscape management plan for a particular area. The Visual Resource Management System thus produces an area map showing visual quality objectives.

Partial Retention (PR). To acheive partial retention, the development should be made subordinate to the features of the characteristic landscape. Attempt should be made to repeat the landscape elements, yet realizing the development cannot completely blend into the landscape. The goal is to make the view acceptable for the observer by maintaining the maximum natural character of the landscape or by complementing this character where it is impossible to completely blend it.

Modification (M). With the use of modification, man's activities may visually dominate the characteristic landscape, but even these activities should borrow as much as possible from the landscape elements of form, line, color, and texture so that it is perceived as congruent with the setting.

Maximum Modification (MM). Man's activities, including alteration of land forms by timber harvesting or major building, may dominate the landscape and may appear somewhat incongruous with the foreground or middleground viewing distances. Yet, when viewed as a background, these forms should blend with the landscape. Thus, viewing distance is important; and the duration of the visual impact should be short term; either by rehabilitation or by enhancement (secondary objectives).

Note there is such a thing as unacceptable modification which does not blend with the character of the landscape regardless of viewing distance. Activities such as contour strip mining and large symmetrical clearcuts often have a lingering effect that cannot be mitigated. Modification or enhancement may improve the visual quality of the activity, but the activity often remains unacceptable. For any situation, unacceptable modification should not be tolerated. Note the amount of "unacceptable modification" around you. If you recognize these on the ground, the picture is more vivid than any photo could reproduce (Fig. 9–18).

Figure 9–18 Unacceptable landscape modification caused by timber harvesting. (Photo by Les Pengelly, University of Montana.)

Landscape rehabilitation is a secondary, short-term, visual quality objective to indicate the need and capability to rehabilitate negative elements in the landscape in order to bring it up to the desired primary visual quality objective. Enhancement, another secondary, short term objective, is aimed at increasing visual appeal by creating variety in a monotonous landscape.

VISUAL RESOURCE MANAGEMENT—
AN INTERPRETATION

We have just discussed a system used by an agency whose interest in land management is multi-faceted. Some modification of the system is obviously necessary at the local level, depending on the perceptions of the user population. A legislative mandate, agency goals, and complexity of programs can also determine the quality objectives that should be selected. Regardless of the agency or situation, there is a basic model that managers can use to arrive at the objectives for a resource management program; the specifics within the model can be modified to suit the individual manager's needs.

SELECTED READINGS

1. Alexander, C., and S. I. Chermayeff. 1964. *Notes on the Synthesis of Form.* Cambridge, Mass.: Harvard University Press.
2. Arnheim, R. 1954. *Art and Visual Perception, A Psychology of the Creative Eye.* Berkeley, Calif.: University of California Press.
3. Birren, F. 1969. *Light, Color, and Environment.* New York: Van Nostrand Reinhold Co.
4. Ekbo, G. 1969. *The Landscape We See.* New York: McGraw-Hill Book Co.
5. Leopold, L. 1969. *Qualitative Comparison of Some Aesthetic Factors Among Rivers.* Geological Survey Circular 620.
6. Litton, R. B., Jr. 1973. *Landscape Control Points: A Procedure for Predicting and Monitoring Visual Impacts.* U. S. Forest Service Research Paper PSW-91.
7. Litton, R. B., Jr. 1968. *Forest Landscape Description and Inventories—A Basis for Land Planning and Design.*
8. Litton, R. B., Jr., R. J. Tetlow, J. Sorenson, and R. A. Beatty, 1974. *Water and Landscape.* Port Washington, N.Y.: Water Information Center, Inc.
9. Litton, R. B., Jr., and R. H. Twiss. 1967. "The Forest Landscape: Some Elements of Visual Analysis," *Proceedings of Society of American Foresters.* Portland, Ore.: Society of American Foresters, p. 212.
10. Lowenthal, D. (ed.). 1967. *Environmental Perception and Behavior.* Geography Research Paper No. 109. Chicago: University of Chicago Press.
11. Mitchell, W. J. (ed.). 1972. *Environmental Design: Research and Practice.* Los Angeles: University of California at Los Angeles.
12. Nighswonger, J. J. 1970. *A Methodology for Inventorying and Evaluating the Scenic Quality and Related Recreational Values of Kansas Streams.* Topeka, Kan.: Kansas Department of Economic Development, Planning Division.
13. Peterson, George L., and E. S. Neamann. 1969. "Modeling and Predicting Human Response to the Visual Recreation Environment," *Journal of Leisure Research,* 1(3):219–237.
14. Rutledge, A. J. 1971. *Anatomy of a Park.* New York: McGraw-Hill Book Co.
15. Shafer, E. L., J. L. Hamilton, and E. A. Schmidt, 1969. "Natural Landscape Preferences: A Predictive Model," *Journal of Leisure Research* 1(1):1.
16. Simonds, J. O. 1961. *Landscape Architecture.* New York: F. W. Dodge Corp.
17. Steintz, C., and D. Way. 1970. "A Model for Evaluating Visual Consequences of Urbanization on Shoreline Landscapes." U.S. Army Corps of Engineers. Washington, D. C.: U.S. Government Printing Office.
18. Tunnard, C., and B. Pushkarev. 1963. *Manmade America: Chaos or Control.* New Haven: Yale University Press.
19. U. S. Department of Commerce. 1966. *Scenic Roads and Parkways.* Washington, D.C.: U. S. Government Printing Office.
20. U.S. Forest Service. 1974. *National Forest Landscape Management,* Volumes I & II. Washington, D.C.: U.S. Government Printing Office.
21. Vernon, M. D. 1962. *The Psychology of Perception.* Baltimore. Penguin Books.

CHAPTER 10

Hazard Management

Hazards are a part of today's life style—the automobile, the hurried approach to life, the attractive nuisances and the last minute decisions. Life may seem more rushed, decisions more complex, and problem issues more numerous, but this does not mean we should merely accept the associated hazardous conditions as part of modern life. On the contrary, they should be enumerated, evaluated, and managed—using elimination (or at least reduction) techniques. This should be a primary goal for any of man's activities, but particularly for those associated with park and recreation settings.[4] When man is participating in any leisure activity, he often lowers his guard to the potential hazards. Perhaps he does not understand or appreciate the potential hazards, or he feels that management has minimized the danger, or his attention is diverted by an enjoyable activity, or he accepts the risk and is possibly attracted by it.

As managers of parks and recreation areas, we should feel some obligation to identify and effectively reduce *known* hazards. How far should we carry this obligation? Do you, as recreation manager, make the area completely free of hazards? Do you selectively choose certain hazards for specific management action, and if so, which ones? If complete removal of a hazard is unwarranted and may be impossible, how do you *manage* it? These and similar questions will be discussed in this chapter.

Ironically, we can view a hazard such as the automobile as being acceptable—even necessary to our life style, but we consider many hazards found in our park areas to be unacceptable. This does not mean we must automatically reduce or eliminate the hazard, but it does point out the need to develop a systematic approach to hazard management. The following steps are offered as just such an approach:

1. *Establishment of objectives* (for the area and the site). The management of any hazard must fit within the framework of the overall recreational management objectives for the area.

2. *Identification of hazards* (natural or manmade—see Fig. 10–1). The next step in the process is to identify all known or potential hazards and locate them on a base map.

3. *Evaluation of hazards.* Each hazard should be evaluated within the framework of the objective and within established guidelines.

4. *Development of management strategies.* The adopted strategies should reflect the previous steps and be coordinated with the overall management plan for the area.

Figure 10–1 Examples of manmade and natural hazards. *A* shows a broken cable on a climbing trail (Photo courtesy of Bruce Farmer); *B*, a coastal storm battering the beachfront (photo by Alan Jubenville).

GUIDELINES FOR HAZARD MANAGEMENT

As managers, we need to establish some basic guidelines for decision making involving hazards. Among the factors to be considered are the following:

Maturity of Participant. This refers to both the *emotional* maturity of the individual — his capacity for rational decision making in the face of risk taking — and the *perceptual* maturity of the individual — how he perceives the particular hazard. The emotional maturity of the individual is usually (but not always) associated with chronological maturity. Perceptual maturity is usually determined by previous learning experiences or, at least by previous exposure to the potential hazard. We should also consider who the primary decision-maker is in a group of participants, since decisions are frequently made by group leaders.

A person may be emotionally mature and still have had little experience with certain environs or recreational activities; thus, he may not understand the significance of the hazards he is facing. Many drownings can be traced to rational decision making by an individual who incorrectly perceived a dangerous situation as having minimum risk.

Type of Activity. The type of activity must be considered; an experience such as technical rock climbing is attractive because of the associated risks. The climber understands and accepts the high risk involved; he also minimizes it through proper instruction, good equipment, and recognition of his individual limitations.

Other concentrated activities, such as picnicking, are considered to be relatively hazard-free and thus should be planned and managed that way. Maximum effort should be made to eliminate, reduce, or modify hazards in the developed recreation site. Intermediate activities, such as hiking and bicycling, may require some reduction of hazards; other hazards can simply be made informationally available to the participant.

Type of Resource. The very nature of the resource may determine the direction that the hazard management program will take. If the resource is unique and worthy of preservation, the hazard reduction program should aim at manipulating the user rather than the environment. On the other hand, maximum modification of the landscape (such as sealing a cave or removing hazardous over-story vegetation) may be more appropriate in reducing some potential hazards. We should also consider manmade developments such as abandoned buildings, pits, mine shafts, and debris, and modify facilities to reduce these hazards.

Predictable Circumstances. If certain circumstances occur on a predictable basis, this information and the location of the events should be used in formulating a hazard management plan. Natural hazards, such as flooding, storms, and tornados, are becoming more predictable. Some, such as flooding, may be predictable on a cyclical basis; others, such as tornados occur on an immediate, emergency basis. Some changes, including possible relocation of facilities, can be done to reduce the effects of predictable hazards. Others would require an emergency plan to reduce the effects of an emergency situation. Unfortunately, if the circumstances are not highly predictable, the manager often overlooks the need to plan for emergency situations.

Accessibility. Possibly, the level of accessibility can dictate the type of hazard management to be used. If the area is somewhat inaccessible, a minimal information program that stresses the potential hazards may be most appropriate. On the other hand, when a hazardous area is made easily accessible so that people can enjoy its unique scenic beauty, maximum safety precautions may be necessary. The overlook at the Lower Falls of the Yellowstone River is an example of this kind of situation. Thus, we are assuming a greater responsibility with increasing accessibility.

Visitor Perception. Perception, although difficult to measure and to respond to managerially, is one of the most significant factors to consider in a hazard management.[1] It is extremely variable; but with sufficient research, we should be able to predict how certain groups of people perceive potential hazards in the recreation environment.[17] With this information, the manager is better situated to. develop an adequate hazard management plan; without it, he is merely speculating on what the normal visitor behavior would be in regard to the hazard. When a real hazard is perceived as being minimal or nonexistent, a much more intensive management program is required.

The question still remains: Where, when, and to what level does the manager involve himself in hazard management. We must first define what is meant by hazard management. It is the purposeful action taken by management to reduce the probability of injury, loss of life, or loss of property occurring to the participant from known or suspected, natural or manmade, hazards, within the recreational environment Notice that a hazard-free recreational setting is not mentioned in our definition. A hazard-free recreational setting would most likely be perceived as being sterile. To enhance the visitor's awareness of the environmental hazards, there may be action taken in the form of manipulation of the environment, regulation of visitor, or education and information programs. A specific management program to fit a particular situation, should take into consideration the six factors we have just discussed.

TYPES OF HAZARDS

The professional manager should be able to quickly recognize the various types of hazards, since recognition is the first step in the process of managing hazards.

NATURAL – LAND

The following is a general list of land hazards:

Cliffs. Cliffs and other places of abrupt relief (such as chasms and pits) that present a hazard to safe movement should be identified and avoided through proper road and trail location. The hazard can also be reduced through adequate site development that includes such items as safety barriers.

Landslides. Local areas of medium to high relief that have unstable soils or rock outcroppings should be avoided. These can usually be identified by early signs of erosion or sloughing. A knowledge of soil types, along with an understanding of geology, would help in predicting the areas of massive soil movement.

Avalanches. Areas of avalanche activity are generally known and identified easily by the old avalanche paths (Fig. 10–2). The environmental con-

Figure 10–2 Avalanche paths evident in the high country. (Photo by Alan Jubenville.)

ditions under which avalanches occur are temporal and must be monitored in order to predict the occurrence. Avalanche areas should be avoided for specific site developments. However, in places where winter sports are offered, the manager can monitor snow conditions to see if avalanches are likely; he can then curtail any activity in the area during that particular time. A remote control monitoring system is being perfected to give more accurate, up-to-date information, eliminating the need for expensive snow survey teams. This work, which utilizes an installed remote probe, which transmits the data to a base station, is being done by a team headed by Dean Sam Hakes of the College of Engineering, University of Wyoming.

Vegetation. Overstory vegetation can be a hazard in developed sites when combined with heavy wind, shallow soils, and high soil moisture. In this case, area planning can help to eliminate those sites where, under certain environmental conditions, the overstory trees could present a hazard to the user. Unfortunately, these conditions occur very infrequently, so that they are sometimes difficult to predict. Die-back (stag-heading) of trees in the developed site can also present a hazard to the user if these trees are not properly monitored and removed.

Others. There are other land hazards such as volcanic action and dust storms that may prove harmful to the recreationist, not just an inconvenience to him. The manager should brainstorm possible approaches to these problems with his staff and incorporate their ideas into the hazard management program including response to emergency situations. In addition, certain forms of wild-life may be considered hazardous if there is potential confrontation between man and beast (e.g., a bison or grizzly bear); consequently, confrontation be-tween the recreationist and dangerous wildlife should be managed.

NATURAL — WATER

Water hazards are probably more obvious but should be enumerated any-way. Any body of water potentially presents a hazard to a terrestrial animal like man, depending on how well he is prepared both physically and mentally.

Tidal changes. Abrupt tidal changes can present a barrier to use. They may cause a person to make irrational decisions that he would not have made under ordinary circumstances.

Currents. Water currents may not appear on the surface but can still be very hazardous to the user. A knowledge of local conditions is essential for un-derstanding and locating water currents.

Water Obstacles. Obstacles to the normal movement of the user over water such as boulders, log jams, rapids, and waterfalls create certain hazards for the user. Some users are qualified to handle these difficult situations; others are not. Certain obstacles are acceptable as part of a given recreational experience (Fig. 10–3), yet they may not be acceptable for another kind of experience.

Flooding. Flooding creates hazards for the user as well as the nonuser; each may suffer if his activity occurs in the zone of flooding. Although these zones are usually predictable, they are also places where a high amount of rec-reational use occurs, and much pressure is placed on the manager to develop and encourage activities within the flood plain.

Others. Other water hazards may include harmful animal life and water pollution. The exact problems will vary with local conditions.

Figure 10–3 Rapids on the Selway River, Idaho. (Photo courtesy of U.S. Forest Service.)

Figure 10–4 Abandoned buildings on public lands.

MANMADE

Manmade hazards are potentially the most difficult to manage, because people often do not realize the danger involved.

Buildings. Abandoned buildings, as shown in Figure 10–4, and similar manmade objects often are visual focal points in a landscape and thus are attractive nuisances.

Road Design. The road design can encourage or discourage certain speed levels, traffic bottlenecks, blind turning, and other problems, such as the one illustrated in Figure 10–5. This is something that is often overlooked, yet much recreational use is auto-oriented.

Altered Landscapes. Altered landscapes refer to the creation of hazards through man's activities, e.g., high walls (from stripmining), wells, and mine shafts similar to the one shown in Figure 10–6.

Figure 10–5 Diagram of secondary road improperly entering the primary road on a major curve.

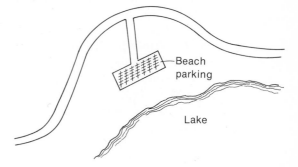

Figure 10–6 A retaining barrier is necessary to protect the visitor from natural sink holes, mine shafts, and similar hazards; or complete elimination by blasting and earth-filling may be desirable (photo by Alan Jubenville).

SURVEY TECHNIQUES

Local hazard surveys must be made in order to determine specific hazards and their potential impact. The following are the primary techniques used in hazard surveys:

Aerial Photo Interpretation.   Stereo pairs of large-scale aerial photos can be used to survey large areas for potential hazards, examples of which are shown in Figures 10–7 and 10–8. Thus, much of the work can be accomplished in the office with a minimum of cost and delay—providing recent photos are available. Fall photos are generally the best for this type of survey, since they tend to maximize detail (because the leaves have fallen) and depth perception (because there is maximum contrast from shadows). This information can be transferred to a base map (a medium-to large-scale topographic map is preferred) and can usually be verified with minimum field sampling.

The two stereo pairs show some of the variables that can be inventoried using aerial photo interpretation. This type of work is usually associated with area planning so that the allocation of land for specific sites can take into account possible hazards. While much of this work can be accomplished in the office, the results should be verified in the field to check the accuracy of the photo information. Also, data on water depth, velocity, obstacles and seasonal changes are better obtained through field studies.

Intensive Field Studies.   Intensive field studies should be done on any prospective, intensive site development to determine the existing hazards and how management may cope with these in the future. Many auto-oriented visitors may not understand the potential dangers involved with hazards that can

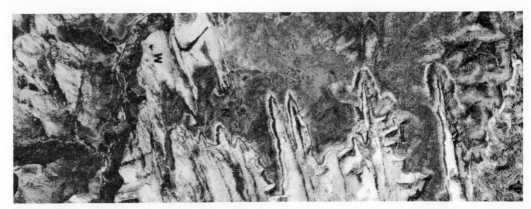

Figure 10–7 Stereopair of Zion Canyon, Zion National Park, showing abrupt topographic changes. (From Scovel, James L., Emmett O'Brien, J. C. McCormack, and R. B. Chapman. 1966. *Atlas of Landforms*. New York: John Wiley and Sons Inc., p. 7.)

casually be visited on a developed site. Thus, the manager should attempt to reduce these possibilities on the site during the planning phase before visitor use begins. On dispersed use areas, intensive field studies may not be necessary; the information needed for alerting the visitor to possible dangers may be accomplished with the use of aerial photos.

For example, a park manager had a site development adjacent to a series of

Figure 10–8 Stereopair of Crater Lake, Crater Lake National Park, showing hazards of abrupt topographic changes and water. (From Scovel et al. *Atlas of Landforms*. p. 61.)

small bluffs overlooking a swift river. Along the base of the bluffs was a tilted ledge. Several drownings had occurred during the previous seasons because people, walking along the water-splashed mossy ledge, had slipped and fallen into the river. Then the manager put up a short, split-rail fence with no signing. He was proud of the job—"We've only lost three people this year."

This type of callousness is unacceptable. A complete physical barrier would probably have solved the problem. Aerial photos could have shown the general problem of use near the swift river, and intensive development could have been directed away from the water. Detailed site studies could have indicated specific actions to reduce the hazards near or within the site development. In most cases, intensive field studies are necessary. Based on the information obtained through these studies, the manager should take action to reduce the hazards.

Seasonal monitoring. For the success of any hazard management program, monitoring seasonal fluctuations is essential. Certain hazards, such as increased water velocity and flooding, may not show up in a measurement taken at only one point in time.

Reconstruction of Past History. While conducting a survey of potential manmade hazards, one should attempt to reconstruct the past history of man's activities in that particular area. This could help to pinpoint potential problems that were left by previous developments. With a sufficiently detailed history, the exact location of hazards such as old mine shafts, covered wells, and building foundations may be made known.

SYSTEMATIC REDUCTION OF HAZARDS

The exact program of hazard reduction may be dictated by the resource (avalanche zones, unique natural areas, and so forth) or by the visitor (such as a demand for beachfront activities). But the manager must deal with a larger problem—the realization that most hazards cannot be removed; they can only be reduced. Thus, this section will emphasize reduction of hazards.

AREA PLANNING

Through the process of area planning, needs are interpreted into specific site developments, which are then given functional locations according to the experience being provided, the resource, and the existing transportation systems. In determining the locations of specific site developments, this same process should account for hazard management. Obviously, this is not an exacting process; we could eliminate use in a given area simply by closing it to the recreationists; this would certainly eliminate the hazards. However, the goal is toward maximizing the opportunities for recreation while minimizing the risks involved. This is akin to the safe minimum standard described by Ciracy-Wanthrup.[7]

As stated earlier in the chapter, there are six variables (listed under Guidelines) that must be evaluated to determine the appropriate action for hazard management during area planning. Once we establish acceptable levels of risk for the various site developments, we can locate them in resource settings that

Figure 10-9 Recreation site design to minimize the hazards associated with visitor use—Inspiration Point overlook in the Grand Canyon of the Yellowstone (photo by Alan Jubenville).

meet the minimum safe standards for the particular development (recreational experience). We would not want to locate a forest campground (a family-oriented experience) along a stretch of the river that is deep, swift, and dangerous, even though it meets all other resource requirements. When a manager locates a family-oriented development in the vicinity of a major hazard, he is asking for trouble in the long run.

Site Planning. Site planning can be used to reduce risks to the user by carefully designing the physical development to fit the human behavior. For some major hazards (such as an overlook or a sharp road curve), proper site design can minimize the risks and still be appropriate for the immediate landscape. In some cases, the safety factor may override the concerns for aesthetics.

In reality, only two methods can be utilized to reduce hazards associated with a particular site. [Assuming that this is the only *logical* place to put it.] The first is a physical barrier that is used to direct people away from the hazard or to restrain them (Fig. 10-9). The second is a psychological barrier that, theoretically, would discourage any visitors—except skilled participants—from approaching the area. For example, a manager is inviting disaster when he allows a road to be built into an area reserved for technical rock climbing. He encourages participation by the casual climber, who does not have the skill or the understanding of the risk involved.

Hazard Removal. Hazard removal is a tool for minimizing the risk of recreation participation. It is simply an eradication of the hazard (e.g., removing buildings, dynamiting mine shafts). This does not necessarily mean it is only to be used as a last resort. It is simply another alternative for the manager to use in particular situations.

Information and Education. Programs can be devised that will raise the

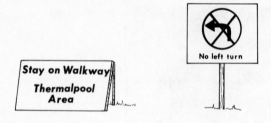

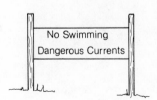

Figure 10–10 Hazard management, using information signs.

level of skill of the individual, increase his awareness of the risks involved, or simply warn him and allow him to make his own choice. Each approach or combination of approaches may be sufficient when used in programs by themselves or in combination with the first three management techniques. Even if we reduce the risk, we should still attempt to remind the individual of a potential hazard by methods such as the use of information signs (Fig. 10–10).

Information programs are often the first step toward hazard management in sites that have already been developed. They are a stop-gap measure to be used until the more sophisticated programs such as relocating a trail, closing out a facility, or establishing a permanent barrier, can be worked out. Information signs should be continued in conjunction with the permanent measures to make people aware that certain dangers still exist. On dispersed use areas, informational programs may be the prime technique for managing associated hazards.

Regulation. Reducing potential risks by regulation can be effective but expensive. Establishing a regulation involves creating a concomitant program for its enforcement. This becomes an expensive procedure. One example of hazard reduction by regulation is the requirement that a raft meet certain design specifications, carry specific safety items (such as life preservers and extra oars) and fill certain on-water safety requirements. To enforce this regulation, we must have qualified technicians to inspect the rafts and boat patrols to ensure that the user complied with on-water safety regulations and has all specified equipment on board.

To reiterate a previous question, How far do you take this? We could perhaps regulate an activity to such a point that it is no longer satisfying to the using public. This type of regulating is mostly reserved for the situation in which there is great potential for loss of life or property. Much depends on the activity, the danger to others, and the general societal values. For example, in order to obtain a hunting license, a hunter safety course is now a requirement in some states. In order to obtain a permit for technical mountain climbing, a statement of experience and qualifications is now necessary in some areas. The number of permit requirements such as the above are increasing. I would first check to see if I had done a thorough job on the first four types of programs before I would begin to establish a stringent regulatory program.

SELECTED READINGS

1. Brockman, C. F., and L. C. Merriam, Jr. 1973. *Recreational Use of Wild Lands* (2nd ed.) New York: McGraw-Hill Book Co.
2. Brown, P. J. 1975. "White Water Rivers: Social Inputs to Carrying Capacity Based Decisions," *White Water River Management Conference,* Moab, Utah.
3. Brown, P. J., B. L. Driver, and G. H. Stankey. 1976. "Human Behavioral Science and Recreation Management," XXI I.U.F.R.O., World Congress, Division VI, Oslo, Norway.
4. Burton, I., and K. Havett. 1971. *The Hazardousness of a Place: A Regional Ecology of Damaging Events.* Toronto: University of Toronto Press.
5. California State Department of Public Health. 1969. *Health and Safety Guide for Development of Recreation Areas.* Sacramento, Calif.
6. Campbell, F. L., J. C. Hendee, and R. Clark. 1968. "Law and Order in Public Park," *Parks and Recreation* 3(12).
7. Ciracy-Wanthrup, S. V. 1965. "A Safe Minimum Standard As an Objective of Conservation Policy," *Readings in Resource Management and Conservation,* Burton, I., and R. W. Kates (eds.). Chicago; University of Chicago Press.
8. David, C. 1966. "Legal Problems and Liability in Outdoor Recreation," *Park Maintenance* 19(12).
9. Forbes, R. D. 1956. *Forestry Handbook.* New York: The Ronald Press Co.
10. Hendee, J. C., W. R. Catton, Jr., L. D. Marlow, and C. F. Brockman. 1968. *Wilderness Users in the Pacific Northwest—Their Characteristics, Values, and Management Preferences.* U.S. Forest Service Research Paper PNW-61.
11. Jubenville, A. 1976. *Outdoor Recreation Planning.* Philadelphia: W. B. Saunders Co.
12. National Park Service. 1975. *Snake River Management Plan, Grand Teton National Park.* Moose, Wyo.: Grand Teton National Park.
13. Paine, L. A. 1966. "Accident Caused by Hazardous Trees in California Recreation Sites," *U.S. Forest Service Research Note* PSW-133.
14. Scovel, J. L., E. J. O'Brien, J. C. McCormack, and R. B. Chapman. 1966. *Atlas of Landforms.* New York: John Wiley & Sons, Inc.
15. Spurr, S. H. 1966. *Photogrammetry and Photo-Interpretation* (2nd ed.). New York: The Ronald Press Co.
16. Van Arsdel, E. P. 1969. "Detection of Hazard Trees in Recreation Areas by Remote Sensing," *Remote Sensing Conference for Recreation and Resource Administrators, Proceedings,* G. R. Harker (ed.). College Station, Tex.: Texas A & M University.
17. Wagener, W. W. 1963. "Judging Hazard from Native Trees in California Recreation Areas: A Guide for Professional Foresters," *U.S. Forest Research Paper* PSW-PI.
18. White, G. F. (ed.). 1974. *Natural Hazards.* New York: Oxford University Press.

PART III

VISITOR MANAGEMENT

Visitor and service management programs are covered in this section. The subjects that are included are distribution of visitor use, informational services, interpretation, concession management, and public safety. Visitor and service management are important as subsystems, but they must also be integrated into the overall management model. Distribution of use is a perennial problem to which there are no easy answers. Many sites and facilities are overused; others are underused. Why? How can we apply redistribution techniques to maximize the efficiency of use of developed sites and minimize the overloading of a few? Should we even try?

Information services are essential for promoting a broader distribution of use. If a person has a large body of information to draw upon in choosing a recreational area, he can make a more rational decision. Theoretically, you enhance the user experience by allowing him to choose the "best" alternative; consequently, this should cause a better distribution of users on an area or regional basis.

Interpretation refers to the principles and methods by which the environment is interpreted to the user. The environment may be natural (national parks and natural areas), historical (historical sites) or cultural (manmade activities). The goal of any interpretive program is an increased awareness of the visitor toward the object or subject; its thrust is the provocation of the individual, encouraging him to seek out information for his own edification. An interpreter can only spend a few minutes with a group of visitors; thus

Figure 11–1   With increasing use, more attention needs to be given to visitor management programs (photo by Alan Jubenville).

the program must be simple and straightforward, but provocative enough to encourage the visitor to seek a greater level of awareness.

Concession management is a very controversial area with regard to the role of the concessioner and the political aspects of controlling concessions through a particular governmental agency. Some people fear the control of private enterprise by government; others fear the encroachment by private enterprise (in the form of tourist development) on the landscape and the experiences that people are seeking. The management should attempt to incorporate both concerns in a concession management program.

Public safety is a comprehensive program to enhance the visitor's enjoyment by improving the existing site conditions to protect the visitor as well as the resource. This includes maintenance (to maintain sites, facilities, and transportation systems for safe, enjoyable experiences), hazard management (to reduce the effects of hazards within the recreational environment), and law enforcement (to protect both visitor and environmental setting).

CHAPTER 11

Distribution of Visitor Use

A reasonable distribution of use over existing recreational areas and sites has always been a management problem. For some reason, people often prefer to congregate at particular locations—to the exclusion of others. The focus of this chapter will be on the problems of dispersed use. The basic principles will be discussed according to priority of application, along with techniques of dispersal.

PRINCIPLES OF DISPERSAL OF VISITOR USE

Dispersal of use must be done on a regional or area basis if it is to be effective. Little can be done on an individual site unless it has been designed initially to allow or encourage dispersal of use. Figure 11–2 shows the three principles of visitor dispersal in ascending order.

If a change in existing use patterns is desirable, one should first attempt to accomplish it by means of voluntary dispersal, either through information programs or through changes in the physical design of the setting. If that approach does not work, dispersal of use may have to be done through regulation—i.e., directing use away from areas of heavy use but not controlling total numbers allowed. When these programs fail to achieve the objective, the manager may still be faced with the limiting of use in order to protect the recreational experience and preserve the environment in which it takes place. When the manager begins limiting use, he also may be detracting from the total user experience. The manager must ask himself, "Is limiting use in this instance a desirable trade-off?" Ultimately, a certain locale may have to be closed to recreational use

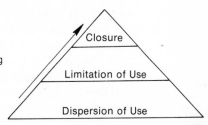

Figure 11–2 Principles of visitor dispersal, in ascending order of implementation.

to allow it to recover or to protect, on a long term basis, its unique, fragile environment.

Dispersion is considered a voluntary redistribution of recreation use over an area. This should really be the manager's first alternative when overuse is occurring on some sites while others are remaining underused. The program should attempt to disperse use voluntarily through information services. This will never achieve optimal dispersal, but it may provide sufficient redistribution to reduce problems of overuse on specific sites. By this approach, we will cause minimal disruption to the normal participation patterns of the visitor. He does not feel *forced* into changing his itinerary; he may even find the other sites more enjoyable. In fact, providing more information on available recreation activities may allow the user an opportunity to choose a more desirable experience than he otherwise may have selected. This helps to eliminate "off-site" uses. For example, some horsemen drove two to three hours from the Butte, Montana, area to the Anaconda-Pintlar area in order to horseback ride. They had been assured that there would be no encounters with noisy trail bikes during their ride. They did not seek a wilderness experience; they only desired respite from trail bikes. One could eliminate this "off-site" user and simultaneously enhance his experience by providing him with information on bridle paths or trails that are zoned for horse use *only* and are also within easy driving distance of Butte.

Limitation is the restriction on the number of people who may participate in a particular activity at a particular location. It involves determining a site capacity limit beyond which use cannot be permitted. For the manager, limiting use is usually a simpler solution than dispersal of use, but it also requires greater supervision. Again, in problems involving concentration of use, one should first apply the voluntary dispersal alternatives before proceeding with limitation programs. There are several ways of limiting use; the most desirable should be one that is closely aligned with the normal behavioral patterns of visitor use. The management objectives can then be accomplished without any major disruption to existing use patterns Perhaps this may seem a somewhat idealistic approach, but often one will find existing social mechanisms that tend to separate users into compatible use patterns—similar to the process described by the theory of cognitive dissonance.[24]

Closure is usually the last alternative for changing recreational use patterns. This may be either temporary or permanent in order to protect the resource base. Permanent closures should be done only when no other means are available for protecting the valued resource, and the size of the area involved should be no larger than necessary to accomplish it. Under certain circumstances, this logically may be the first alternative. As an example, perhaps you have located a pair of nesting bald eagles along the river in your park. You may wish to close the general area to recreational use and not allow people to get out of their boats along this stretch. You also may want to limit the number of people or the size of the craft on this portion of the river. Through your information program, you may even attempt dispersal of use voluntarily to other rivers and streams or to other portions of the same river. Thus, all levels of visitor redistribution may be employed in a recreation area or focused on a specific problem. As the preceding example illustrates, the problem for management becomes much more complex when one tries to incorporate resource and social variables into the decision; therefore, it is important to follow the desired hierarchy of principles involving the distribution of recreational use.

TECHNIQUE—DISPERSION

There are three techniques for obtaining voluntary dispersal—regional and area planning, regional information management, and area information systems.

Regional and Area Planning. On a regional and an area basis, the patterns of use will be determined by the transportation systems—primarily by the system of roads and trails. Since nearly all recreational use is associated with road or trail access, the type, character, and location of either one generally will determine the type and the amount of recreational use a given place will receive. When you do not want recreational use to occur in a particular place (assuming it is for some legitimate reason), do not place a road or trail nearby.

The type and character of road and trail may encourage or discourage certain recreational uses. For example, a scenic road would be a type that is designed to slow people down so that they can enjoy a view of the surrounding landscape. If we design the scenic road for high-speed, through traffic, we may be encouraging undesirable use and creating conflict between users. Even if the road has been properly designed in terms of speed, its character must still be considered. The presence of large cuts and fills or of widely cleared areas for rights-of-way may detract from the character and discourage use of the road. The location can also influence use—whether a road is located to capture a maximum variety of scenery or to mask negative land uses (e.g., dumps, junk yards).

Although the above may not be the best example, it does indicate that road and trail layouts can encourage or discourage certain use patterns that promote the dispersal of recreational use. It is hoped that we will use a positive approach to encourage dispersal by proper regional and area planning, rather than by exposing visitors to the negative elements of the landscape or to a poorly designed road and trail system. We could allow use to just build up to such a point that the site would no longer be desirable as a recreation space (socially or environmentally). People would then move on to other sites that had not yet been overused. This is reminiscent of the early days of farming—when the soil was "worn-out," the farmer would simply move on to new lands. However, the amount of space that is available for various recreational opportunities is scarce. Thus, we must maximize use of the existing space, and this requires a positive approach to dispersal.

Given a particular transportation system, the type, character, and location of specific site developments will determine the patterns of recreational use. The types of site developments—even if they are substitutes for the opportunities people are really seeking—will determine primary use. Each person has his own preference for specific site developments. If all of these are reasonably available, the individual will choose the one most suitable to his needs. The problem often is a lack of variety that forces a person to choose a less desirable alternative.

The character of the development will force the camper to make a choice—for example, a primitive auto campground versus a modern one. The character is really the quality that distinguishes one development from another, given a specific type of site development. The character of the development can thus encourage or discourage certain types of uses.

Also, location of the development can directly affect use patterns.[13] If they are poorly located in terms of the normal behavioral patterns of visitors, substitutes may be sought. As an example, a transient campground that is located away from the main through-route will not be used for the purpose it was originally intended. Informal, transient camping usually takes place near the access to a through-route. This is also true for a family picnic unit occupying the same area. It may encourage en route picnicking solely because of its location.

Regional Information Management. After development, the most effective management tool for obtaining voluntary dispersal is an information system that reaches the individual recreation area visitor before he arrives at his destination. Ideally, one should reach the recreationist while he is planning his trip so that he will have sufficient information on which to base a legitimate decision. Often, contacting the visitor on the site is too late to obtain a better dispersal of use, since his plans are less flexible at that point.

There are problems in implementing a regional information management system, and assumptions must be made in developing such a system. These will be discussed in detail in Chapter 12.

Area Information Systems. Area distribution or redistribution can be accomplished through the use of specific visitor information programs and visitor services. Information programs at the area level are aimed at direct visitor contact through signing, information centers, on-site contact, and brochures.[3, 13] By making specific information available to the user, the manager does have a say in the distribution of people over the area; he may also influence redistribution of visitor use by making information available on existing use patterns, points of overuse, and conflicts. A current research project by Robert C. Lucas* is testing the value of this information in causing redistribution of use. A brochure showing existing use patterns, deteriorated campsites, and other problems has been made available to the hiker in the Stevensville District of the Bitterroot National Forest (Fig. 11–3). The results as yet are not available, but many people feel that this is socially a more desirable approach to redistribution than through limitation or closure programs. Other visitor services that may affect the distribution of use include public safety, type of concessions, and type of accommodations.

TECHNIQUE – LIMITATION

Limitation of use is predicated on the determination of capacity limits, or the carrying capacity, of a site. Physical carrying capacity refers to the durability of the site to sustain a given level of recreational use with minimal permanent resource deterioration. Wagar[25] has used simulated trampling to establish the durability limit after which permanent damage will occur to the vegetation. Then it becomes a matter of establishing the criteria for judging unacceptable damage to the resource.

Social carrying capacity is often equated with the perception of crowding.[16] However, there are other factors to consider—such as the visitor's perception of the environment in which the activity takes place and the normal behavioral patterns of the user.[23] Regardless of the variables, the purpose of social carrying capacity is to *maximize* the enjoyment of the particular experience to the indi-

---

*This study is being sponsored by the Wilderness Research Project, Forest Science Laboratory, Missoula, Montana.

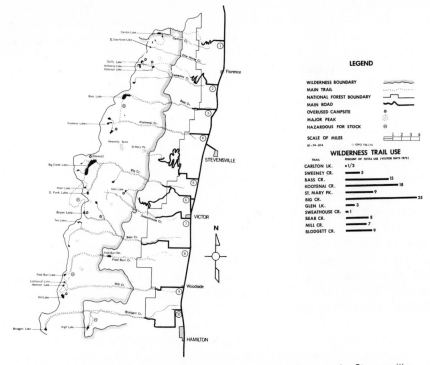

Figure 11–3 Informational map showing existing use patterns on the Stevensville District portion of the Selway-Bitterroot Wilderness Area. The concept is to aid in redistribution of use through information.

vidual. Since there are many kinds of users who are seeking a "quality experience" on the same land and since there possibly are conflicts of interests, perhaps it would be more appropriate to call it *optimization* rather than *maximization.* We should try to make the experiences optimal within the content of the management objectives for the area and with the realization that some experiences may be eliminated or shifted to other areas if they do not fit management objectives.

Service carrying capacity is the maximum limit of developed facilities in terms of visitor needs. This is commonly called head count or bed count, depending on whether it is to be used as a service facility (such as a restaurant or visitor center) or as an overnight accommodation.

Any one of these capacities could be a limiting factor in terms of handling visitor loads. Ideally, we would first determine the social carrying capacity (in terms of numbers of people) that could be accommodated on a site without lowering the quality of the recreation experience. Then, the physical carrying capacity should be established to determine if the resource can sustain the level of use indicated in the previous step by the social carrying capacity. If it cannot, the capacity must be reduced to a level that the resource can sustain. The service capacity is determined by the ability of the facilities to provide for a given number of visitors. Since the service capacity is often inadequate because of budget constraints, it creates additional management problems of enforcing capacity limits and site renovation.

Recreational Use Zoning. This is probably the most common form of limiting use—and also one of the most appropriate.[24] This method consists of clustering compatible recreational uses in selected zones. It is being used more and more to limit kinds of recreational uses, to disperse incompatible uses, and to protect the resource base. If certain activities are not compatible with existing recreational uses or are not within the capability of the resource, they would be more appropriate located elsewhere.

This type of zoning has been employed successfully on large bodies of water in order to separate motorized and nonmotorized boating, to separate boating from swimming activities, and to separate two incompatible activities (such as fishing and water-skiing).

Perhaps this should be the first step, since this is essentially what is meant by area planning — i.e., allocating space for specific recreational uses and locating that space, based on some pattern or zoning system, within the specific area.[13] Next, one could look at other ways of obtaining dispersal such as the more sophisticated techniques of density and time zoning.

Time Limitation. Time zoning is a means of controlling use during peak periods, reducing conflicts between users, and ensuring adequate turnover rate so that opportunities are available for all users. The actual time limitation can be daily, weekly, seasonally, or annually. The time frame that is chosen will depend on the activities, the season of use, the concentration during certain periods, and the efficiency level that one wishes to attain in managing the area.

Where competition for open space is high, time zoning can assist in redistributing use by limiting visitor stay. This forces some users to seek other desirable alternatives. If the program is to be reasonably successful, these alternatives must be available for visitor use. Ideally, time zoning would fit the normal behavioral patterns of the users as closely as possible.

For example, a small lake near the coast of North Carolina was being used by fishermen and water-skiers. Conflict was occurring between users, since the lake was oval and not large enough to handle both types. An observation study showed that the fisherman typically used the lake from daybreak until about 9:00 A.M., returning around 5:00 P.M. until dark. Water-skiers usually arrived around 10:00 A.M. and stayed until 4:00 P.M. The conflict arose over the times when the fisherman stayed late and the water-skier arrived early. The final decision limited the fisherman to a time period from daylight to 9:00 A.M. and from 5:00 P.M. until sunset; water-skiers were allowed on the lake from 9:00 A.M. to 5:00 P.M.

Most situations are not that simplistic; regardless of the problem, one should consider the existing behavioral patterns of the users. Time zoning is better adapted to the shorter time frames, such as daily or weekly. Seasonal or annual periods of time are usually too long to effectively redistribute use for either ecological or sociological purposes.

Space Limitation (Use per Unit Area). Space limitation, or density zoning, is a relatively new concept that has been applied to surface waters and roadless areas.[1, 12] Desirable density levels are functions of the type of experience, the durability of the resource, and the perception of the user and are established as the upper limit for various management zones. Once these densities are reached, use is shifted to less populated zones. To be effective, this measure requires a well-supervised permit system. Ideally, we would encourage voluntary redistribution through an information program and then limit use through a space limitation program that sets up well-defined zones.

Grand Teton National Park has a program that establishes the density of overnight use for certain critical backcountry zones. Several Midwestern lakes have recently been zoned and their use limited to certain density patterns, which are based on the resource, the activity, and the perception of the user. There are no standards of desirable density because of the variable inputs of the three elements previously described—type of experience, durability of the resource, and perception of the user.

Quota or Service Limitation. Quota limitations are established for developed sites based on the ability to handle a given number of people at any one time. This may be limited by the size of the facility, by the service loads of the supporting facilities, or by legal means such as state fire codes. Often the quota system is referred to as the "bed count" (for overnight facilities) and the "head count" (for day-use facilities). If no overflow camping is allowed, the service limitation is the total number of camping units located in the developed sites. Camping is usually regulated on a unit basis rather than by the number of individual campers.

When maintenance of aesthetics and environmental protection are important for a developed site with a given number of service units, the manager has a mandate to limit use to the existing service capacity. By this method, use can again be more evenly redistributed by directing the overflow to underused sites, rather than allowing crowding to occur at a few sites.

For any particular area, any, or all, of the three techniques for limiting use just described may be used at the same time. Thus, each situation in which the limiting of use is required must be handled on an individual basis, with a program specially designed for that situation.

Physical and Psychological Barriers. The purpose of this approach is not to *eliminate use* but to restrict it by creating certain barriers. It is a way of managing use by design—by limiting it to a specific corridor, rather than employing a permit system. One such barrier may be a rustic fence to keep vehicle use on the road; another may be an unmaintained trail in a roadless area. If you wish to travel on foot and enjoy the hiking experience, you must be willing to scramble over fallen timber along your route. This forces the individual to assess his own motivations for participation. If he is not interested in that kind of experience, he is "forced" to seek a less challenging hiking opportunity. However, if you psychologically force someone out of an area, there should be alternative opportunities available.

TECHNIQUE—CLOSURE

Closure means to close the area for recreational use. No matter what the reason is behind its use, the manager needs to identify the closure as temporary or permanent, since these are entirely different management programs.

Temporary Closures. Temporary closures are implemented on a particular site for specific objectives and for a given amount of time. The primary purpose is to renovate a worn out site or to protect a site during a period of maximum vulnerability—such as seasonal closures during high precipitation periods.

Obviously other techniques to reduce visitor concentration should be employed before a temporary closure program is attempted. When this approach is being used, a concomitant information program is also mandatory so that people understand the situation (i.e., what you are attempting to do) and are aware of available alternative sites. Without this program, you may face a greater, long term problem—dissatisfaction of the visitor toward any new management program because of a lack of confidence in the management. This lack of confidence often stems from poor communications between user and manager.

Seasonal closures are generally done to relieve pressure from visitors on the resource during the critical periods which usually occur during the earlier part of the growing season (vegetation impact) and when high precipitation and soil saturation affect heavy soils (a combination of soil compaction and subsequent loss of vegetative cover and surface erosion). Many times, the situation is a self-correcting one, since periods of high precipitation often will discourage visitor participation. Some activities, such as four-wheel driving and hunting, may not follow this trend. Ultimately, the manager may have to make the unpopular decision to close the area or site during a particular season. In doing so, he realizes the need to sustain resources over time rather than having them depleted by visitor use over short periods of time. These measures do not necessarily have to be obtrusive. For example, the road leading to a campground located in a subalpine zone was plowed of snow during the early camping season so that people could use the site. Because of the semi-open forest cover, the campground was free of snow, but the soil was saturated by the snow melt. Early use was causing problems such as soil compaction, loss of vegetation, and sheet erosion of the soil surface. The decision was made to discontinue plowing, since the timing of the natural snow melt on the road would allow the site to dry out before the campers could get into it. This was less obtrusive than a method that continued the plowing—with only a sign stretched across the entrance stating that no camping would be allowed until after July 1.

Probably the most sophisticated temporary closure technique is the *rest and rotation* system. In this method, certain sites or portions of sites are programmed on a rotating schedule to remain inactive so that the vegetation can be maintained at some acceptable level. This has to be included in area and site planning processes so that there are sufficient, alternative opportunities available to the user during any particular rest and rotation period. In the initial resource inventory for area planning, if one foresees a need for a rest and rotation program because of low natural site productivity, sufficient sites could be located and developed to accommodate such a program.

Possibly a more widely used approach is to have a site that is developed as a series of approximately equal *subsites*, which then can be rested and rotated. An example would be the multi-loop campground where one loop is closed each year for site renovation.

Permanent Closures. Permanent closures may be needed to protect the individual from environmental hazards or to protect a very sensitive resource from any recreational use. The need for such a measure is determined during the area planning process. Generally, problems requiring closure are more easily handled by not locating road, trail, or site development near the suspected areas; i.e., avoiding them. Locating the new sites, road, and trails away from suspected problem points, creates more of a psychological barrier than a physical one. More significant problem locations (such as sink holes or rare or endangered vegetation) may still need physical barriers to close the location to general recreational use.

ECONOMIC RATIONING

Since our social system is based primarily on some form of economic rationing, we could limit use through employing user fees—a demand schedule of consumption rates at various prices. The price would be adjusted until the desired levels of use are reached. Clawson and Knetsch[6] described demand schedules for various park units, based on differential pricing, as being potential management tools. This can be seen in the hypothetical demand curves shown in Figure 11–4. The user fees that are charged (including entrance fees and service charges) would represent the "price" of the experience. As user fees rise, demand for various recreation opportunities decreases; this is a form of rationing using economic criteria.

Many people disagree with the idea of applying economic rationing to recreation; they feel it should be free and open to all. In reality, the participants in most forms of outdoor recreation are middle class Americans, and already a form of rationing exists in terms of equipment, travel expenses, and so forth. Thus, economic rationing should be an acceptable means of managing use patterns, since it forces the user to make choices concerning his recreational participation. Adjustments could be made to include the economically disadvantaged; however, rationing generally should not affect participation by the *poor* person, who was already out of the game well before the addition of user fees.

SUMMARY STATEMENT

Regardless of the nature of its pattern, *distribution* of recreation use *per se* is not the problem. Rather, the *effects,* both social and environmental, create the problems. Once these problems have been isolated, we then can look at programs and techniques to adjust the patterns of use in order to better meet established, long range objectives.

No matter what the solution is, we should carefully consider the effects of

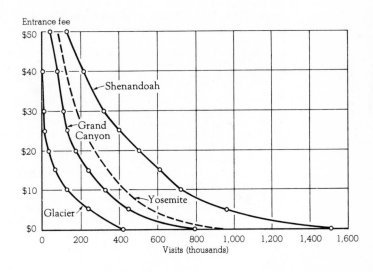

Figure 11–4 Estimated visits under various entrance fee schedules for Yosemite, Glacier, Grand Canyon, and Shenandoah National Parks. (From Clawson, M., and J. L. Knetsch. 1966. *Economics of Outdoor Recreation.* Baltimore: The Johns Hopkins University Press, p. 83.)

the program and the techniques because, in attempting to redistribute use, we may create greater problems by forcing social changes or environmental changes at points that have not been hardened sufficiently to sustain a given level of recreational use.

The suggested initial approach for obtaining redistribution of use is through voluntary dispersal, primarily by means of informational programs. This does not imply the equal distribution of use over an area. It involves the redistribution of use from "problem" points to places that are durable or site hardened enough to sustain it. In essence, it is a matter of concentrating use where it would be acceptable. That is the primary reason for agency coordination in the redistribution of use effort; often we may force the problem out of our jurisdiction and onto some other agency's property without really solving it.

The other techniques of limitation and closure also are desirable solutions and should be applied where needed, but they should not be the first alternatives. It seems that we have allowed ourselves to be trapped by the "carrying capacity syndrome" — i.e., to establish some magic number as a level of use and then to maintain this level without much concern for the effects of such a decision. Even then, we may just be forcing the demand for that type of recreation onto other, less durable and less desirable areas.

Other alternative techniques that have not been discussed in this chapter are hardening of sites to sustain higher levels of use, developing more sites to handle the increase in demand, providing more variety in opportunities available to the visitor, and developing "substitute" experiences. These could all be clustered under the term *planning and development;* each could help to alleviate problems caused by existing use patterns but it would generally require large scale development of sites and facilities. However, for any development, there are realistic and pragmatic levels of use where ultimately one must utilize the three basic programs of use distribution — dispersal, limitation, and closure.

The answers to the complex problems of visitor distribution are not easy. In fact, one should thoroughly document the existing situation and brainstorm and analyze any alternatives (including trade-offs) before making a decision.

SELECTED READINGS

1. Brooks., L. 1963. "Zoning as a Step in the Planning of Natural Parks." *Second Federal–Provincial Parks Conference Proceedings,* Ottawa: Canadian National and Historical Parks Branch.
2. Brockman, C. F., and L. C. Merriam, Jr. 1973. *Recreational Use of Wildlands.* New York: McGraw-Hill Book Co.
3. Brown, P. J., and J. D. Hunt. 1969. "The Influence of Information Signs of Visitor Distribution and Use," *Journal of Leisure Research* 1(1):69.
4. Burch, W. R., Jr. 1964. "Two Concepts for Guiding Recreation Management Decisions," *Journal of Forestry* 62(1):707.
5. Bureau of Outdoor Recreation. 1966. *National Conference on Policy Issues in Outdoor Recreation.* Washington, D.C.: U.S. Department of Interior.
6. Clawson, M., and J. L. Knetsch. 1966. *Economics of Outdoor Recreation.* Baltimore: The John Hopkins University Press.
7. Cowgill, P. 1971. "Two Many People on the Colorado River," *National Parks and Conservation Magazine* 45(11):10.
8. Douglass, R. W. 1969. *Forest Recreation.* New York: Pergamon Press.
9. Gilbert, K. 1967. "Resources Management and Operation," *Proceedings of Recreation Management Institute.* College Station, Tex.: Texas A & M University.
10. Godfrey, E. B., and R. L. Peckfelder. 1972. "Recreation Carrying Capacity and Wild Rivers: A

Case Study of the Middle Fork of the Salmon," *Western Agricultural Economic Association Annual Meeting.*

11. Held, R. B., B. Brickler, and A. T. Wilcox. 1969. *A Study to Develop Practical Techniques for Determining the Carrying Capacity of Natural Areas in the National Park System.* Ft. Collins, Colo.: Colorado State University.
12. Jackson, R. 1971. "Zoning to Regulate On-Water Recreation," *Land Economics* 45(4):382.
13. Jubenville, A. 1976. *Outdoor Recreation Planning.* Philadelphia: W. B. Saunders Co.
14. LaPage, W. F. 1968. The *Role of Fees in Camper's Decisions.* U.S. Forest Service Research Paper NE-118.
15. Lime, D. W., and G. H. Stankey. 1971. "Carrying Capacity: Maintaining Outdoor Recreation Quality," *Recreation Symposium Proceedings.* Northeast Forest Experiment Station.
16. Lucas, R. C. 1971. "Hikers and Other Trail Users," *Recreation Symposium Proceedings.* Northeast Forest Experiment Station.
17. McEwen, D., and S. R. Tocher. 1976. "Zone Management: Key to Controlling Recreational Impact in Developed Campsites," *Journal of Forestry* 14(2):90.
18. McGill, A. W., "Dispersal of Recreationists on Wildlands," *Outdoor Recreation Research: Applying the Results.* U.S. Forest Service Technical Report NC-9.
19. Myles, G. A. 1970. *Effect of Quality Factors on Water-Based Recreation in Western Nevada.* Reno, Nev.: Agricultural Research Station, University of Nevada.
20. O.R.R.R.C. 1962. *The Quality of Outdoor Recreation: As Evidenced By User Satisfaction, Study Report 5.* Washington, D.C.: U.S. Government Printing Office.
21. Prausa, R. L. 1971. "Multiple Use Management for Recreation in the East," *Recreation Symposium Proceedings.* Northeast Forest Experiment Station.
22. Schlatter, J. 1972. "Great Smokies Trails: The Backpacking Permit System," *National Parks and Conservation Magazine* 46(9):13.
23. Siecker, J. 1951. "The Future of Forest Recreation," *Journal of Forestry* 49(7):503.
24. Stankey, G. H. 1973. *Visitor Perception of Wilderness Recreation Carrying Capacity.* U.S. Forest Service Research Paper INT-141.
25. Travers, R. M. W. 1967. *Essentials of Learning.* New York: Macmillan Co.
26. U.S. Forest Service. 1969. *Management Handbook, Boundary Waters Canoe Area.* Superior National Forest, Duluth, Minn.
27. Wagar, A. 1964. *The Carrying Capacity of Wild Lands for Recreation: Forest Science Monograph 7.*
28. Wilson, G. T. 1969. *Lake Zoning for Recreation: How to Improve Recreation Use of Lakes.* American Institute of Park Executives.

CHAPTER 12

Information Services

Information services are necessary to increase the visitor's awareness of those opportunities available to him, to inform him of any restrictions placed on that use, and to maintain open communication with the user (Fig. 12–1). However, this does not include the use of facilities to promote special interest groups or to release propaganda to the public. These programs serve to provide information for the visitor and to promote his general welfare and that of the resource setting where the activity takes place.

The specific information services will vary depending on whether they are offered on a regional or an area basis. Regional informational programs are aimed at reaching the individual before he arrives at his destination, while the goal of area programs is to inform the individual after he arrives. The communication portion (feedback) encourages open, two-way interaction between agency and public. It is important to maintain open channels of communications.

Figure 12–1   For the larger parks, one of the primary informational programs is the visitor contact at the entrance stations (photo by Bruce and Debbie Maxon).

REGIONAL INFORMATION SYSTEM (RIS)

Ideally, regional information systems would reach the visitor *while he is planning his recreational trip.* This is a new concept—to reach the individual while he is making certain choices about his recreational participation. Usually, we consider a regional information system as a "hit or miss" tactic employed in reaching the visitor through centers located along his travel route. Although information is provided on regional recreation opportunities, it frequently is fragmented and thus not effective. Often, people have developed their itinerary before they receive the information, so that they are unwilling to alter it. Thus, to be effective, we must reach the individual while he is still planning his trip—the difficulty is in reaching the person.

Under present conditions, most regional information management efforts are doomed to failure because of the limited scope of application. It is usually done on an agency basis so that the information is extremely well defined. In some instances, the information is limited not only to a specific agency but also to a specific activity, such as the campground reservation system of the National Park Service. In order to be effective, the regional information system should include all agencies (public or private) and activities and should be easily accessible to the visitor. Excluding some agencies will leave tremendous gaps in the available information. Denying easy accessibility to all users would create a differential effect in the available information. This type of system presently exists on a limited basis (such as American Automobile Association, AAA); but to be effective, it would have to be expanded and would have to have the confidence of the people.

Information Management—A Two-Way Street. The concept of information management is shown in Figure 12–2. It is essential that the information be updated continuously in terms of general use patterns and that new information be fed back to the visitor so that he knows not only what resources are available but also how other people are using them. This is a two-way street in which all agencies contribute to the information on the available opportunities and to the feedback about specific visitor use patterns. The feedback system is useful in updating information to the visitor as well as in changing management strategy in other programs

In order for the feedback to be useful, more sophisticated techniques of monitoring recreational use will be necessary. Much of the user statistics are based on limited observations, often with very little statistical validity. Too often the reported statistics are based on educated guesses or at best on limited samplings. Yet we use computer programs to manipulate the data in order to

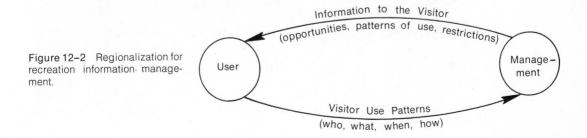

Figure 12–2 Regionalization for recreation information management.

give it a degree of credibility and then present the results as legitimate. Perhaps this may seem overly critical; the point is that we use statistics in our information management program without any concern for their validity.

In order to overcome the problems of validity, we need to improve monitoring techniques and sampling procedures.[9] Probably, it is more important to establish adequate sampling procedures, since without them the information gathered and disseminated is nearly worthless. In sum, an information system is only as good as the information.

Regionalization. It seems important to gather and disseminate information on a regional level in order to minimize discrepancies in data collection methods, units of analyses, and modeling of actual participation.[5] Many people will agree on this point; however, the problem becomes one of defining regional boundaries. Some feel that each state should be divided into regions; however, this does not seem to be a large enough geographic area for describing the normal travel and behavioral patterns of the users and for disseminating this information to the using public. The geographic area should be larger—*much* larger. Since use patterns and demands for information often exceed the state and even multi-state boundaries, the regional boundaries should be extremely large (6 to 10 states), and the regions should be interconnected so that the information can be exchanged between regions. Probably the best way to delineate boundaries is based on the primary physiographic areas of the United States that have been adjusted to the political boundaries of the states (Fig. 12–3).

Since the purpose is to collect and disseminate information to the recreationist, it is important to include all opportunities, public or private. This means that many agencies will be contributing to the information pool, and this may potentially cause many operational problems.

Figure 12–3   The major physiographic provinces in the United States, (excluding Alaska and Hawaii). These represent general recreational opportunities.

System Operations. Probably as important as any single phase of the regional information system is the actual operation. Other systems usually have been limited to a single agency that does not give the visitor the total spectrum of available opportunities. Consequently, the visitor will have limited information on which to make a choice.

This would require a constant updating of the information to be given to the participant if the system is to be effective. This means that every agency would have to use the same system, the same units of measure, and so forth in order to feed in information. The operation would have to be computer-based because of the large volume of information and the need for constant updating.

There are already some broad-range systems in operation (such as that used by AAA and Woodall's Trailer Guide); however, these are simplified information systems to generally inform people about the recreational opportunities in a given area. A more sophisticated operation may be devised for a nationwide chain store system, whereby an individual may go to his local branch, plug in his computer card, and obtain all the information he needs for his visit to southern Florida during December.

Drawbacks to the RIS. There are many drawbacks to a regional information system:

1. Overloading an individual with information.
2. Lack of participation by agencies and organizations.
3. Present availability of much of the information, although it is often in fragmented form.
4. Competition from existing private endeavors.
5. Lack of acceptance by the public.
6. Trying to reduce uncertainty when it is really a part of the recreational experience.[5]

The RIS does reduce voids in information so that the user has an opportunity to make better decisions about participation choices. What type of information should be made available and to what degree of refinement? Should this system be controlled or manipulated by a governmental superstructure? Is reduction of uncertainty in personal decision making a realistic goal? If we ensure that the individual has more information to work with, will we alter desirable use patterns to those that are not acceptable to either the user or the management?

Do we already have good RIS? Do people use them? Would a new governmental superstructure be necessary and desirable? Are we really just trying to control for control's sake? Are we trying to usurp states rights? I suppose it all boils down to what the benefits are and who gets them!

Many people are looking closely into the regional information system for use in outdoor recreation management. It is a contemporary concept and a very controversial one. I think it is worth considering, but I also feel we should proceed slowly. The individual needs information for his decision making, but should take some precautions in regard to the RIS.[2]

1. Do not openly manipulate, process, regulate, order, etc. the people through the RIS.
2. Do not impose the heavy hand of government to get the job done.
3. Allow for maximum feasible exercise of individual choice.

AREA INFORMATION SYSTEM

This is an information system for a specific area, usually under the management of a single agency. It is a more manageable situation through contact with the visitor, and the information is more easily updated and transmitted to the user. There are several means of transmitting the detailed information to the using public and of receiving feedback.

Visitor Centers. Probably the more traditional means of transmitting information to the visitor is through on-site contact at the visitor center. The visitor center is usually located at the main access point to the area so that it is easily identifiable and accessible to the visitor as he enters the area, or it is located at some critical point in the visitor's travel (such as near a mountain pass) where he might seek information about several surrounding areas.

On a cost-efficiency basis, the visitor center is probably the most effective means of disseminating information. It is readily available to those who seek information, it is stationary, and it is easily located by the visitor. Plus, it is not disruptive to visitors who are not interested in using it—provided that the site planning does not create traffic problems and the facilities are visually congruent with the landscape. Based on observations, it is amazing how traffic flow (auto and pedestrian) and the appearance of the visitor center affect visitor participation. A center that is properly located along main access routes, that is easy to get to and from, and that fits the surrounding landscape is more casually and continuously used than one that does not possess any of these characteristics. Thus, the original planning may have a tremendous effect on the visitor center's success.

As indicated in earlier chapters, information is an important part of other visitor and resource management programs. Thus, we should attempt to reach as many people as possible, and the visitor center can accomplish much of this dissemination. Too often, visitor centers are either understaffed or closed because of low funding; yet the success of other management programs often depends on information dissemination. Thus, by not keeping the visitor center open, the overall operation of the resource may be affected; consequently, it seems advisable to put more money and effort into informational services, particularly into visitor center programs.

As indicated by Figures 12–4 and 12–5, the facilities should fit the situation. They may be very simple or complex; yet often we think of expensive facility developments for visitor centers. A simple, one-room building with parking facilities may be sufficient in some situations; other situations may call for a major complex to handle visitor loads. Additional services may be offered along with information services at the visitor center, such as comfort stations, emergency phones, interpretive programs, overnight accommodations, and reservation systems. This makes other services more available by increasing their accessibility; and by having them together in a single facility, it is also more economical to provide a combination of services.

Area Signing. Signing can be used to provide the visitor with information as he travels through the area. An area sign or a map showing the road and trail systems, the available recreational opportunities, and the developed facilities may be placed strategically at major access points to familiarize the visitor with the area (Fig. 12–6). This type of area information sign is becoming more popular in relatively large areas, where no visitor information center is located. This

Old Faithful Visitor Center

Figure 12–4   Old Faithful Visitor Center in Yellowstone National Park.

gets the basic information across with minimum inconvenience, then the visitor can also receive additional information through signs, publications, radio contact, and on-site contact as he passes throughout the area.

Signs may be used for informational, educational or warning purposes, but use and location should be carefully scrutinized. There are some rules of signing

Figure 12–5   A small Visitor Center at the Snowy Range access to the Medicine Bow National Forest (photo by Alan Jubenville).

Figure 12-6 Area information signs can give the visitor a quick orientation to the area and the available opportunities (photo by Alan Jubenville).

Figure 12-7 An information sign with a simple but effective message.

that the manager should follow:

1. There should be an identified need at a specific location.
2. Do not overload the visitor with informational signing.
3. Each sign should present only one idea, and the message should be made as simple as possible (Fig. 12–7).
4. Where possible, use international information signs (Fig. 12–8). These are being adopted by most major park systems.

Publications. Publications are important sources of information; however, one should follow the basic rules of signing—don't overdo it. An agency should consider conducting follow-up studies to determine the effectiveness of publications, particularly those that are not sold at publication cost. Often we spend considerable amounts of money on publications that are used very little by the visitor. Brochures passed out at entrance stations tend to be wordy and difficult to read, so the visitor just scans and discards them. Thus, the use of brochures frequently is not an effective information technique. This would indicate that people generally are not interested in doing extensive reading while pursuing their leisure activities. They would prefer a minimum of inconvenience during their leisure time. Assuming this is true, the manager must seek more innovative means of getting the *necessary* information to the visitor. Sometimes the agency seems more concerned with meeting legal and administrative requirements in their publications than with answering the needs of the visitor. Thus, as previously indicated, don't oversell the role of the publication. At the same time, a brochure that is done well, such as the one in Figure 12–9, can be very effective. If the use of a publication is desirable, it should meet the following criteria:

1. *Overall appearance.* The overall appearance should be inviting to the user. Too often, we are more concerned with the technical aspects of the message without regard to whether or not the message will be read.

2. *Attractive cover.* The cover creates the initial impression of the brochure. If it is done well, it may encourage the visitor to open the brochure and to read further. A poorly done cover will discourage further reading. The title should be placed tastefully to indicate the subject matter that is being presented.

3. *Proper size and shape.* Proper size and shape can encourage continued use. For the backpacker to refer to a brochure on his trip, it should easily fit into his shirt pocket; otherwise it will not be convenient to use. If it is to be mailed to the visitor prior to his arrival, it should be the right shape for mailing. A crumpled brochure that has been folded for mailing is not well received.

4. *Conciseness.* Use as few words as possible to present the message. People are on their leisure time and are generally not very receptive to lengthy messages.

5. *Pictures and diagrams.* Pictures and diagrams can be used to easily present the necessary message with minimum distortion, regardless of the audience. In addition, you reduce the amount of time needed to read and understand the message.

6. *Eliminate agency rhetoric and bias.* Don't try to impress others with technical jargon and artificial eloquence. Also, try to be factual, eliminating agency bias and personal values.

7. *Local contact.* Give a local contact if desirable. Too often, we attract people's interest only to frustrate them by not including address, contact, or schedule for those who wish to pursue the matter.

Symbol with red
slash mark indicates
activity is prohibited.

Land Recreation

Horse Trail
Bicycle Trail
Hunting

Playground
Interpretive Auto
Trail
Tramway

Trail Bike Trail
Hiking Trail
Stable

Recreation Vehicle
Trail
Amphitheater
Interpretive Trail

Water Recreation

Motorboating
Marina
Diving

Water Skiing
Swimming
Sailboating

Rowboating
Fishing
Surfing

Scuba Diving
Launching Ramp

Accommodations/Services

Picnic Shelter
Lodging
Trailer Sites

Telephone
Trailer Sanitary Station
Men's Restrooms

Handicapped
Campground
Post Office

Campfires
Food Service
Picnic Area

Trailer Shelter
Women's Restroom
Vehicle Ferry

Viewing Area
Lockers
Gas Station

Parking
Airport
Restrooms

Bus Stop
Showers
Mechanic

Sleeping Shelter
Grocery Store
Kennel

First Aid

General

Firearms
Tunnel
Fish Hatchery

Trucks
Smoking
Lighthouse

Dam
Bear Viewing Area
Information

Pedestrian Crossing
Automobiles
Lookout Tower

Deer Viewing Area
Environmental Study
Area
Ranger Station

Pets on Leash
Falling Rocks
Drinking Water

Winter Recreation

Ski Jumping
Snowmobiling
Sledding

Cross-Country Skiing
Winter Recreation Area
Downhill Skiing

Ski Bobbing
Ice Skating

Figure 12–8 International signs used by major park systems. (From U.S. Department of Agriculture. 1973. "Symbols." *Forest Service Bulletin* PA1030. Washington, D.C.: U.S. Government Printing Office.)

FLOATING THE SNAKE RIVER
IN
GRAND TETON NATIONAL PARK

THE NATIONAL PARK SERVICE
U.S. DEPARTMENT OF THE INTERIOR

MILEAGE LOG AND TRAVEL TIME. The following chart gives the river mileage between all major landings. The location of these landings is shown on the Snake River map.

Major Landings	Jackson Lake Dam	Pacific Creek	R.K. O. Site	Deadmans Bar	Lower Schwabacher
Jackson Lake Dam	0				
Pacific Creek	4.5				
R. K. O. Site	8.5	4.0			
Deadmans Bar	15.0	10.5	6.5		
Lower Schwabacher	20.0	15.0	11.5	5.0	
Moose	25.0	20.0	16.5	10.0	5.0

Travel time on the river is highly variable depending on many factors, such as rate of water flow, type of craft, speed and direction of wind and rate of rowing and paddling. Suffice to say that the entire 25 mile trip from Jackson Lake Dam to Moose can be made in one day under all but the most unfavorable conditions.

Figure 12–9 A simple but effective brochure. (National Park Service brochure, illustrations by Scott M. Coburn.)

8. *Management problem.* If the brochure focuses on a management problem, indicate the regulations that were developed to alleviate it, but don't dwell on the subject. Also, indicate the reasons for these actions and the *rewards* to the user.

Radio Gadgetry. Special radio programs are used to provide information to the visitor. The mobile visitor may receive information on his auto radio from a remote transmitter (usually within a one mile transmitting radius) or through the use of a headset receiver. The remote radio transmitting is done through a pretaped program that is easily changed at the site (see Fig. 12–10). It is usually a relatively short and concise presentation because of the time limitation as the person passes through the transmitting radius.

For the walking visitor, the headset receiver operates from a very short distance—sometimes less than 100 feet. Usually, these gadgets are used in well-developed, controlled sites, such as historical sites or museums. There are also on-call radio transmitters on which an individual pushes a button and receives information over an open speaker.

On-site Contact. On-site visitor contact is a very personal and, often, very necessary means of transmitting information—for example, special management programs in which the information given is an integral part of another program, such as visitor safety or visitor dispersal. However, on-site contact, as a general area information program, tends to be ineffective and inefficient. In this approach the visitor seeks and accepts information while he participates in an activity on a

Figure 12-10 Remote transmitters are being used to reach the auto-oriented visitor through recorded information programs (photo by Bruce and Debbie Maxon).

particular site. The probability is low that someone will be available when a person is seeking information; thus, few people are contacted, and little information is transmitted. In sum, on-site information contacts by park personnel are usually secondary objectives that are achieved while the personnel are performing other services.

OTHER FORMS OF VISITOR INFORMATION

Group Contact. Continuous contact with groups—conservation, recreational, business, or otherwise—is an excellent means of communicating. Today more people belong to various organizational groups or to special interest groups and participate with them recreationally. It is important to maintain open communications with them in an attempt to understand their motives and concerns. At the same time, you can express the concerns and contemplated actions of your agency.

Many groups, if they have had some input into the decision making, will be more willing to police themselves rather than being policed by an agency during recreation participation. This does not mean that the groups are allowed to get their own way; the contact between agency and group simply provides a forum for open discussion. This type of interchange can only help, not hinder, the agency in achieving its management decisions. These contacts can also assist the organizational groups in formulating their own programs.

Group contact is often spurned as having no real benefits for the agency or is envisioned as "consorting with the enemy." If such contacts have been made, they should be kept up on a continuous basis with a variety of organizations in order to maximize the information exchange and maintain the confidence of the group toward management. Being extremely selective in the choosing of groups to contact would be self-defeating because, in doing so, you would lose the respect of other organizations and individuals. It would appear as though you were listening only to those groups whose ideals you personally agree with.

Public Hearings.   Public input into decision making has been covered in Chapter 4. It should be emphasized that public hearings are excellent opportunities for communication to take place; however, too often they are handled as a one-way information flow rather than an interchange of ideas. At such meetings, any unfounded concerns can be cleared up, and any misinformation can be corrected. As indicated in Chapter 4, people often take polarized views because they do not understand the views of others. Public hearings should alleviate some of this by presenting objective information and by encouraging interchange of ideas.

Mass Media.   The use of mass media such as radio, television, and newspapers is a legitimate means of disseminating information to large numbers of people. Too often this is deplored as being impersonal and consequently is not used. However, this may be the only way to reach large numbers of people. In addition, many people do not consider this method to be impersonal, since much of the daily information that we receive comes through mass media. Whenever media are used, the receiver should be aware of *channels* of personal communication so that he may follow up the information if he wishes.

Often, timing and reaching the desired amount of people are the two factors that will determine the appropriateness of using mass media. Sometimes legal requirements require that certain information be disseminated through mass media.

COMMUNICATIONS

Sometimes we forget that information management involves communications—a continuous interchange of information. The interchange is used by both agency and visitor to reassess and adjust their own programs, modes of behavior, and so forth. The interchange can be formal (such as at a public hearing) or informal.

Communications, when used in the public sector, is sometimes dictatorial and is done without regard as to how the public will receive it and respond to it. When this happens, the channels of communications become restricted, and the public loses confidence in management. These channels are only re-established after the public agency has done something to redeem the public confidence.

In summary, the following communications should be encouraged:

1. Information to the user on the available recreational opportunities and feedback from the user on the quality of the experience.
2. Information to the user on existing use patterns, and feedback from the user on patterns of use in order to update plans and further information going to the user.
3. Information and feedback on major problems or proposed plans being considered by the agencies.
4. Open channels for continuous interchange of information. This is vital to the organization and to the public. It is important that all people feel they can use the *open channels;* otherwise, we may discourage the interchange that we wish to encourage. We already have too many people talking to those who agree with them and not enough people talking to those who do *not* agree with them.

SELECTED READINGS

1. Berlo, D. K. 1960. *The Process of Communications: An Introduction to Theory and Practice.* New York: Holt, Rinehart & Winston, Inc.
2. Bleiker, H., and A. Jubenville. 1977. "The Freedom of Choice Issue in Outdoor Recreation." Laramie, Wyo.: University of Wyoming, unpublished.
3. Budd, R. W. 1972. *Approaches to Human Communications.* New York: Spartan Books.
4. Burch, W. R., Jr. 1970. "Recreation Preferences As Culturally Determined Phenomena," *Elements of Outdoor Recreation Planning.* School of Natural Resources, University of Michigan. Ann Arbor, Mich.: University of Michigan Press.
5. Burdge, R., and J. Hendee. 1972. "The Demand Survey Dilemma: Assessing the Creditability of State Outdoor Recreation Plans," *Guideline* 2(6)65.
6. Clawson, M., and J. L. Knetsch. 1966. *Economics of Outdoor Recreation.* Baltimore: Johns Hopkins Press.
7. Eisenberg, A. N., and R. R. Smith, Jr. 1971. *Nonverbal Communications.* New York: Bobbs-Merrill Co., Inc.
8. Hendee, J. C., and R. J. Burdge. 1974. "The Substitutability Concept; Implications for Recreation Research and Management," *Journal of Leisure Research,* 6:155.
9. Jubenville, A. 1975. *Outdoor Recreation Planning.* Philadelphia: W. B. Saunders Co.,
10. Lerbinger, O. 1972. *Designs for Persuasive Communications.* Englewood Cliffs, N.J.: Prentice-Hall, Inc.
11. McGill, A. W. 1974. "Dispersal of Recreationists on Wildlands," *Outdoor Recreation Research: Applying the Results.* U.S. Forest Service General Technical Report NC-9.
12. National Park Service. 1968. *Design.* Washington, D.C.: Park Practice Program.
13. Ross, T. L., and G. H. Moeller, 1974. *Communicating Rules in Recreation Areas.* U.S. Forest Service Research Paper NE-297.
14. Schram, W. L. 1973. *Men, Messages, and Media.* New York: Harper & Row, Inc. Pubs. Inc.
15. Stankey, G. H. 1977. "Some Social Concepts for Outdoor Recreation Planning." *Outdoor Recreation Advances in Application of Economics.* U.S. Forest Service General Technical Report WO-2.
16. Wagar, J. A. 1971. "Communicating with Recreationists," *Northeast Forest Experiment Station Recreation Symposium Proceedings.*

CHAPTER 13

Interpretive Services

It is not so much what we see in nature but how we interpret what we see.

John Burroughs

Interpretation may have many meanings; in park management, it essentially is the act of demonstrating to the public the meaningful relationships occurring among the natural phenomena around us. Tilden[28] considers interpretation to be more than the mere communication of information; it is "an educational activity which aims to reveal meanings and relationships through the use of original objects, by first hand experience, and by illustrative media, . . ." He further states, "The chief aim of interpretation is not instruction, but provocation." These statements summarize the role of interpretation. Through interpretation, the meaning of natural phenomena is revealed to the visitor on a first-hand basis, using common, easily understood examples to illustrate the interrelationships among phenomena. In addition, it is hoped that these examples will provoke the individual into searching for greater meaning and understanding concerning nature.

Interpretive services are required to adequately tell the story of the park, the ecosystem, or the animals (e.g., bison). Interpretation is a total program designed to portray a whole story; but usually, it is put together from many programs that tell parts of the story and that are intended to reach a variety of audiences, even within the particular park (Fig. 13–1). *Variety* is a key word; we must use many different methods and media to reach the total user population, since they have diverse interests and ways of using the park. Most failures in interpretive programs can be attributed to *a lack of understanding toward the role of interpretation and alack of sufficient variety within the total program.*

Sharpe lists three objectives for interpretation programs:[23]

The first or primary objective of interpretation is to assist the visitor in developing a keener awareness, appreciation, and understanding of the area he or she is visiting. Interpretation should help to make the visit a rich and enjoyable experience.

The second objective of interpretation is to accomplish management goals. It can be done in two ways. First, interpretation can encourage thoughtful use of the recreation resource on the part of the visitor, helping reinforce the idea that parks are special places requiring social behavior. Second, interpretation can be used to minimize human impact on the resource by guiding people away from fragile or overused areas into areas that can withstand heavier use.

Figure 13–1 General interpretive programs are done through visitor contact at the visitor center (photo by Bruce and Debbie Maxon).

The third objective of interpretation is to promote public understanding of an agency and its programs.

The first objective—to promote awareness and understanding—is the primary one. The second—to accomplish management goals—is a secondary objective that may be achieved through the visitor's greater understanding of the situation. But the third—promoting the image of the agency—is not really a goal of interpretation. Any program aimed at promoting its own image most likely will reduce the effectiveness of the total interpretive program because many visitors will find that this type of atmosphere is less than exciting and detracts from their interest in the total program.

A PHILOSOPHY OF INTERPRETATION

Although the opening section may be written in a fine academic style, it is hindered by the same problem that affects some interpretive programs—it fails to be stimulating. What is needed is a basic guiding philosophy. Others have expressed this same opinion.

Some one [sic] said this is an interpretive center, and that I could get my questions answered here. I don't know what an interpretive center is, but I do need some information.

Russell K. Grater

Our interpretive efforts must be designed to complement an area, to tell its story, and at the same time utilize the purpose and values of the area to stimulate better understanding and the appreciation of this place—earth—our home,

Tom D. Thomas

To excite curiosity, to open a person's mind—there is a challenge for anyone who seeks to communicate ideas. I know of no one more sensitive to the challenge than the interpreter, for he is a teacher in the purest sense of the word. He works with people who are at leisure, at the special places of beauty and history which have been dedicated and set aside. He seeks to translate, vividly, the language of the earth, and of the earth's inhabitants.

Freeman Tilden

Do not try to satisfy your vanity by teaching a great many things. Awaken people's curiosity. It is enough to open minds; do not overload them. Put there just a spark. If there is some good flammable stuff, it will catch fire.

Anatole France

It is not so important that we be taught but that we be given the wish to learn.

Anonymous

When technology has nothing more for man, then nature will go on showing him her wonders.

Eduardo Arango

There is the world around us, the complex society we live in, and the increasing detachment from nature. Then there is the interpreter—for him, it is a real challenge.

BASIC INTERPRETIVE MODEL

The basic interpretive model is presented in Figure 13–2. The park is the microcosm in which the interpretation takes place, and it is hoped that the effects of the program will extend beyond that microcosm. Interpretation was perceived as necessary for people's understanding of the natural phenomena. From this need evolved the principles of interpretation. Methods were established to facilitate the art of interpretation—personal services, self-guiding programs, and (later) electronic gadgetry. The media associated with these methods also became more sophisticated—such as the modern interpretive center, the interpretive trail, and the use of radio and television. Programs were fitted together to offer specific interpretations for the various types of park visitors. Then special programs were developed—programs for children, environmental education for public schools, junior ranger, urban awareness, and so forth. We must remember that interpretive programs are for people, not for parks or administration. When the programs become stale, the manager should contemplate the message of the preceding section on philosophy. Finally, it is hoped that the visitor will be able to relate this information to the world in which he lives.

PRINCIPLES OF INTERPRETATION

Tilden summarized the principles as follows[28]:

1. Any interpretation that does not somehow relate what is being displayed or described to something within the personality or experience of the visitor will be sterile.

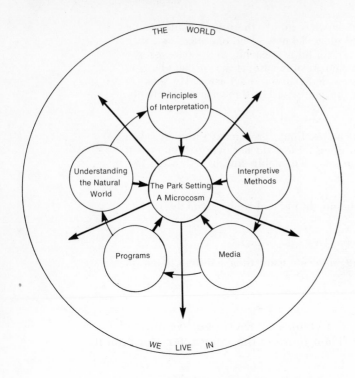

Figure 13–2   The Interpretive Model.

2. Information, as such, is not interpretation. Interpretation is revelation based on information, but they are entirely different things. However, all interpretation includes information.

3. Interpretation is an art which combines many arts, whether the material is scientific, historical or architectural. Art is in some degree teachable.

4. The chief aim of interpretation is not instruction, but provocation.

5. Interpretation should aim to present a whole rather than a part, and must address itself to the whole, rather than any phase.

6. Interpretation (say up to age twelve) should not be a dilution of the presentation to adults, but should follow a fundamentally different approach. To be at its best, it will require a separate program.

These principles are self-evident, to a certain degree, but personality characteristics of the interpreter also affect the quality of the program. Even then, principles and methods of interpretation can be taught. Yet, too often, the young interpreter apparently wants to bypass the basic philosophy and principles in order to get to the methods and media. He certainly cannot achieve success unless he understands what he is doing and why he is doing it.

METHODS

There are three methods of interpretation:

1. *Personal services,* which includes talks, demonstrations, and walks.

2. *Self-guiding,* by which the visitor is directed through the program with special self-guiding materials and facilities.

3. *Gadgetry,* by which the interpreter uses electronic devices to communicate to the public.

PERSONAL SERVICES

Personal services are programs that are personally attended and presented by the interpreter. Communicating directly with the visitor is important; these contacts may be formal or informal. The informal interpretive program is conducted by all park personnel—from the information person to the law enforcement officer. Visitors expect all park employees to be able to answer questions about the area, and the employee ideally should be able to respond to these questions. If he is unsure, he should refer the visitor to a place where his question can be answered.

The informal contacts usually occur on a one-to-one basis at an entrance station, in the visitor center, on developed sites, on point duty at overlooks, at unique scenery, or during roving duty. The person on point duty also may be contacting large groups. Point duty generally consists of answering questions; but in the process, there is an opportunity for interpreting the surrounding wildlands.

The formal programs that we tend to rely on in our total interpretation include talks, demonstrations, walks, and the interpretive center.

Talks. As indicated by Riske,[23] the interpretive talk is the

> ... translation of technical and often complex language of the environment into nontechnical form, with no loss in accuracy, so as to create in the listener sensitivity, awareness, understanding, enthusiasm, and commitment.

These talks are directed toward the level of understanding of the audience and are usually more effective when illustrations or real examples are used in addition. It is much more effective to show a weathered replica of an early horse-drawn wagon that depicts life on the trail during westward expansion than to merely describe it. Talks may take place at the amphitheater, around the campfire—wherever the message can be best delivered and still be convenient for the visitor (Fig. 13–3).

Demonstrations. These can enhance the understanding and the awareness of visitors about the subject under discussion. They can be used to inform people by *re-creating* history; for example, a living history program can illustrate the life style and hardships of the Indian and the early settler. When using this technique to show a natural ecosystem, it is preferable to have a model on display so that the audience can see the entire system and any changes that you may wish to demonstrate.

Walks. The guided, interpretive walks are what we consider to be the classical interpretation approach. It is probably the most interesting and motivating form for the visitor because he can learn through first-hand experience and ask questions about what he sees. The personal interactions are greater on interpretive walks because of the informality and the small group size. Also, having along a capable interpreter is reassuring to many people who are visiting a new and strange environment for the first time. Being at ease, they can focus more attention on the environment around them.

Interpretive Center. Interpretive center programs are both formal and informal. The informal one is through the point duty at the information desk. The formal programs include publications available at the interpretive center, audio-visual presentations, museum displays, and reference collections. The center itself, as shown in Figure 13–4, is often the hub of park activity; thus, in

Figure 13–3 An interpretive walk gives the visitor an opportunity to experience nature through all five senses (photo by Bruce and Debbie Maxon).

Figure 13–4 Interpretive center at Big Hole National Battlefield, Montana.

order to reach large numbers of visitors, the manager should emphasize interpretation at these centers.

The museum, when used, is usually combined with an interpretive center. The size and number of displays in the museum are usually determined by what is to be interpreted at the particular park.

SELF-GUIDING

Self-guiding refers to unattended, interpretive programs that usually are designed to interpret a particular landscape, environmental variable, or unique species. Self-guided programs are done through printed brochures or signs. Typically on the long walks, a brochure is provided to interpret the natural phenomena for the visitor. For point-specific opportunities, such as an overlook, the interpretation is usually done through signs and displays.

GADGETRY

Interpretation has reached the age of advanced communications. We are now using radio contact from remote stations, short-distance radio contact requiring headsets, electronically controlled moving displays, and educational television. This type of gadgetry has made it easier to reach more people. The questions to ask are, How far do we go, and at what price?

INTERPRETIVE MEDIA

Although some of these have been mentioned previously, this is an appropriate place for enumerating and discussing the various media available to the manager.

Interpretive Center. The interpretive center usually is relatively accessible to all park visitors and is connected to a variety of other services (such as an information area, a rest stop, possibly a special permits center, a transportation center). It is listed as the prime medium in which interpretation takes place because, as a complex, it is usually the focal point of the visitors' itinerary.

Interpretive Trail. The interpretive trail is the medium that facilitates the nature walk (Fig. 13–5). If it is purely an interpretive trail, it will be designed to enhance the interpretive program so that each stop along the way will tell part of the story. When the walk is completed by the visitor, he will have the entire message that you wish to convey.

Signs and Displays. Signs and displays are ways of reaching the visitor along his route—road, trail, or water. Signs and displays as illustrated in Figures 13–6 and 13–7, are very effective for presenting a simple idea to the visitor, particularly at points where it would be difficult or inefficient to have an interpreter. The only word of caution is to keep the message simple, since there is no one to answer any follow-up questions about the phenomenon.

Publications. Brochures and lengthier publications have been used as primary media since the beginnings of interpretation. Possibly millions of dollars are spent annually on informational and educational publications related to the use of our parks, recreation areas, and open spaces; yet little effort is spent on evaluating these programs.

Figure 13–5   A self-guiding interpretive trail.

Figure 13–6   Interpretive signs such as this are important in reaching large numbers of visitors.

Figure 13-7 Roadside interpretive display showing the geological history of Larmar Valley, Yellowstone National Park (photo by Alan Jubenville).

Too often, we have immersed ourselves in the natural history of an area without regard to effective communication of these ideas to the visitor. First, we need reliable communication techniques in our publications; second, we should periodically evaluate how well the public is receiving and using the information. (For guidelines on development of publications for visitor use, see Chapter 12.).

Radio, Television, and Other Special Devices. These are being used more and more as interpretive media because they can reach large numbers of people quickly and efficiently. Radio and television have some limitations as interpretive media. Usually the receiving range is limited; and at times, one may have to restrict the range even further to reduce possible overlap during transmission. There also are some legal concerns involving the overlap with commercial frequencies. With more public education channels, these concerns should be minimized.

Special devices would include a tape series that a visitor could use while driving around the park or a battery-operated headset that could pick up short-distance, continuously playing radio programs—as one passed from one point to another on a trail or historic grounds, a new message would be received. New gadgetry is continuously being developed, especially for interpretation purposes. Watch the market in the next few years, as we enter the space age of communications.

PROGRAM PLANNING

Many factors must be consdered in planning interpretive programs, and all of these should be considered very carefully. The success or failure of a particular program will depend on how carefully the program prospectus is developed. Grater[14] offers the following outline of the prospectus.

Interpretive Prospectus Outline

1. Interpretive statement defining basic values of the area of subject to be interpreted. These values will determine scope of the plan to be presented.
2. Statement summarizing objectives of the area's interpretive program, defining the major interpretive goals this particular area hopes to accomplish.
3. Factors influencing selection of interpretive means.
    a. The environment.
        (1) Weather and climate.
        (2) Location of the area.
        (3) Geography of the area (if pertinent).
        (4) Natural history values of the area (geology, biology, ecology).
        (5) Historical values of the area.
        (6) Archeological values of the area.
        (7) Other values.
    b. The visitor.
        (1) Origin (his home).
        (2) Type (economic level).
        (3) His background.
            (a) National origin.
            (b) Educational level.
        (4) Visitor use patterns.
        (5) Interpretive activities of other nearby agencies or organizations.
4. The interpretive program.
    a. Present (describe activities and facilities in some detail).
        (1) Visitor center.
        (2) Wayside exhibits.
        (3) Interpretive signing.
        (4) Self-guiding devices.
        (5) Personal services.
            (a) Conducted walks, hikes and tours.
            (b) On-site assignments.
            (c) Off-site assignments.
            (d) Demonstrations.
            (e) Amphitheater and campfire programs.
        (6) Audiovisual facilities.
        (7) Publications available to visitor.
        (8) Reference library.
        (9) Reference collections.
    b. Proposed facilities and activities (summations of the same items as given above).
        (1) To be developed in some detail, giving thoughts behind each proposal.
    c. Summary chart, showing present and proposed activities and facilities, and locations and manner of treatment of each activity or facility.
5. Content of the proposed program.
    a. The visitor center.
        (1) List what it is to contain and how the building is to function.
        (2) Function of the various rooms.
            (a) Lobby and contents.
            (b) Exhibit room contents. Indicate the stories to be told.
            (c) Audiovisual room.
            (d) Library.
            (e) Work and storage rooms.
            (f) Other (rest rooms, offices, etc.).
    b. Wayside exhibits.
        (1) List locations and basic stories to be covered, and describe how each is to be accomplished.

    c. Interpretive signing.
        (1) List and describe how each is to be accomplished.
    d. Self-guiding devices.
        (1) List and describe what each is to accomplish and how it is to be done.
    e. Personal services.
        (1) Information desk at visitor center or museum.
        (2) Conducted walks.
        (3) Conducted tours (building, archeological site, auto, etc.).
        (4) On-site assignments.
        (5) Off-site assignments.
        (6) Demonstrations.
        (7) Campfire and amphitheater programs.
    f. Audiovisual facilities.
    g. Publications available to the public.
        (1) Folders, maps, etc.
        (2) Publications relating to the area and its features.
        (3) Self-guidance leaflets or booklets.
        (4) Other.
    h. Reference library.
        (1) Contents. General statement.
        (2) How used.
    i. Reference collections.
        (1) List types and scope of collections (biological, geological, historical, archeological, other).
6. Studies supporting the interpretive program, list of studies made, or being made of value to interpretive plan and program.
7. Staffing requirements.
    a. Present staffing.
    b. Proposed staffing.
8. Cost estimates for the proposed program. Follow breakdown of facilities and activities as given in item 5 above.
9. Map of area showing locations of all present and proposed facilities and activities.
10. (Added by author.) Review and evaluate each major program on a periodic basis.

Effectiveness should be determined by how well the message was received and reacted to, within the stated management objectives. Logically, the evaluation should be done by applied research and reviewed by an outside team. The on-site interpreter often cannot be considered objective enough to do this evaluation, since it was his "brainstorm" in the first place.

Evaluation of programs can be done using unobtrusive techniques, such as measuring attention spans at exhibits,[10, 24] numbers of visitors, and rates of erosion and accretion (described by Webb, *et al.*[30]). This can only indicate the patterns of visitor use in the program. More is needed to determine the effectiveness of the communication and visitor's reaction to it. Obviously, each park program should be closely scrutinized, but generic studies at various geographic locations can help answer the questions related to problems of communications. Base-line data on any program are essential to a long term evaluation of that program.

SPECIAL PROGRAMS

The following are special programs that have been recently developed.
1. *Environmental education.* Environmental education is designed to use

park properties as educational areas and to promote programs on environmental subjects in the local and regional school systems. Usually, a staff position is assigned to develop and promote the program.

2. *Junior Ranger.* The Junior Ranger program, although initiated under the National Park Service, now is being adopted by many state and regional park systems. The purpose is to promote interest and knowledge of the important natural and cultural values of the park on the part of the young park users. Additional emphasis is placed on having the parents help in the supervision of the program. Generally, some type of certificate indicating the activities the youngster has participated in and a sew-on patch are awarded for successful completion of the program.

3. *Facilities and programs for the physically handicapped.* Improved facility development allows the physically handicapped to participate in all park programs, including interpretation. Often simple facility design changes can make activities and programs available to the physically handicapped. At times, special facilities may be necessary, even special programs. Special facilities (such as interpretive trails for the blind, hardened surfaces, redesigned rest rooms, and ramps) should be considered in the future planning of a site. Possibly a physically handicapped interpreter could be employed to handle on-site visits because of his understanding of the special needs of the handicapped.

4. *Traveling interpreter.* The future may bring arrival of the traveling interpreter. The visitor of the future may come to our major parks via mass transit. Each group of visitors, as they enter the park are assigned a natural history interpreter. This interpreter travels with the group on their visit, interpreting the landscape and answering questions.

A FINAL THOUGHT

There are two final concerns:

1. Evaluate what you are doing. (This already has been discussed.)

2. *Don't overdo it!* Too often we feel we must reach the public with our programs. People are participating in our park setting during their leisure time. Many wish to have minimal "interference" in their leisure activities, and they may rebel at someone who is overtly trying to "force" them into enjoying nature. This is exemplified by a recent master plan for Yellowstone National Park in which the primary theme of interpretation was "to get people out of their cars and into nature." I am not sure nature is ready for that.

Perhaps we should allow people to seek their own level of enjoyment through maximum freedom of choice. The drive from Banff to Jasper through the Canadian National Parks is an example of maximum freedom of choice. There is a paved parking lane on each side of the road that allows the visitor to stop anywhere and enjoy the beauty around him—the pine tree, the mountain, the flowers in the meadow, and the rock outcropping. In most U.S. parks, we program what the visitor will enjoy by our placement of turnouts, parking lots, and so forth.

SELECTED READINGS

1. Ashbaugh, B. L. 1963. *Planning a Nature Center.* New York: National Audubon Society.
2. Ashbaugh, B. L. 1963. *Trail Planning and Layout.* New York: National Audubon Society.
3. Baker, D. R. 1969. "Nature Interpretation," *Trends* 6(2):14.
4. Boulanger, F. D., and J. A. Smith. 1973. *Educational Principles and Techniques for Inter- preters.* U.S. Forest Service General Technical Report PNW-9.
5. Boulanger, F. D., and J. A. Smith. 1971. "Principles, Methods, and Techniques for Teaching in Recreational Areas: A Primer for Interpreters," Project Report, Pacific Northwest Forest and Range Experiment Station.
6. Cahn, R. 1968. *"Will Success Spoil Our National Parks?" Christian Science Monitor.*
7. Canter, S. G. 1963. "Winter Comes to Yellowstone," *Yellowstone Library and Museum Associ- ation.* Yellowstone National Park.
8. Collins, J. 1968. "The Braille Trail," *Trends* 5(2):1.
9. Conway, M. R. 1968. "Petersburg—Living History," *Trends* 5(4):1.
10. Dick, R. E., E. Myklestad, and J. A. Wagar. 1975. *Audience Attention As a Basis for Evaluating Interpretive Presentations.* U.S. Forest Service Research Paper PNW-198.
11. Erskine, D. J. 1964. "A–V Materials in the Interpretive Programs," *Trends* 1(1):11.
12. Food and Agricultural Organization. 1976. *Planning Interpretive Programs in National Parks.* Rome: United Nations.
13. Gantry, J. 1968. "Touch and See Trail," *Science and Children* 6(2):20.
14. Grater, R. K. 1976. *The Interpreter's Handbook.* Globe, Ariz.: Southwest Parks & Monuments Assn.
15. Grove, H. J. 1971. "Interpretation in the National Wildlife Refuge System," *U.S. Department of Interior.* Washington, D.C.: U.S. Government Printing Office.
16. Mahaffey, B. D. 1968. "Interpretation—The Missing Ingredient?" *Trends* 5(3):9.
17. McCurdy, D. R., and L. K. Johnson, 1967. *Recommended Policies for the Development and Management of State Park Systems.* Southern Illinois University Agric. Pub. No. 26. Car- bondale, Ill.: Southern Illinois University Press.
18. Michigan Department of Natural Resources. 1969. *Interpretive Services Procedures Manual.*
19. Moore, W. R. 1974. "America Needs a Land and People Ethic." (Speech to Montana Wilder- ness Society on December 7, 1974.)
20. National Education Association. 1970. *Man and His Environment.* Washington, D.C.: National Education Association.
21. National Park Service. 1970. *Grand Teton Environmental Education Center—A Proposal.* Moose, Wy.: National Park Service.
22. Pile, J. 1962. "Enjoyment and Understanding," *First World Conference on National Parks.* Washington, D.C.: U.S. Government Printing Office.
23. Sharpe, G. W. 1976. *Interpreting the Environment.* New York: John Wiley & Sons, Inc.
24. Shiner, J. W., and E. L. Shafer, Jr. 1975. *How Long Do People Look at and Listen to Forest- Oriented Exhibits?* U.S. Forest Service Research Paper NE-325.
25. Shoman, J. J. 1968. *Manual of Outdoor Interpretation.* New York: National Audubon Society.
26. Sutton, M. D. 1976. "Interpretation Around the World," *Interpreting the Environment.* Sharpe, G. W. (ed.). New York: John Wiley & Sons, Inc.
27. Thomas, T. D. 1968. "The Challenges of Interpretation." *Proceedings, Recreation Management Institute.* College Station, Tex.; Texas A & M University.
28. Tilden, F. 1967. *Interpreting Our Heritage.* Chapel Hill, N.C.: The University of North Carolina Press.
29. Wagar, J. A. 1974. "Interpretation to Increase Benefits to Recreationists," *U.S. Forest Service General Technical Report,* NC-9.
30. Webb, E. J. 1971. *Unobtrusive Measures: Nonreactive Research in the Social Sciences.* Chicago: Rand McNally & Co.

CHAPTER 14

Concession Management

The objective of concessions management, as we view it, is to see that the park visitors' needs for food, lodging, transportation and other services are identified and provided at reasonable rates and at acceptable quality.

Our role as concessions managers is, I believe, to use the tools of management—policies, plans, contracts, standards, evaluations, etc.—to achieve the objective. Social change, however continually presses us to restate policies, redesign facilities, and redefine standards, etc. Concomitantly, technological change gives us new opportunities to feed, house and move more visitors with diverse needs and aspirations better and faster and more efficiently. We believe that the concessions manager—whether he comes from the public or the private sector—will play a larger and more vital role in the planning, development and management of parks than he has in the past.[8]

Concession management refers to the planning, development, and supervising of the visitor services that are designed to create or enhance the recreational experience. The manager first must decide what services are needed and where they should be located. This is critical—to decide *what* is needed and *where*.

Too often we assume that any service the public may wish to have should be provided. However, we need to evaluate each service by a set of criteria so that we, as park and recreation area managers, are able to determine whether or not we should provide those services. In evaluating a service, the basic criteria proposed in this text are *necessary* and *desirable*. Each service should be necessary to the enjoyment of the outdoor recreational experiences we wish to promote. Necessary, in this case, refers to something that absolutely is required in order to participate in the various activities (e.g., overnight accommodations, food service, winter sports site). Next, any service should meet the test of desirability—is it sufficiently desirable to be developed within the park boundaries, or should it be located outside park limits?

As an example, in a park unit, it is necessary to have overnight accommodations and food service for the park visitor to enjoy his stay; the historic Old Faithful Lodge (Fig. 14–1) is a good example. These services are necessary because of the normal travel distance to park and the length of visitor stay. However, because of the large numbers of visitors to a relatively small park, any major

Figure 14–1   A major park concession development is often necessary to provide needed visitor services (photo by Alan Jubenville).

development would detract from the total experience, since it would disrupt many of their day-use activities. Thus, although these services are necessary, they may not be desirable. In this case, the solution may be to encourage the private sector to develop these services outside the park and to maintain maximum visitor activity space inside the park.

The desirability test may also include the environmental effects. Perhaps a needed service is to be located in an alpine zone, which is an environmentally fragile area. The decision may be that it is not desirable to provide the service at that location and that it must be moved elsewhere.

PROVISIONING FOR CONCESSIONS

In the United States, development is often diffused throughout the parks, although it is controlled. Some countries have used the enclave concept in the development of visitor services within the parks. Enclaves are established in places where intensive development can handle the needs of the visitor, and the other portions of the parks are maintained with minimum disruptions. Banff National Park is a good example in which concessions (in terms of intensive development) are encouraged within the town site of Banff (Fig. 14–2).

There are three primary steps in the provisioning for concessions:

AREA PLANNING

One of the concerns in area planning is the determination of what is needed and where it is needed. Area planning allocates space for the development and properly locates it in relation to needs, visitor flow patterns, and environmental concerns.[15] The service must be located where it is needed;

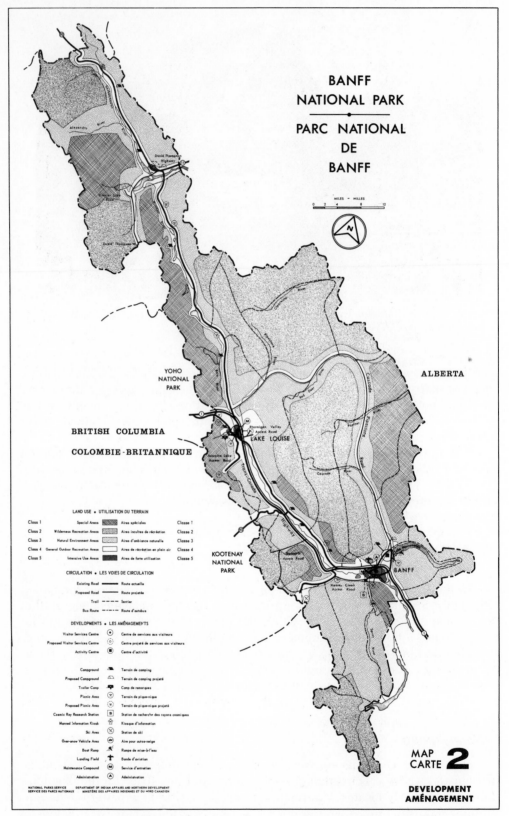

Figure 14-2 A map showing the townsite of Banff and Lake Louise as the primary Visitor Service Center.

otherwise, people will not use it or will use it for other than the intended purpose.

Ideally, we should try to cluster visitor services where they will be used. By clustering, we often are able to provide more services in a more economical way, with a decrease in loss of open space and in total environmental effects. Clustering has been used in some national and state parks; probably it will be used increasingly as the rise in recreational participation places more demands on the limited parkscape. The first step in this process of course is to determine the normal travel patterns and activity participation for the particular park and to locate and develop those facilities that are *necessary* and *desirable* to facilitate or enhance travel or activity patterns. (Please note that what is *necessary* and *desirable* must be evaluated in regard to the specified long range objectives of the park—e.g., the service or concessions center would be part of those facilities.)

The second step is to develop the facility for ease of access and use and for visual harmony with the landscape. Some facilities may have the proper location but are difficult to reach from the main road—consequently, are not efficiently used. For most park units, there is an understood requirement that the development be blended with the landscape. Yet there may be pressures from the concessioner to allow some deviation from this requirement. It is important to maintain the integrity of the visual environment for the visual enjoyment of the visitor and the protection of the resources.

The third step is cooperation with the private sector over area planning. This is essential if we are to offer a wide spectrum of services that will satisfy the interests of all visitors. We, as managers, frequently try to provide all services within the park. On the other hand, we may ignore certain legitimate service needs. We cannot continue in this way. If we are to do a reasonable job in providing these services, we must recognize the role of the private sector, outside the park, and cooperate with them through the area planning process.

TYPE OF OWNERSHIP/OPERATION

After we have determined *what* is needed and *where* it is needed within the park, we must determine *who* will develop and operate the concession.

Government Ownership and Operation. This means that a governmental agency will develop and operate the concession service. Generally, this has not been a desirable alternative because the manager may have difficulty in setting regulations for himself. The pressure may become so great for tourist development that we forget the basic planning criteria of *necessary* and *desirable*. I know of a situation that occurred in a county park, where the local park district developed and operated a short-order restaurant located adjacent to a park beach. In the first year, the restaurant netted nearly eight thousand dollars, which was used for park operations. Because of the initial success of the restaurant and the scarcity of appropriations for park operations, the decision was made by the park district to add other short-order restaurants near the remaining beaches. This decision illustrates what can happen in concession development when one does not really evaluate the specific service needs and alternatives to meet those needs.

Government Ownership and Private Operation. This is a reasonable alternative in which there is a large investment in the development with the prospect of a marginal return. The agency develops the facility and then leases it for operation to the private concessioner. This is sometimes the only way in which to get the needed services if one does not choose to have the agency operate it. In this case, the agency should evaluate thoroughly the need for the concession service, since a large investment is required for developing a facility that may be serving only a small number of visitors. There must be some criteria for determining the limit beyond which no facilities will be provided.

Private Ownership and Private Operations. This has generally been the most desirable direction to take in developing a service, since it involves no government investment and less government control. Generally the agency goes through the area planning process to determine what is needed within its own area boundaries and then develops and distributes the concession prospectus to all potentially interested private investors. The prospectus should indicate what is needed and where it is needed and then should allow the private individual to respond with a specific proposal on facility development and services to be offered. The proposals from the entrepreneurs are evaluated in terms of meeting the service needs of the visitor as well as protecting the environment. The individual selected then would be offered a concession lease based on the original proposal or a modified version of it. It then would be the responsibility of the manager to oversee the provisions of the lease.

Quasi-Public Corporation. Sometimes, certain services are needed, and the private sector is not interested in responding to these needs. In this case, if agency operation is not desirable, the development of a quasi-public corporation to handle the operation seems to be a solution. In this way, the agency does not try to regulate itself. This is an interesting way to provide necessary concession services, but one should carefully evaluate service needs in regard to actual costs. The real question is how are those corporations to be subsidized? With public monies? Special tax exemptions?

THE CONCESSION LEASE

The concession lease is the legal document that determines the basic relationship between concessioner and the agency management. It is an explicit statement of role for both the concessioner and the agency in terms of the services to be offered, the administration of the operation, any special considerations (such as pricing and advertising) and the monitoring of the operation.

Everything that is expected of the concessioner and the way in which his services will be evaluated must be a part of the lease contract. This protects both parties and leaves little doubt as to roles and performance standards. For a small operation in a single park, the contract may be very short with a minimum of requirements; on the other hand, a large, diverse operation may require a very detailed and complex contract. No matter what the operation is, we must recognize the lease contract as the vehicle that establishes the quantity and quality of services to be provided by concessioners in any park or recreation area.

Unfortunately, many services have been allowed to develop and grow within our park and recreation areas without management direction. Perhaps while they are small, they are of little concern; however, they later may reach a point where they create problems and seem "unmanageable." A detailed concession lease would eliminate this uncontrolled growth and would maintain only the necessary and desirable services at specified levels.

CONCESSION VARIABLES

The following are variables that should be considered in the development of the concession:

COMPETITION

It is important to consider competition. Should we encourage it as a means of regulating prices and quality of services? In America, where competition is usually encouraged, the answer in the context of park concessions is not clear. The general principle relates to the "necessary and desirable" concept, in which the park attempts to develop specific services that are deemed appropriate and then to control the service and costs through *regulated* monopolies.

The primary interest is to provide services at a reasonably fair price so that the typical park visitor can enjoy them. For pure competition to exist, there must be sufficient business for two or more companies "to operate at something approximating lowest possible cost."[14] If insufficient business exists, costs will be high; this will drive prices up, or one or more of the operations will go out of business, perhaps leaving a building to weather and become a blight on the landscape. Since the amount of available recreational space already is limited, it seems prudent to minimize the space needed for services and to try to maximize the actual activity space for recreational use. Thus, regulated monopolies are usually adopted to meet identified service needs, minimize spatial needs, protect important park features, and maintain buildings, grounds, and quality of service in a manner acceptable to the public and the agency.

We have many existing, regulated monopolies (e.g., utility companies); it is not a unique concept to park and recreation areas. The concession, unlike other regulated monopolies, is often faced with real competition from areas immediately adjacent to the park. This may cause some real problems, since the concessioner is not allowed to quickly adjust his business to meet his competition. Sometimes we have regulated a concessioner out of business. It could be argued that he should not have been there in the first place; yet we attracted him and encouraged the development. Most likely, we will adjust the lease in order to keep the concessioner going. We then should ask ourselves, "If there was that much competition from the outside, why did we try to develop the same service inside our park?"

There are no simple answers; obviously, conditions change. For example, during the early development of our national parks, there was a greater need for maximum overnight accommodations because of the limited mobility of the visitor within the park. Large hotel complexes were built to accommodate the visitor; otherwise, he would not have had a place to stay. With the increased mobility of the modern traveler, these service needs no longer have to be provided within the park. In addition, developments have sprung up outside the parks to meet the changing behavioral patterns and service demands. It is not surprising to see more long range plans for moving a concession service outside the park, where they can compete within the private sector. This will require maximum coordination between the public and private sectors.

Frequently, what appears to the public to be a stable economic operation is only marginal in terms of profit-making; consequently, it often is difficult to encourage large money lenders to invest in such a conditional operation.

ECONOMY OF SCALE

Scale of operation is important to management efficiency and economic soundness of the concession operation. A development should consider scale of economy in the initial planning so that it will be attractive to potential concessioners, particularly those you may wish to have operating within your park.

The small family operation may be the most desirable; but because of the inefficiencies in regard to its size, this type of venture may be doomed to economic failure or inflation. How do you balance economy with both visitor needs and protection of park values? The answer is simple: you just do it. Certain value judgments have to be made based on the present conditions, and adjustments will have to be made later as the conditions change. Possibly systems analysis or simulation modeling can help to determine where the services should be located and the effects on management (concession and park) of various scales of development. This can give us more objective kinds of inputs into decision making. Ideally, we would attempt to project these inputs into the future so that we have a better understanding of potential changes in visitor use patterns and the need for associated developments. Otherwise, the development should be planned to be as flexible as possible — to expand or reduce the scale as conditions dictate.

Also, the manager should consider clustering concession services in order to increase management efficiency and to make a concession attractive to the private developer. Campgrounds are good examples. Most campgrounds on public lands are small and scattered over large areas; this makes them uneconomical in terms of management. If they were clustered at desirable locations, they may be operated economically and consequently, become attractive to the entrepreneur. The problem that we must solve becomes one of the trade-offs — are the campgrounds properly located to provide the required overnight accommodations? What have we done in terms of changing the "camping experience" from the small, scattered camp to the large, centrally located one? What are the acceptable trade-offs?

CONDITIONS OF LEASE

The following factors should be considered in the development of a concession lease.

Roles and Responsibility. The roles and responsibilities of each party entering into the lease, as indicated in the previous paragraphs, must be explicitly stated in the lease agreement; nothing should be implied. Any loopholes or misunderstandings over the wording in the contract can lead to strained relationships and ultimately to a decline in the very service the agency wished to offer to the public. It is only fair to both parties of the contract to fully develop roles and responsibility — in a moral sense, in terms of service management, and in a legal sense, in terms of protection of both parties.

Location and Level of Development. The location and level of development should be completely agreed upon by the two parties. The basic decision on this is made by the agency, with possibly negotiations between the two parties in considering changes. Thus, the location and level of development (with negotiated changes) both become parts of the lease. Included in this would be a phasing-in schedule so that each party would be aware of the actual timing of each phase of the development. However, some provision should be made for

Figure 14–3 Canyon Village in Yellowstone National Park—a major development that embodies the clustering concept.

extending the deadlines, if necessary. Each party should have some flexibility involving future commitments; therefore, there should be some provision in the lease for future expansion if needed. The provision may be nothing more than a statement of the management philosophy—i.e., to attempt to cluster developments (Fig. 14–3) or add to existing ones, if future conditions demand it.

Utilities and Energy Conservation. Energy conservation is extremely important from both an economical and a philosophical standpoint. If we are trying to promote conservation as well as protection of many of the natural resources of this world, every phase of this operation should foster these ideals. The type of utility needed and the long term effects should be considered in regard to the scarcity of energy resources. Possibly we should consider an alternative source of energy, such as solar energy, and use the parks and open spaces as areas where man and nature can live in harmony. I suspect that in times of critical energy shortage, many park and recreational facilities will be denied energy resources to operate utilities. A real step forward is represented by the solar energy–operated visitor center at the Bighorn National Recreation Area (Fig. 14–4).

Maintenance, Sewage Treatment, and Refuse. Maintenance of the area and of the buildings within it is essential to the overall aesthetic appearance of the park. Besides good appearance, we also need to concern ourselves with the problems of sewage treatment and solid waste disposal in order to protect the recreation environment and the well-being of the visitor. Ideally, we would utilize regional sewer systems. This would minimize problems of trying to maintain on-site treatment facilities and maximize the treatment area at the lowest possible cost. In solid waste disposal, it is essential to use a properly developed sanitary landfill. This will usually mean cooperating with the local

Figure 14–4 Solar-heated buildings may become more important in providing various visitor services. The building shown is the new visitor center for the Bighorn Canyon National Recreation Area (photo by the National Park Service).

government to use existing facilities. Whatever the course, the requirements and role of each party should be specified in the lease.

Quality of Service. Quality of service is a must if the visitor's needs are to be satisfied, but quality *per se* is a nebulous term. Since the concession lease is the document that initiates the needed service, the quality expected to provide that service should be stated in realistic, measurable criteria. Included in these criteria would be agency as well as federal, state, and local requirements established by law. There is sometimes included in the statement on quality of service a provision for the availability of low cost services so that even low-income people can use them. The standards and systems of monitoring the quality of service should be stated so that the concessioner can maintain an acceptable level of operation.

Franchise or Lease Fee. The annual fee that is paid to the government for the concession lease (i.e., for the right to operate a concession) may be a flat rate or a percentage of the gross receipts. The choice of fixed versus percentage is a matter of management preference. To some managers, the charges basically are designed to cover supervision of the lease. Others feel it is a means of obtaining additional operation monies for other programs. Still others feel it is a way of evaluating the demand for a service. The fixed rate is usually used for small operations in which a full accounting of receipts would not be necessary. For larger concessions, the percentage of gross receipts method requires the full accounting of receipts. Thus it is a measure of changes in participation from year to year, adjusted for yearly increases in cost of service. However, a more modern concept is the division of profits.[14] This simply means that a "break even" point is determined for the business, and a percentage fee is assessed for gross revenues above that point. The concept is one of providing service first, then assessing a fee on the excess profits. In this way, the concessioner gets his expenses and a reasonable return on his investment (including making up for unprofitable years and giving him some incentive for efficient management). This ensures a reasonable profit, in the long run, to better stabilize the business; thus it is comparable to income averaging for tax purposes. In the past, the concessioner would not have received a break during lean years and would possibly have been charged an excess profit fee during good years — he could not win either way.

Length of Lease, Guaranteed Renewal, and Exclusive Rights. The length of lease should be commensurate with the investment by the concessioner; this should make the investment more financially attractive. The ordinary length of a lease is equal to the expected life of the facilities — i.e., the number of years over which they will depreciate. Typically, this has been a maximum of 30 years, but it can be as few as one to five years (with little investment needed in the facilities). The agency should employ the minimum length of contract necessary to attract a desirable lease, yet maintain flexibility to allow for change in the future.

The idea of a guaranteed renewal clause in a concession contract is controversial. Many people feel that all the contract options should remain with the agency. On the other hand, people may be reluctant to invest their money and effort into developing a concession when there is no guarantee that they will continue in operation after the lease expires. This does not mean that, if we are guaranteed renewal, the old contract is automatically renewed. The concessioner has to meet the terms of the original lease; then, under the guaranteed renewal clause, he would have first option on the new lease. Provisions may change in the negotiated contract in terms of facilities, maintenance, services, and so forth because of changes in service needs, legal requirements, and management philosophy. This type of clause may be the best way to attract and keep good concessioners.

Under ordinary circumstances, use patterns, management philosophy, or service needs will not have changed sufficiently to drastically alter the new lease; consequently, a renewal clause seems a logical solution in terms of continuity of the concession. The renewal of the lease should not be used simply as an administrative prerogative to get rid of "bad" concessioners. If the lease contract is well written and the provisions are properly monitored, the administrator should be able to get rid of "bad" concessioners because they did not fulfill their contract obligations. He should not have to wait unitl the lease renewal comes up. Furthermore, experience has shown that many long term concessioners have great respect toward the park or recreation area where they are located and for the ideals under which they are managed. Consequently, they support and protect many of the public values associated with the particular landscape.[14]

Exclusive right is a guarantee to the existing concessioner that he will receive the first option on future concessions that may be developed. This is usually done in the interest of reducing competition and increasing the economy — possibly even incorporating the new service inthe existing facilities. The new concession service is simply an "add on" to the original concession without the need for a formal selection process. Also, the manager does not have to worry about whether or not the new service will be large enough to attract a new investor.

Season of Operation. The seasonal length of operation or the provision for annual negotiated dates should be stated in the lease so that the agency has some reasonable control over the period of service availability. In this way, the early or late season visitor at least can have minimal services available; otherwise, they may only be available during the peak season (in order to maximize profits). A change in local conditions, such as year-round public schools, also may dictate a different length of season for operating a concession in a local or regional park. Another example is the changing winter recreational use patterns that have caused a change in the length of season for many concessions.

Architectural Styles and Building Materials. Controls on architectural styles and building materials ensure a reasonable harmony between the natural landscape and the existing development. A pleasant manmade environment will provide the visitor with a more desirable experience by emphasizing the prime park values, including the perception of open space, while it also is subordinating the man-induced changes. This can be done effectively even in a relatively heavy developed parkscape.

The types of materials used also may affect the visual harmony of the development. The use of native timber and stone can be very desirable yet expensive to use in construction and long term maintenance. If it is desirable to use those materials, perhaps an adjustment can be made that will compensate the concessioner.

Possessory Interest. Possessory interest means the right of ownership to the buildings and related real property, if they are located on public lands. Possessory interest in the developed or acquired facilities should be stated in the lease in the event the lease is legally terminated or not renewed. Even if the facility is located on public land, the concessioner usually is given possessory rights if his money went into the development or acquisition of it. This usually means that he will be justly compensated for such a facility at the termination of the lease. Just compensation can mean "book value" (original cost less depreciation) or "present market value" based on an appraisal. The method to be used should be so stated.

Insurance and Bonding. The concessioner should be required to carry a reasonable amount of insurance for fire, public liability, employee liability, and other business hazards.

Bonding should be required to guarantee the construction of proposed facilities and the "faithful performance of other obligations under the contract."[20]

POLITICS

Concession operations within our parks and recreation areas come under a great deal of political scrutiny. Some politicians feel we are being too lenient to the concessioner; others feel we are being too harsh in our control of concessions, and often there is only a fine line distinguishing between the two.

A manager shouldn't be continually looking over his shoulder, waiting for the "axe to fall." You should invoke a positive approach to concession operations by planning, developing, and supervising needed concessions. Decisions relative to the operations should be based on facts and sound judgment. Your ego should not be involved—i.e., "me" and "my" park become substitutes for the real role of caretaker of the public's park. We also must realize that most of the important decisions that influence the job of manager are made in the political arena through the legislative process—as it should be!!!

MANAGEMENT CONSIDERATIONS

The following is a summary of those considerations through which the manager can exercise rightful control over the concession:

PLANNING

Basic service philosophy. A basic service philosophy must be adopted before one can conceivably develop a management program. This would be the overall guiding doctrine in determining service needs and consolidating those needs into specific concession operations. We are all affected by our beliefs and attitudes in developing management programs. This is especially true of a controversial program like concession management. Consequently, it is important to enumerate this basic service philosophy, then compare it to the agency management guidelines and the normative behavior of the visitor. If trade-offs are to be made in providing concession services, what are you, as the manager, willing to sacrifice?

Area and site planning. As indicated in the beginning of this chapter, area planning, which incorporates the basic service philosophy, can determine specific visitor needs (including concession needs), allocate space, and select the proper location for a needed facility development. This is the most important step; if these facilities are not developed to meet the needs of the visitor or are not properly located, they will not be used adequately.[15] Consequently no matter what decisions are made subsequently, much of the service needs of the visitor may go unmet. Without planning, there may be an increase of certain services without regard to the overall needs and how they may be fulfilled.

Good site planning will blend the development to fit the landscape and will make it functional in terms of people using the site. I remember a well-located camp store that was not well utilized, primarily because of difficult access to it from the main road and the poorly designed parking lot, which often created a safety hazard to the pedestrian and motorist alike.

Prospectus. The prospectus is the document by which we make known service needs and how they are to be handled and encourage the private sector to provide these services within the public lands. It is a response to the concession questions of what, where, when, and how, and it should include:

1. Needed service facilities, their location, and details of operation.
2. All provisions discussed under Conditions of Lease, at least in summary form.
3. Statutes and regulations under which the concessions will operate.
4. A description of area, including location, transportation systems, climate, existing use patterns, projected demand, and other data pertinent to the particular project.
5. How to submit offer. It is usually desirable to allow the prospective concessioner maximum design choice in submitting a proposal in response to the prospectus if the facilities are to be developed by the private individual.
6. The criteria by which the applicants will be judged. Special criteria

are usually used in selecting the successful applicant—i.e., how appropriate is the proposed development, how well can the service be provided, and how financially stable will the operation be? Competitive bidding in terms of the lease fee that one is willing to pay is important but generally not a prime criterion. Thus, it is a good practice to require a background résumé and a complete financial statement from each applicant.

ASSESSING ENVIRONMENTAL IMPACTS

After a proposal has been selected as the one that best meets the criteria, the total project then should be assessed in terms of its environmental effects. Mitigating measures must be developed to alleviate the environmental problems, or the project should be modified to reduce the environmental impacts. If the impact cannot be reduced to an acceptable level another alternative is to move the location.

SUPERVISING

Once the project has been given final approval, concession management (if the concession is to be privately owned or operated) is a matter of supervision—starting with the groundbreaking—and includes the following:

1. Construction of facilities to ensure that they meet the specifications set forth in the plan.
2. Monitoring of services to ensure that they meet specified minimum requirements.
3. Monitoring of potential environmental effects in order to adjust programs if problems arise.
4. Maintenance of site to ensure the adequate protection and the appearance of the facilities.

SELECTED READINGS

1. Bissonette, J. F., and D. G. Wright. 1966. "Vending Machines—A Survey of and Manual for Park and Recreation Department." Wheeling, W. Va.: National Recreation and Park Association.
2. Brockman, C. F., and L. C. Merriam, Jr. 1973. *Recreational Use of Wildlands.* New York: McGraw-Hill Book Co.
3. Buchinger, M. 1968. "Concessions and Service Arrangements in Various Parts of the World," *Canadian National Parks: Today and Tommorrow.* Nelson, J. G., and R. C. Scace (eds.) The National and Provincial Parks Association of Canada and the University of Calgary.
4. Cahn, R. 1969. "Will Success Spoil the National Parks?" *Christian Science Monitor.*
5. Chamberlain, C. J. 1970. "A Profitable Concession," *Parks and Recreation* 5(3):29.
6. Darling, F. F., and N. D. Eichhorn. 1969. "Man and Nature in the National Parks: Reflections on Policy," *National Parks Magazine* 4:13.
7. Everhart, W. C. 1972. *The National Park Service.* New York: Praeger Publishers.
8. Flynn, T. F., Jr. 1968. "The Management of Concessions in National Parks in the United States," *Canadian National Parks: Today and Tomorrow.* Nelson, J. G., and R. C. Scace (eds.). The National and Provincial Parks Association of Canada and the University of Calgary.
9. Green, P. D. 1963. *Souvenir, Gift and Novelty Shops—A Manual and Survey on Operation in Public Parks and Recreation Areas.* Wheeling, W. Va.: American Institute of Park Executives.

10. Green, P. D. and M. Schack. 1966. "Souvenirs and Novelties," *Revenue Resources Management School,* National Recreation and Park Association, Oglebay Park, Wheeling, W. Va.
11. Gray, M. T. 1950. "Park Concessions," *Parks and Recreation* 3:12.
12. Hileman, R. 1957. "Concessions vs. Direct Operation," *Parks and Recreation* 4:151.
13. Illinois State Department of Conservation. 1970. *Park Ranger's Handbook.*
14. Ise, J. 1963. *Our National Park Policy: A Critical History.* Baltimore: The Johns Hopkins Press.
15. Jubenville, A. 1975. *Outdoor Recreation Planning.* Philadelphia: W. B. Saunders Co.
16. McKim, W. 1968. "Townsite Administration and Management in Canadian National Parks," *Canadian National Parks: Today and Tomorrow.* The National and Provincial Parks Association and the University of Calgary.
17. Memmel, B. G. 1963. *A Manual on Concession Contracts for Park and Recreation Executives.* Wheeling, W. Va.: American Institute of Park Executives.
18. National Park Service. 1972. *Provisional Master Plan for Yellowstone National Park.*
19. *National Park Service. 1970. Marina Food Service and Merchandising Prospectus, Arbuckle Recreation Area, Oklahoma.*
20. National Park Service. 1960. *Concession Management Handbook.* Washington, D.C.: U.S. Government Printing Office.
21. National Park Service and National Conference on State Parks. 1964. "Guidelines" *Park Practice Program: Concessions.*
22. Oehlmann, H.. 1955. "A Concessionaire Talks Back," *American Forests* 6(7):13.
23. Parent, C. R. M., and F. E. Robeson. 1974. *Economic Aspects of Concessionaire Regulation: A Case Study in Grand Teton National Park.* Logan, Utah: Utah State University Press.
24. Reid, L. M. 1959. "Food and Merchandise Sales in Public Parks," *Cooperative Extension Publication.* University of Michigan Agriculture Experiment Station. Ann Arbor, Mich.: University of Michigan Press.
25. Rubini, F. F. 1969. "Fees and Charges, Leases and Contracts, Other than Food," *Proceedings, 19th Annual Great Lakes Park Training Institute.* Angola, Ind., p. 83.
26. Rubini, F. F., and V. Brackett. 1970. "Specifications and Contracts with the Concessionaire," *Proceedings, 20th Annual Great Lakes Park Training Conference* Angola Ind., p. 136.
27. Stanford Research Institute. 1976. "The Concession System in National Parks: Background, Services Performed, Public Attitude Toward, and Future Considerations," *Stanford University Research Report.* Stanford, Calif.
28. U. S. Congress. 1965. National Park Service Concession Policies (P. L. 89–249).

CHAPTER 15

Public Safety

Public safety is a broad concept that concerns the safe use of public lands. Too often, the manager has adopted a paternalistic approach, attempting to eliminate all potential safety problems and control the behavior or use patterns of the participants in order to ensure adequate safety. This may result in a very sterile environment for the recreationist because a choice in terms of his own behavior has been taken away from him. We assume by this approach that man is not rational and cannot make a reasonable choice when faced with personal risk; in some instances, this may be true. In doing this, we may modify the setting to such degree that it is no longer desirable for that particular activity.

We are responsible for public safety, but we should be reasonable in our developing of programs to do this. It becomes a matter of balancing the safety of visitors with the sophistication of the participants, the type of activity, and the potential consequences of the decision. The activity itself should dictate a general safety program. Certain activities require maximum safety standards; others, such as wilderness recreation, require only minimum programs (usually informational). The level of knowledge or experience that is required in a particular activity also should be considered. Those with less experience would be encouraged to participate with more experienced people until they developed the necessary skills. Possibly, in potential, life-threatening situations, only those individuals possessing the requisite skills would be allowed to participate. However, it is often difficult to define that level of expertise with any accuracy. In a more common approach, programs focus on the feeding of up-to-date information to the user and allow him to make the decision.

Since programs also must focus on protecting the resource from deliberate abuse and destruction by the visitor, public safety is really a two-way street. We try to provide a safe, enjoyable experience for the visitor, but also must protect the natural resource base and the developed facilities from visitor abuse.

Public safety, as a management objective, is often implied and consequently is not stated as a separate program. To ensure adequate safety control, it may be better to state objectives for public safety and to develop specific safety programs, which eventually must be integrated into all the other programs.

Three categories of public safety will be discussed: law enforcement, maintenance, and hazards. We often think that law enforcement is the main concern of public safety, but protection from natural hazards and proper maintenance of existing facilities are also important.

LAW ENFORCEMENT

Law enforcement, as a management program, is purposely included under the category of public safety, since it is a primary goal of any public safety program, especially in relation to outdoor recreation. As managers, we try to reduce violations of the park regulations by visitors and improve the way in which the visitor treats the landscape. It may be wiser to use the term public *safety*; too often, people are "turned off" by the term *law enforcement* because of an association with police action after a *crime* has been committed. The term *public safety* is more acceptable because it connotes a genuine interest in the visitor and in the protection of those values that originally attracted him to the site.

Each park or recreation area generally has its own public safety problems. Thus, the actual number of law enforcement programs reflects particular needs. Consequently, there will be several types, or levels, of law enforcement operating within a given management structure.

LEVELS OF LAW ENFORCEMENT

There are three primary levels of law enforcement for park and recreation agencies:

Hard Core. Hard-core programs are designed to supervise and enforce existing laws and regulations. This may involve the monitoring programs—e.g., road and trail patrols, facility surveillance during periods of visitor use, and a communications network for receiving and responding to distress calls. It also may include investigation, apprehension, and assistance in prosecution of criminals. This is equated by the public with the typical police action of most city police forces; however, it is absolutely necessary in light of the many deliberate law and regulation violations within most park and recreation areas. Because of the highly specialized requirements, the actual investigation and follow-through on major crimes (felonies and high misdemeanors) are usually handled by a staff specialist or an outside law enforcement agency—depending on who has legal jurisdiction.

This type of management program is frequently interpreted by the manager as requiring emergency flashing lights, special law enforcement uniforms, and sidearms. In some cases, this may be warranted, but in others it may not be necessary or even desirable. Certainly, it is not in keeping with the primary goal—i.e., protecting the visitor and the park values. A visitor can identify a law enforcement person by a uniform, which also promotes a visitor's respect (Fig. 15–1). An official must uphold the law and the agency regulations, but too much identification with law enforcement programs outside the park may reduce the overall effectiveness of public safety within. It is a fine line to clearly distinguish between the two, and one that varies with the particular agency and its legal and administrative mandates; but it is not a trivial matter to consider when building an effective program.

Soft Core. In soft-core programs we try to either encourage or discourage certain types of visitor behavioral patterns through management by design, continuous monitoring and improvement of safety conditions, or improved visitor cooperation. If we can anticipate problems of visitor conduct during the

Figure 15–1 Law enforcement is becoming an increasingly important function of the outdoor recreation manager (photo by Bruce and Debbie Maxon).

planning phase, we may be able to design a road, a trail, a recreation site, or even an entire system (such as a river system) so that it will promote the intended types of use and discourage others. In this respect, we often are our own worst enemy. We create a lot of management problems when we develop a poorly designed site and then implement an intensive, hard-core law enforcement effort to alter use patterns on this site. To even a casual observer, this appears to be a rather expensive way to make a poor design actually work. On-site enforcement is very expensive and is often difficult to implement without good facility design.

I have examined trails and trail heads leading into wilderness and backcountry areas, where considerable illegal and uncontrollable vehicle use was taking place along with vandalism (Fig. 15–2). At first, the agency attempted to catch the culprits; when that proved to be nearly impossible, they asked the nonvehicular traveler to report any violations (the agency would follow up any reports). When this approach also did not work, the agency was ready to give up on the problem. In most cases, the real problem was caused by poor design. The designers had widened the trails, lowered the gradient, removed all barriers, and casually placed occupancy sites (campgrounds, picnic sites, and so forth) adjacent to the trail head. They encouraged casual trail bike use that could have been discouraged by better design.

We also can manipulate the social environment in dealing with problem situations. We can separate conflicting and competing uses to reduce tension. Possibly, we can limit the size of parties, require them to register, and work with interest groups to plan their itinerary in order to have a more manageable situation. The visitors could even police themselves. For example, a state park was having trouble with large motorcycle gangs abusing the parkscape and har-

Figure 15-2 Vandalism of facilities is increasing at an alarming rate. Note the bullet holes in the newly installed solid waste container (photo by Alan Jubenville).

assing other users. The park agency developed a plan by which all large groups were required to register 24 hours in advance so that facilities could be reserved. In addition, a group member was to serve as trip leader. Problems from the gangs diminished drastically because of the reasonable controls exercised by the manager. Ultimately the "gangs" were able to police themselves. Continuous monitoring of potential problems and the development of contingency plans for law enforcement are necessary if the manager is to maintain law and order in the parks.

Educational. The educational approach is an attempt to improve the *quality of use* by making people aware of the important park values and the individual's role in protecting these values. As an example, the very survival of the grizzly bear in Glacier National Park may depend on educational programs to reduce the number of encounters between man and bear. In such an encounter, the bear will ultimately lose to the man. We can issue citations for violation of the rules (e.g., camping in the wrong area, leaving food to attract the bear), or we can locate our trails and campsites to reduce the probability of an encounter. We still must educate the user, or the total program will not be effective. We must have all levels of law enforcement in order to have a total program; however, to protect the parkscape, we must work with the user before a violation has been committed — in a positive approach that emphasizes education and environmental design.

We should consider the establishment of other related public safety programs for emergencies and search and rescue. Both are important and require good management and good planning to be effective; facilities, well-maintained equipment, skilled personnel, and good communications are all necessary for the programs to succeed. These must be considered in a management plan so that we know how to respond before a problem situation arises. It is easier to be logical and objective in decision making without the tension and pressures of the emergency situation.

ORGANIZATIONAL FRAMEWORK

You manage the way you are organized for management; this axiom is especially true of law enforcement. You have to be prepared to respond to specific law enforcement problems rather than just react to particular circumstances. The organizational framework is the first step in management planning. If you are not organized properly, you will not be very effective no matter what you do. These plans should be thought out well in advance; then the full scale operation can be tested to see if it is properly organized, with serviceable equipment and trained personnel.

The problems of poor organizational framework are shown in the following example. A state park division was part of the state Department of Natural Resources. It was organized into seven districts, each with a district supervisor. The conservation law enforcement division of the department was not organized into districts but into small areas in which a conservation law enforcement officer reported directly to the division chief at the state level.

If a problem arose, the park superintendent had to call the district supervisor, who then relayed the problem to his division chief at the state office, who in turn would ask the law enforcement division chief to respond to the problem by calling the local field officer. Needless to say, there was much inefficiency, and many problems received no response. In fact, the situation became so frustrating that the state park division chief armed and trained his own personnel in some of the troublesome parks. Because of the difficulty in getting the proper authority to respond, these park personnel, with limited training and experience, took over the primary hard-core law enforcement program. Some park personnel became so "gun-happy" that many of the charges they brought against violators were dismissed, and people became upset and angry. Because of the officials' behavior, all management programs suffered.

In delegating responsibility within your organization, you should separate the areas of responsibility as follows:

Crime (Felonies and Major Misdemeanors). A person in a staff position should handle this area. The individual would have to investigate, arrest, and assist in the prosecution of major crimes that occur within the park. He would need all the training and experience that are required to handle this type of law enforcement.

Minor Misdemeanors and Rule Violations. This would be the responsibility of the management staff assigned to patrol duty, with emphasis on reducing park violations and handling emergency situations, as well as on educating and informing the public in order to improve the quality of use. Issuing of citations would be secondary but necessary in certain situations.

The park staff members are usually the first officials at the scene of a crime or an accident. Although they may be directly handling the problem, they still should be supervising (e.g. to seal off the area, to detain people) in proper legal fashion until the staff law enforcement officer arrives. Thus, all management personnel should have at least minimal training in law enforcement procedures and should be familiar with the standard operating procedures of the agency.

General Safety Management Problems. All staff members, including those in the lowest position, should have some public safety training, including law enforcement, first aid, and public relations. Many times it is the maintenance worker or similar technician who is present when a problem arises. He should have minimal training to handle the situation until other assistance arrives on the scene.

Perhaps your organization is large enough to have staff diversity in public safety. Still, you should think along the lines of the three law enforcement functions and try to organize yourself to respond accordingly. Even then, you must define the legal responsibilities and maximize your legal role while working in coordination with other agencies that may have specific law enforcement functions within your park. For National Parks, these functions are defined in the enabling act for each park by designating which responsibilities are delegated to the federal government and to state or local law enforcement agencies. These are shown in the U.S. Codes. If all responsibilities for law enforcement are delegated to the managing agency, it is called *exclusive jurisdiction*. A problem may arise at the state or local level if a statute establishing a park or recreation area does not specify what agency is responsible. Subsequently, it may be difficult to get the proper authority to respond.

A CONCEPTUAL PROGRAM

Based on the previous discussion, a law enforcement program should be divided into two phases—crime and park violations.

Crime. Crime is an important part of the total program, particularly in our larger parks and recreation areas. Many of these areas have tremendous crime problems that have been difficult to combat. Thus, much of the management budget for those areas has gone toward crime prevention efforts. However, the law enforcement staff must be made aware of and properly trained for several other, related programs.

Crime Prevention. Crime prevention is very important and includes roving and point patrol, installation of building and recreation site security equipment, and public information/education efforts. Through information and education the visitor can be utilized, to a degree, to discourage or report suspected crime.

Detection and arrest procedures. Detection can be accomplished through direct observation by law enforcement personnel, electronic surveillance, and reports of violations by the visitor. This requires the manager to identify and concentrate on potential crime areas, yet he must also be able to respond to crime in all portions of the park or recreation area.

Arresting someone requires a knowledge of proper arrest procedures. This involves warning the person of the charge on which he is being held and advising him of his rights. The person making the arrest should be careful not to use excessive force; at the same time, he should be extremely cautious about his own personal safety while making the arrest.

Criminal investigation. Successful prosecution of a crime depends upon good investigation. This begins as soon as the first park staff member arrives at the scene of the crime. The area should be sealed off immediately, and the names and location of all potential witnesses should be recorded. If this does not occur, evidence may be destroyed or testimony may be lost. The handling of evidence and the interviewing of witnesses should only be done by qualified investigators. Investigations may take weeks or even months; thus, the staff investigator must have time to pursue the problem.

Assistance in prosecution. The investigation is not finished until the prosecution is completed. The management personnel and the investigators must understand court procedures and be able to properly present testimony in court.

Coordination with other agencies. Coordination with other law enforcement agencies is essential to the development of a viable program. The coordination must be planned so that it can be immediately implemented at the local level. In that way, the criminal can be apprehended with minimal delay. Sometimes the coordination is stated in the federal, state, or local statutes or through written cooperative agreements, but at no time should it be merely implied or assumed as understood.

Park Violations.   There are really three subprograms involving park violations and types of protection:

People from people. We should try to maximize the enjoyment of each visitor, this often requires the development and enforcement of rules to reduce conflict between users. Through management, we minimize conflict, harassment, and confrontation between different types of park users. This is becoming more important as the number of visitors increases. With more people, there is more social contact and greater diversity of interest. This can lead to social conflict if we try to provide too much variety in too small a space. Thus, a feasible area and site design can reduce tension between user groups.[7] Still, enforcement of rules is necessary to minimize social tension.

People from the park. We can encourage or discourage certain types of use patterns in order to minimize potential harmful effects to the visitor—whether from grizzly bears, hot springs, or automobiles.

Park from the people. This is an important, traditional role of law enforcement. It is necessary to develop a set of rules for visitor conduct and to make the visitor aware of these rules. If he breaks them, it can potentially destroy many of the values for which the park is established and maintained. Try to remain objective and respond according to the actions of the visitor, the consequences of his actions, and the idea behind the action. The intention of the act may not be as significant as was first imagined, and it may have been done out of ignorance or, at least, from a lack of awareness. Don't over-react. Don't be too hasty or too harsh—but be firm in your handling of the individuals involved. The agency will generally provide some general guidelines, but how a particular situation is to be handled is left to the individual. Remember that this is an opportunity to informally educate the visitor on the effects of his behavior. If you can change the person's behavior, you also have increased the quality of use of the landscape.

A FINAL THOUGHT

The four DO's in the development of a park or recreation law enforcement program are the following:

1. *Do* emphasize management by design. If we can alter the physical environment to encourage or discourage certain behaviors, we may need to rely on

little or no direct control through enforcement. This would leave maximum choice to the individual and minimum appropriations for direct law enforcement.

2. *Do* maximize education and information efforts that will increase visitor awareness and, subsequently, the quality of use. If we are to improve the etiquette of the user to protect the prime park values, we must educate visitors about these values and how their behavior affects them.

3. *Do* delineate staff and other agencies' roles and responsibilities. These roles must be delineated and coordinated so that an effective, total program can be created.

4. *Do* maintain immediate response capability in terms of both crime prevention and emergency treatment. We must maintain an adequate staff and an ability to respond to any emergency on a 24-hour basis.

MAINTENANCE PROGRAMS

Maintenance of facilities is listed because of its immediate importance for the protection of the *unaware visitor*. Once we develop a facility, we are obligated to maintain it—whether it is a building, a foot bridge, or a road. The underlying assumption by most participants is that the facilities are maintained in reasonable condition in relation to the expected use. Visitors usually focus their safety concerns on either the nature of the activity or on the use of the facility and not on the facility itself. For example, a visitor is hiking through a narrow canyon. Where the trail crosses the river, the visitor concentrates on hiking (and possibly on any associated hazards such as talous slopes or slippery rocks) and on crossing the narrow, rustic foot bridges; he gives little consideration toward the possibility that the bridges may be unsafe. He assumes that someone checks them periodically for safety.

There are two ways of implementing a facilities maintenance inspection program—on a scheduled or a nonscheduled basis. Both should be implemented simultaneously if the maintenance program is to be really effective. The scheduled inspections are done on a regular basis, and records are maintained concerning these inspections (Fig. 15–3). A master schedule is kept at headquarters to ensure that the required inspections have been accomplished. If a safety problem is noted, it is corrected immediately, or a stop-gap measure is used until the problem can be completely resolved. These inspections also act as a preventive measure to correct a situation before it becomes a major problem.

The maintenance inspection form should have specific guidelines and criteria for the inspection. This reduces guesswork and ensures that each inspection of a particular facility will be done in a consistent manner. These guidelines cannot be printed on the inspection form but may be included in the handbook used by the inspectors.

The unscheduled maintenance inspections are accomplished by all personnel. Each employee is encouraged to become aware of the potential safety problems in his area and to report any suspected problems. In this way, the manager can be on top of any problem situation that might arise. Too often the employee is subtly discouraged from reporting unsafe conditions because it

Annual
_____
(Frequency of Inspection)

Foot Bridge
_____
(Facility)

Warm Springs Trail at Stewart Creek
_____
(Location)

1963
_____
(Year of Development/Renovation)

20 Years
_____
(Expected Life)

Date	Component	Condition	Signature of Inspector
8/11/77	Abutment 1	O. K.	*P. S. Smith*
	Abutment 2	Minor crack in lower wall.	*P. S. Smith*
	Substructure	Needs protective paint; no cracks.	*P. S. Smith*
	Bearing Surface	Three surface boards need to be re-placed (marked w/red paint).	*P. S. Smith*
	Railings	O. K.	*P. S. Smith*

Figure 15–3   Sample Maintenance Inspection Form.

Figure 15–4   Driving hazard caused by poor road maintenance.

puts the agency in an unfavorable light and often requires a shift in personnel and appropriations. However, if we are truly dedicated to providing quality recreational experiences and to protecting the visitor, it is important that all facilities be in reasonable repair.

Also, there are legal obligations in terms of inspection and repair of facilities to protect both the agency and the manager. If you can show through maintenance inspection records or employee reports that the inspections were made and the deficiencies were corrected, there is little cause for legal concern. On the other hand, if repairs were done but not reported, there is no documentation to support their completion.

PUBLIC HAZARDS

The first step in hazard management is the identification of potential hazards within the park, possibly through brainstorming with your staff personnel. It is important to get an initial list, clear it of unnecessary items, and then divide the remainder into two categories—*significant* and *routine*. Each item also should be rated as *modification* or *preservation*. Modification means that it is acceptable to modify the landscape or the facility to mitigate the hazardous condition. An example of this might be to add a rustic handrail along a boardwalk surrounding hot springs. Preservation means that modification would generally be unacceptable; consequently any mitigating measures would involve manipulating the visitor or at least warning him of the dangers involved.

Significant hazards would receive priority in the programs developed to manage the potential effects of hazards. The rating of modification or preservation would indicate the direction that the program should follow. The routine ones would receive less priority in terms of amount of effort that is extended; however, it may be possible to immediately implement a program to reduce some routine hazard without the need for a great deal of analysis.

After the identification and rating process, the manager must formulate specific programs. These programs will offer some balance between the maintenance of a desirable landscape/facility and protection of the visitor. An example of poor action is a case in which the superintendent of a state park failed to seal off an attractive water-splashed rock ledge along the river near the main parking area. There had been several drownings as a result of people accidentally slipping off the ledge into the water. He constructed a one-rail, 3-feet high fence; the following year, the drownings dropped from six to three. It would have been sufficient to tastefully (in terms of architecture) seal off the ledge, and hopefully the number of drownings would have dropped to zero.

In sum, safety is important; however, we often do not develop specific objectives in relation to public safety. It is usually an implied objective; I would suggest making it a written objective. In this way, we ensure that the specific programs are aimed not only at providing certain types of recreational experiences and protecting the environment but also at providing *reasonable* safety to the visitor. The importance of safety programs will probably increase as the numbers of visitors increase and as more people arrive in areas that are poorly prepared or lack the necessary safety precautions.

SELECTED READINGS

1. Bard, M., and R. Shellow. 1976. *Issues in Law Enforcement: Essays and Case Studies.* Englewood Cliffs, N. J.: Resten Publishing Co.
2. Beckman, E. 1977. *Law Enforcement in a Democratic Society: An Introduction.* Chicago: Nelson-Hall Co.
3. Brockman, C. F., and L. C. Merriam, Jr. 1973. *Recreational Use of Wild Lands.* New York: McGraw-Hill Book Co.
4. Campbell, F. L., J. C. Hendee, and R. Clark. 1968. "Law and Order in Public Parks," *Parks and Recreation* 3:28, 51.
5. Ceracy-Wanthrup, S. V. 1965. "A Safe Minimum Standard As an Objective of Conservation Policy," *Readings in Resource Management and Conservation,* Burton, I., and R. W. Kates (eds.). Chicago: The University of Chicago Press.
6. Davis, C. 1966. "Legal Problems and Liability in Outdoor Recreation," *Park Maintenance* 19 (12).
7. Doell, C. E. 1963. *Elements of Park and Recreation Administration.* Mineapolis, Minn.: Burgess Publishing Co.
8. Gilbert, D. L. 1964. *Public Relations in Natural Resource Management.* Minneapolis, Minn.: Burgess Publishing Co.
9. National Park Service. 1975. "Law Enforcement Program," Grand Canyon National Park, Arizona: Horace M. Albright Training Academy.
10. National Recreation and Park Association. 1971. *Manual and Survey for Public Safety,* Management Aid Series No. 20.
11. National Recreation and Park Association. 1973. *Park Police,* No. 32.
12. National Recreation and Park Association. 1975. *Litter Control,* Management Aid Series No. 53.
13. Smith, F. E. 1966. *Politics and Conservation.* New York: Panthenon Co.
14. Snarr, R. W., and L. N. Craft. 1976. *Student Programmed Learning Guide and Introduction to Law Enforcement and Criminal Justice.* Springfield, Ill.: Charles C Thomas, Publisher.
15. Somerset County Park Commission. 1962. "Park Police Personnel Manual," Summerville, N.J.: The Somerset County Park Commission.
16. Wicks, R. J. 1974. *Applied Psychology for Law Enforcement and Correction Officers.* New York: McGraw-Hill Book Co.

PART IV

MANAGEMENT APPLICATION

This part focuses on the general application of the concepts and principles developed in the previous sections. You must realize that there are no absolute answers; any work must be tempered with good judgment and imagination.

Probably the greatest concern that I have as a recreation manager is the need to maximize the recreational experience for the individual. I also realize that, ultimately, certain limits or restrictions *may* have to be placed on user participation patterns. All of this must be accomplished according to the objectives of the particular area. It seems that the manager often overestimates the visitor's need for solitude, natural environment, and physical challenge—i.e., he fulfills the needs of the "purist" rather than those of the average user. Consequently, he attempts to control the recreational environment (social and physical) in such a way as to protect the experience for the purist. Yet the manager may be eliminating a large portion of the spectrum of participants and possibly may be reducing the total experience for even the purist. If we were really interested in protecting the experience—initially for the purist and ultimately, for the entire participant spectrum— we would want to maximize freedom of choice for the individual. We can do this by *management by design, variety of opportunity* (within specific objectives), and *good informational and educational programs.*

Management by design refers to the development of a recreation system that is essentially self-regulating. The decision to participate is left to the individual; the environment in which he participates is manipulated to encourage or discourage certain use patterns that are within the objectives for the area. For example, an objective for a backcountry area is to maximize hiking in the day-use zone and to minimize conflict between the hiker and the horseman user for social and environmental reasons. It would be easier to simply eliminate the horseman or to limit his participation to those portions of the site that are visited by the hiker. Perhaps a system of access roads, trail heads, and trails could be developed in the day-use zone to subtly encourage hiking and discourage horseback riding. Concurrently, riders could be directed toward a different area by developing the horse facilities at other trail heads and by having the trails pass directly through the day-use zone into the extended participation zone.

You can encourage use patterns according to the type and the location of the facilities. A hiking area should be reasonably accessible to the main attractions of the site, such as lakes, if you wish to encourage day use. To discourage horseback riding, do not manicure the trail and do not provide horse facilities. Unfortunately, it is not always that simple, and no system managed solely by design will be perfect. Yet is is an ideal that we should strive for—that is, the self-regulated system. If we try to manage by design, we will never achieve optimum distribution of users in terms of maximizing the social experience or minimizing environmental impact, but at least we can move toward that goal. We can achieve a reasonable proportion of acceptable recreational experiences while maximizing alternatives for the participant and minimizing environmental damage. A desirable outcome, which is acceptable (but not perfect), can be achieved for less cost by this process than by overt control.

Yet it seems we have lost perspective of what we are trying to achieve. The direction (from recent discussions, readings, and symposia) is toward the application of overt control to create and maintain the perfect system. We attempt to manage people, their behavioral patterns, and impact. That is an admirable goal, but it is not achieved through overt control. Many of the problems of overcrowding, adverse behavioral patterns, and negative environmental impact have been created by the location and the design of our roads, trails, recreational sites and by the information we have distributed. We need to correct these mistakes to alleviate the problems. Ultimately, we may have to exercise direct control, but it is hoped that this will only be necessary after we have exhausted every alternative.

We do not like to be controlled by others except when it is absolutely necessary, and we should respect this feeling in our relations with others. Theoreticians tell us that when we participate in recreational activities, we are less restrained by normal societal roles than at any other time. This includes more freedom of choice to the individual.

The next three chapters are not intended as "how to do it" check lists for good management techniques. The problems of good management are not easy ones. The principles and techniques that have been presented, combined with personal experience and imagination, will help in solving complex problems for which there are no stereotyped answers. The next three chapters will present some of the problems facing today's outdoor recreation manager. They will be drawn from the previous discussions in the book. Sample problems will be presented in order to challenge the reader with some possible situations.

CHAPTER 16

MANAGEMENT OF INTENSIVE-USE SITES

Intensive-use sites are classified as occupancy sites, winter sports sites, waterfront site complexes (Fig. 16–1), and historical/cultural/educational sites. Management programs should reflect the objectives that have been established for the area. A major variable affecting this is ownership (public versus private or a mixture of both).

OCCUPANCY SITES

Occupancy sites, which include campgrounds and picnic areas, generally receive medium- to high-level use. Consequently, they present a real challenge to the manager. A significant problem has been the distribution of users in relation to the sites. Many sites are overused, while others are underused. Merely controlling overuse so that resource damage does not occur is not a satisfactory answer. Overuse is a symptom of the problem. Probably, the real problem is the distribution of people in proportion to the distribution of occupancy sites.

Figure 16–1 Management of intensive use sites—the waterfront complex. In this example, boats and swimmers have been separated to reduce hazards and conflicts.

If we recognize the problem, we can focus on the causes—a poor location, design, or informational program (or perhaps the program is too good). We can never solve the problem until we isolate it and attack the causes—not the symptoms.

We can encourage good distribution through our informational programs by making the visitor aware of the available opportunities and the existing use patterns at the various occupancy sites. The assumption is that the visitor will make rational decisions based on the available information. Theoretically, a good informational program should encourage an even distribution of use; nevertheless, there will be some unevenness, since the choice has been left to the individual. We then can look at our site locations and designs. Since times and individuals change, we should analyze our designs to see if they meet the present needs of the visitors. Various designs obviously are needed to satisfy the different user groups. Location can encourage or discourage use, too. This means that we may have to make some difficult and expensive decisions to redesign or relocate a number of the existing occupancy sites.

The problems of resource deterioration, including landscape aesthetics, are similar to those of site distribution—poor design, poor location, and poor quality of use. Good design can very subtly direct use to those portions of the site that are more stable or have been hardened to handle a higher level of use. Even good design is of little importance if the site is not durable enough to sustain the intended level of use.

There will still be some site deterioration caused by the careless visitor—mainly through his lack of awareness of the consequences of his actions. Ideally, an educational program that is designed to communicate this awareness should upgrade the quality of use of the site as well as reduce the overall deterioration.

This point of view is intended to present some alternatives to the way we now conduct our business. We need some regulations and direct control. As recreational use spirals and natural resources decrease, the need for regulations and direct control mechanisms will increase. However, there are other available alternatives. Regulations and direct control are often easy to develop, implement, and even justify. But this implies managing the *perfect* system, which does not exist. The near perfect system would be one in which the decisions were made by the individual, as much as possible. Our economic system of free enterprise also is not perfect; however, freedom of choice for the individual is much more desirable than a "perfect" management system that controls individual choice. What if the government told you that only blue cars would be for sale instead of blue, green, or yellow cars? What if you wanted to move to California but were told that California was closed to immigrants because of the high rate of unemployment? Take a look at your own operation. Does management by design (including a variety of opportunity and a well-managed information system) appear to be a more desirable direction for management to take than direct controls?

In the following case problems, see how you react, and try to analyze your reactions. The problems are expressed in general terms so that you can use your own data or alter the problem to resemble a local situation. Use the problem analysis format presented in Chapter 3.

Problem 1. Overflow Camping. This problem, which most managers face, has both social and environmental implications.

A schematic map of the area, including developed campgrounds, is shown in Figure 16–2. There is a reasonably high use of Campgrounds 1 and 2. Many units are unused; but in Campground 3, there is usually an overflow — people camping in between developed units — even though it is not allowed (Table 16–1). Recently, more overflow camping has occurred in the overlook parking area and in several places in the subalpine zone south of State Highway 24 and east of the Livermore River. Loss of vegetation, erosion, and conflicts with day users are beginning to occur in and around Campground 3 and the places of informal camping.

You don't want the situation to get out of hand, and you are dedicated to protecting the scenic natural wonders of the park. What is the problem? What would you do? Would you . . .

1. Put in artificial barriers to keep people from camping in the subalpine zone?
2. Reroute the road?
3. Add more campgrounds? (Where would you locate them?)
4. Zone the subalpine zone for day-use only?
5. Close the park gate after the campgrounds are filled and turn other camping parties away?
6. Allow use to continue as it is?

Brainstorm other approaches to the problem. Don't confine your answers to the alternatives that we now use to handle such problems. Possibly, you would eliminate all camping or would remove the road. Just remember that there may be more information needed in order to make the best possible decision about

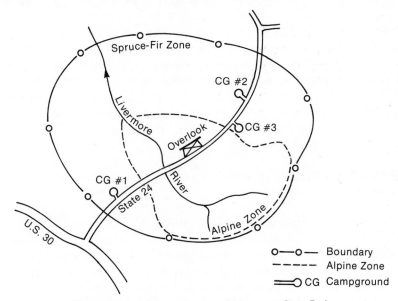

Figure 16–2　Schematic map of Livermore State Park.

TABLE 16–1　CAMPING USE AT LIVERMORE STATE PARK

Campground No.	No. of Units	% Occupancy (Avg. Summer Day°)
1	68	55
2	32	38
3	43	110

°Averaged over the last four years.

the problem. What additional information would you like to have about the particular situation, and how would you expect to use it in your problem solving?

Problem 2. Soil Compaction. You are manager of a regional park in the Piedmont region of an Eastern state. You have two major campgrounds; both are located on heavy clay soils (including clay subsoils). The use season begins in the middle of May and extends through October; however, the rainy season occurs in the spring and usually lasts until about June 10. The soil does not become reasonably dry until approximately July 1.

People still come during the wet season; consequently, the pattern of camping has caused considerable compaction of the soil in the upper 3 to 5 inches, and the ground vegetation is almost completely gone. Gravel surfacing and mixing sand into the upper 5 inches have been tried, but neither method has alleviated the compacted conditions; consequently, sheet erosion still occurs. Furthermore, the camp units become exceedingly dustier later in the summer.

What are the symptoms? Can you define the problem? What are the causes of this problem? What are the available alternatives if you are to attack the causes?

Problem 3. Dust Hazard. You are the private owner of a campground-marina complex on White Lake. You own only the land that is presently developed. No other land is available. The soil is sandy (with some silt) and supports an overstory of 35-year-old loblolly pine with a crown density of about 80–85 per cent. The trees are still healthy, but their growth rate has been slower in the last five years. There is some pine litter in places where little use occurs; otherwise, most parts of the area are completely bare. The campground is about eight years old.

Many visitors complain about the large amount of dust. They feel something should be done, or they will be forced to camp elsewhere. You have tried to reduce the problem by short, periodic waterings during the low-use periods, but this method has not worked. You also know that every other camp operator is having the same problem and has not been able to solve it. What are the symptoms, the subproblems, and the main problem? Be imaginative, and brainstorm some new approaches to this continual problem.

WINTER SPORTS SITES

The primary activity at winter sports sites is downhill skiing. This requires an intensively developed site, including the base area, and has created very important management problems. There has been a proliferation of new winter sports sites, many of which are only marginally profitable. Thus, the first concern of the manager is the marketability of the skiing opportunity in relation to the potential user population, the transportation systems, and the type of resource (snow conditions, vertical relief, and so forth). Even if the complex has been in existence for a long time, it is still possible that poor attendance is based on its lack of marketability, particularly if local market conditions have changed.

Since most potential large ski areas are located on public lands which are committed through a long term concession lease, the manager has a responsibility to determine the marketability of a proposed winter sports site complex.

There are competing values for a lot of this land; thus, the manager should determine what values should be emphasized in the management planning. Once these lands have been committed to intensive development, it often becomes difficult to reclaim a defunct site. More often, we try to resurrect the business, or we abandon it—perhaps to become a hazard or a visual blight on the landscape.

Beyond these problems, there are other on-site management concerns: queuing, maintenance, safety, and quality of service. Queuing problems at the lifts have caused some loss in business. Redistribution of use can help to reduce queuing. Ultimately, updating the ski lift capacity and designing a better base area may be the only ways to reduce the queuing problems associated with the lifts, and to improve the quality of service. Maintenance inspections of facilities must be conducted continually to ensure a safe and satisfying experience for the visitor. Maintenance, in terms of both appearance and safety, is often lacking on the lifts and in the buildings. Within the last few years, accidents have been occurring on lifts at major ski resorts that theoretically have a supervised maintenance inspection schedule. If this occurs at major winter sports sites, one wonders what the problems and situations may be like at local sites. The appearance of many of these facilities also is deteriorating.

The quality of the recreational opportunity is decreasing at many of the site complexes; however, others are doing quite well. In fact, some developments are flourishing while other segments of our economy are at a standstill. The long-term answer to the problem facing the ski industry must be solved through market research and a tightly guarded leasing program. The leasing requirements must be enumerated in the initial lease, since it is unlikely that renegotiations will occur.

Problem 1. Winter Sports Site Development. The case study of North Snow Park Winter Sports Site shows some of the preceding problems. North Snow Park Winter Sports Site is located on public domain lands northwest of North Snow Park. In 1974, it went bankrupt at its present site. It is located in A county and is generally isolated from more populous areas because of travel time. It offers some good beginner to advanced intermediate skiing.

An individual bought the ski area and hired a consulting firm to do a market analysis and a preliminary plan to move the site around to the main Snow Park area (the base of which is privately owned). According to the marketing study, about 20,000 skier visits would be generated from A, B, and C counties. The managing agency of the ski area hired another consulting firm to do their own market analysis. The inclusion of B and C counties in the regional market proved to be inaccurate because of travel problems (i.e., amount of time involved and poor winter travel conditions) and the proximity to higher quality skiing opportunities within the counties. This left A county, with a population of about 15,000 as the market place. A liberal estimate of potential skier use was one-third of the original one done by the consultant for the private developer. Furthermore, it was projected that a large portion of the skier population in A county would travel elsewhere, since there was a nationally famous winter sports site within a two-hour drive of Snow Park, and other excellent skiing opportunities were located within driving distance for weekend trips. In addition, the population of A was expected to double within the next decade because of the increased mining activity, which would primarily attract blue collar workers (non-skiers).

By moving the site about one-half mile from the existing one, the variety of skiing opportunities would be increased, and more base area facilities and services would be available. Potential problems involve the base area, which will be located in a natural bog, and one of the proposed ski runs, which will terminate in a V-shaped, eroded gully.

Is this overstating the problem? Don't be hasty to agree or disagree, since you may be faced with a similar situation. What other information would you feel you need? What about the verification of existing information? How would you use the given information in your calculations? What factors would have more weight than others?

If you really want to try your hand at decision making, insert *specific* data (such as travel distance, competition, quality of skiing, and so forth) into the problem,[6] now change the data, and try it again! Try inserting some outside variables. For example, your local field manager promised in public forum that the people of A county would have their new winter sports site. Perhaps the developer assured the county commissioners that it would add hundreds of thousands of dollars to the county tax base, or the county planning board approved an associated summer home development but stipulated that no subterranean sewer systems would be allowed. It is difficult to develop a simple program to handle all these situations. How would you handle it?

Problem 2. Public Values. Assume that a major winter sports site was proposed for development on public lands, and this would disrupt or destroy some of the values associated with the existing landscape. These considerations may include scenic qualities, destruction of wintering grounds for big game, and the reduction of prime habitat for a rare or endangered species. Develop your own problem around that theme. Choose a course of action to solve the problem, and defend that position, with legitimate arguments. Perhaps you could divide your group into three committees: the first would specify the details in the problem; the second would respond through problem analysis; and the third would critique the decision-making effort. Then these roles could be rotated (with new data).

WATERFRONT SITE COMPLEXES

The interest in water-based recreation is spiraling. Yet the water resource base (depending on the particular locale) either is remaining constant or is diminishing because of changes in adjacent land use and water pollution. Besides the obvious problems of supply and demand, there are many legal concerns in relation to access, riparian rights, and safety.

The primary management problems seem to center on access (too much or too little), conflict between activities, safety, and stabilization of the riparian environment. Access has particularly been a problem at major beach areas. Too little access to public waterfront discourages use, even though the demand may be high; too much access can encourage overuse or indiscriminate vehicle use that destroys the riparian environment. Other social problems arise from too much access—e.g., conflicts between activities, competition for the limited amount of space, enforcement of safety regulations, and just mass confusion.

Management by design would be a good approach, since the problems of waterfront management are usually a combination of problems that cannot be easily separated. Management by design can direct people away from sensitive areas, control access, and separate uses according to access, facilities, and services. Experience indicates that it is necessary to combine management by design with administrative zoning that fits both the needs of the visitor and the durability of the resource (according to the volume of participation). This must be coupled with a public safety program that protects both the visitor and the resource. Ancillary public safety programs are mandatory, including law enforcement, information and education, hazard reduction, search and rescue, and public relations.

This overview is an attempt to dissect the primary management problems—to unravel a complex situation and isolate the management issues. Perhaps the following problems will better demonstrate the interrelationships involving those issues.

Problem 1. A profile of the ecosystem at a seashore is shown in Figure 16–3. Many recreational use patterns along this portion of the sea coast have been allowed to evolve over decades, with little concern for managing the visitor or the resource. Visitors could enter with vehicles through selected access points and then drive across the wet, hard-packed sand until they reached their destinations. However, in the last five years, the number of visitors has doubled, and the amount of off-road vehicle use has tripled.

The real stability of the ecosystem comes from the wetness of the sand in the wet zone and from the beach grass and sea oats in the dune zone. Severe loss of dune vegetation affected by increasing and often indiscriminate off-road vehicle use has caused tremendous wind erosion. It is hard to design and maintain a facility, including parking, without dune stability. Furthermore, a major storm could completely wash away the beachfront if the dunes are not stabilized.

A social problem exists because of the conflicts between various activities. The worst of these conflicts appears to be between the dune buggy and four-wheel user and the casual hikers and swimmers—i.e., users without vehicles. Any management program must attempt to resolve the two issues: resource damage and conflicts between users. Within this framework, create a specific problem, and change these data to make new situations. You could even show the situation over a specified time period. You may want to sketch road networks, indicate public/private ownership, and identify specific geographic points as problem areas. Regardless of how you do this, look at your entire system and try to determine the interactive effects of subsystems. Set up a trade-off sheet so that you can identify what you may get and give up if a particular management alternative is selected. The ultimate success of your management plan may well depend on citizen participation in the planning process. If so,

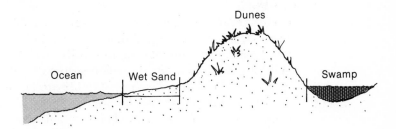

Figure 16–3 Profile of a seashore ecosystem.

decide on the objective for citizen participation (CP). Choose an appropriate CP technique, and conduct your own CP session!

Problem 2. Because of the demand and the competition for water-based recreation, there must be several important management problems that you can identify within your immediate vicinity. Develop a *real* problem with *real* data. This approach often helps the student to better understand the problem-solving process and gives him an opportunity to immerse himself in the process without being pressured to come up with an immediate solution. He also may find out that good solutions can come from involving others, even citizen-recreationists. Good decisions are not made in isolation; the professional does not have a monopoly on the "good decisions market." Don't let training (and ego) limit your perspective in terms of expected outcomes. This is the reason for the brainstorming phase of problem solving. Try to accumulate an array of alternatives before you begin the evaluation process. The professional might use the same techniques. We all are students to a degree, and can learn much in that role. If you have a problem that you cannot solve, you may be too close to it. Look at a similar problem outside your own agency to see if you can develop alternative solutions. You can then evaluate them without bias. Perhaps you then can step back into your agency role and solve a similar problem. Possibly you may benefit from an informal association with other professionals within your region for the purpose of sharing problems and potential solutions. Don't overlook the people around you — your packer or outfitter, your secretary, even your maintenance person. Ask them; the results may surprise you.

HISTORICAL SITES

There are three primary concerns in managing historical sites: stabilization of the buildings and grounds, protection of buildings and artifacts while maintaining accessibility, and educational enrichment. Stabilization and protection of the buildings and grounds are important if we are to provide an authentic historical setting. Walls and flooring of historical buildings may have to be reinforced and foundations reworked in order to preserve the building in its present condition. Wood may have to be treated to prevent further weathering. Even without a high level of visitor use, a historical site needs to be stabilized and protected from the effects of climate. This hardens the site; however, one still must maintain the authentic appearance of the site. Modifications may occur in internal reinforcing and protective surfacing that will not change the historical value of the site. If the buildings are of different time periods, some determination must be made about the time period to emphasize — particularly in the historical interpretive program. The buildings and grounds may be preserved in the existing conditions, renovated to show the life style of a particular historical period, or reconstructed.

Once the site has become stabilized, the buildings and artifacts must be protected from vandalism and theft yet remain accessible to the public. One way is through management by design. In this case, it refers to directing use through the buildings and grounds by encouraging a flow of traffic to minimize congestion, maximize visual enjoyment of the historical site, and reduce theft and vandalism. By reducing congestion, more people can visit the site with minimum disruption. Sometimes this is difficult to achieve because of the original layout of

Figure 16–4 Bannock City, Montana—former territorial capital and abandoned gold mining town. The buildings and grounds have been preserved and, in some instances, restored to the early gold mining period.

the site—such as an old historical mining town (Fig. 16–4) or the floor plan of a specific building. Even with these limitations, one should strive to facilitate traffic flow patterns.

The visitor may wish to handle and inspect the furnishings, clothing, firearms, and other artifacts. Because of the fragility of antiques and in the interest of preserving these items for posterity, it seems prudent that they be only visually accessible to the public. The overall historical interpretation is dependent on the arrangement of the artifacts to indicate relationships and to tell the story of the historical site. One cannot allow irreplaceable artifacts to be handled casually or to become lost by accident or theft; but the other extreme—complete isolation or limited private showings—may not be a desirable solution. One must carefully consider whether the visitor's feeling of detachment from the historical setting is so great that it detracts from his interest, enthusiasm, and empathy for the historical setting. Much of this can be resolved by an educational enrichment program that interprets the setting and the important events associated with it. Some sites have developed over several periods in history and can be interpreted to the public only with great difficulty. In those cases, the manager must determine the most significant period and develop his program around it. In this manner, the visitor can better understand the historical background of the site. Simplicity of the message should increase the awareness and understanding of the visitor for the time period that you wish to emphasize.

Living history programs greatly increase visitor awareness by portraying specific events, daily routines, and so forth for a specific time period. By using live actors, the site "comes alive," and the visitor will have greater empathy for the history associated with the site. Living history programs are difficult to develop, since it is not just any seasonal employee who will succeed as an actor

Figure 16–5   Living history interpretation at Ft. Laramie, Wyoming (photo by Douglas Johnson).

re-creating history. Costumes, personalities, and acting ability—along with training and practice—are the basic ingredients for a successful program. These elements must be coordinated so that they tell the total story (the objective in terms of historical message), or you may destroy the very effect you wish to create. If you wish to portray the daily life of the foot soldier at a fort, such as that shown in Figure 16–5, let that be your guiding theme. Focus the spotlight on him, and let the contact with the other types of people (settlers, Indians, officers) be incidental to what you wish to portray.

   Problem 1.   Site Stabilization and Protection.   Select a nearby site that has regional or local historical significance and is not presently being managed as a historical site. Research the history of the site; sketch in all buildings and developments in their present condition. Develop a map of the visual corridor (what you can see from the site). With this base-line information, you can construct the problem in any number of ways. Try to develop an interdisciplinary study team to handle the scope of the problem. Using the generic terms (such as architect, engineer, historian, and so forth), list your team members, and justify why each one is needed.

   Problem 2.   *Historical Significance.*   With the same site as in Problem 1, trace the steps necessary for placing it in the National Historic Landmark Registry.

   Problem 3.   *Interpretation.*   Develop a program that interprets the site for the visitor. This program may vary in its approach—from simple signs to an elaborate living history program. The choice is yours, but it should be appropriate for the site, the managing agency, and the type of visitor.

   Bonne chance!

SELECTED READINGS

1. Alden, H. R. 1973. "Systems for Analyzing Impacts of Outdoor Programs on Environmental Quality," *Outdoor Recreation and Environmental Quality*. Foss, P. O. (ed.). Ft. Collins, Colo.: Colorado State University.
2. Bleiker, A., and H. Bleiker. 1977. *Citizen Participation Handbook*. Laramie, Wyo.: Institute for Participatory Planning.
3. Dickerson, R. 1974. "Management Challenges for Parks," *Proceedings of the Recreation Management Institute*. College Station, Tex.: Texas A & M University.
4. Fogg, G. E. 1974. *Park Planning Guidelines*. Washington, D.C. National Recreation and Park Association.
5. Grater, R. K. 1976. *The Interpreter's Handbook*. Grand Canyon, Arizona. Southwest Parks and Monument Association.
6. Jubenville, A. 1975. *Outdoor Recreation Planning*. Philadelphia: W. B. Saunders Co.
7. McEwen, D., and S. R. Tocher. 1976. "Zone Management: Key to Controlling Recreational Impact in Developed Sites," *Journal of Forestry* 74(2):90.
8. McGill, A. W. 1974. "Dispersal of Recreationists on Wildlands," *U.S. Forest Service General Technical Report* NC-9.
9. Mackie, D. K. 1966. "Site Planning to Reduce Deterioration," *Proceedings of the Society of American Foresters,* p. 33.
10. National Park Service. 1960. *Concession Management Handbook*. Washington, D.C.: U.S. Government Printing Office.
11. Orr, H. R. 1971. "Design and Layout of Recreation Facilities," *Recreation Symposium Proceedings,* U.S. Forest Service.
12. Orr, H. R. 1967. "Analytical Approach to Design," *Park Maintenance,* 20(2):34.
13. Outdoor Recreation Resources Review Commission. 1962. *The Quality of Outdoor Recreation: As Evidenced by User Satisfaction,* Study Report No. 5. Washington, D.C.: U.S. Government Printing Office.
14. Pressman, J. L. 1970. "Decision-Making and Public Policy: the Perils and Possibilities," *Elements of Outdoor Recreation Planning,* Driver, B. L. (ed.). Ann Arbor, Mich.: University of Michigan Press.
15. Rosse, T. L., and G. H. Moeller, 1974. *Communicating Rules in Recreation Areas.* U.S. Forest Service Research Paper NE-297.
16. Tocher, S. R., J. A. Wagar, and J. D. Hunt. 1965. "Sound Management Prevents Worn Out Recreation Sites," *Journal of Forestry* 48(3):151.
17. Wager, J. A. 1965. "Cultural Treatment of Vegetation on Recreation Sites," *Proceedings of the Society of American Foresters,* p. 37.

CHAPTER 17

Management of Dispersed Recreation Areas

The management of dispersed recreation areas has taken on greater significance in the last two decades. Use has spiraled during this time. At first it was oriented toward travel on foot; then it shifted to off-road vehicle activity. Now, with the increase in both foot and vehicle travel and the keen competition between vehicle and non-vehicle users, management problems have become even more numerous and complex; plus at the present time, more and more land is being allocated for uses other than recreational. Thus the manager must become more sophisticated in the development of ways to alleviate these problems.

The chapter is divided into types of dispersed recreational activities so that management problems can be discussed generally or specifically—i.e., in terms of a particular use. For example, a general problem appears to be conflict between vehicle and non-vehicle users; however, even if you separate them, there will still be management problems associated with each of the activities.

DISPERSED RECREATIONAL ACTIVITIES (NON-VEHICLE)

Most of us are familiar with summer dispersed recreational activities—hiking, backpacking, 4-wheel driving, trailbiking, and riding RV's, i.e., recreational vehicles—and the potential problems associated with them. Rather than just focusing on potential problems, we will be examining the expected behavioral patterns associated with the various activities so that we may try to maximize the experience for the participant. *Then* we can focus on the social and ecological conflicts that may occur. If the goal is to provide recreational experiences, management should attempt to describe the behavioral parameters associated with each specific activity. The manager should attempt to maintain these parameters even if use patterns must be altered to maintain the desirable social and ecological environment of the area. It would be poor management to merely restrict use without really understanding the consequence of that decision. Thus, it is imperative that the manager be totally familiar with the three management subsystems—resource, visitor, and management—and how they interact. Restrictions should be made only after a thorough review of the problem. For example, it may be in the best interest of the public to protect particular environmental conditions. By understanding the consequences of such a decision, we can feel secure that our strategy not only will protect the existing conditions but also will minimize the disruption to normal behavioral patterns of the user. A problem such as competition between two recreational activities can disrupt the social environment or the social patterns of recreational use. When this occurs, the manager may have to take immediate action, such as zoning the area for a variety of experiences. Otherwise, the more primitive form of participation will be overwhelmed by the more modern form. This is based on the assumption that when two activities overlap spatially, the one with the more modern form of transportation will prevail.

HIKING

Hiking, an important day-use activity, has not been studied to any great extent; consequently, we know very little about the normal behavioral patterns. There is a tremendous variation in hiking participation—from the urban trails to the wilderness and backcountry area. Thus, the specific microbehavioral patterns must be influenced, in some way, by the setting in which hiking takes place. However, there also seem to be some general management problems regardless of the setting. The first problem is the lack of clear objectives that state the purpose for specific hiking areas or trails. We often try to make each area provide a great variety of hiking opportunities, some of which may be incompatible. It would be better to provide variety by establishing a variety of roadless recreational experiences. Perhaps larger areas could be zoned to maintain the integrity of specific opportunities (see Fig. 17–1). The objectives for each zone, in terms of recreational opportunities and environ-

Figure 17-1　Hiking in the Snowy Range Scenic Area—an intermediate type of roadless recreation experience.

mental protection, should guide the manager in the development of appropriate strategies. Other general problems that exist are the following:

Problem 1. *Failure to recognize hiking (day use) as being a separate activity.* We have tried to increase management efficiency on public lands by closing many miles of trails and directing use toward well-maintained trails. This has been done to increase the efficient use of the management dollar. However, while demand has increased at a phenomenal rate, supply has decreased, creating tremendous competition for the remaining trails. This forces a greater variety of trail uses on fewer miles of trails. Actually, we may have aggravated the situation by closing off trails in the nonwilderness areas and increasing maintenance of trails in the wilderness area. This has reduced the availability of casual hiking experiences in the pastoral landscape where it is more likely that more use could be sustained, both environmentally and socially. It appears that we have "forced" the user who is looking for casual hiking experiences into the wilderness setting—a setting that generally is more sensitive to environmental changes. It also is the retreat of the recreation "purist" seeking less social contact.[14] Thus, in several instances, we have employed management techniques that have reversed the roles of wilderness and nonwilderness hiking areas to such a degree that even the manager is confused. If the manager is confused, think of the identity problems that the poor hiker must have!

Problem 2. *Off-site hikers (a corollary to Problem 1).* Different objectives are achieved through hiking experiences—physical fitness, transporation, enjoyment of aesthetic surroundings, solitude, and so forth. Some of these uses may be mutually exclusive; others may be very compatible. If we encourage all types of hikers in a single area, we may end up with many "off-site" hikers. These individuals, attracted to the trail because of access, facilities, and design, become disappointed in the activity because it is not the type of experience they were really seeking. If we are to reduce the number of off-site users, we must provide different types of hiking experiences as well as inform the public about what is available. In this way, the individual has a choice. In addition, the location and design of the trails should communicate to the user the type of experience that he can expect along the trail within the roadless area.

Problem 3. *Too much emphasis on national trails.* This is similar to the situation described in the book *Tragedy of the Commons;* i.e., we place great emphasis on the development and management of extensive trail systems that are isolated from the general population while we all but exclude the high-density systems situated close to urban centers.[10] The national trails obviously make the headlines, but shorter, simpler trails that are closer to home may be better utilized on a regular basis by a larger number of visitors. The appropriate approach may be to have a system of different trails[8] and to have the level of development and maintenance commensurate with the type and level of experience being offered.

BACKPACKING

Backpacking involves the overnight use of a roadless area by the hiker. Some of the problems of hiking also apply to backpacking. However, the potential impact of the backpacker, both socially and environmentally, is much greater, since he spends more time in the area, uses it as living space as well as recreational setting, and is often sedentary in his camping habits. All these factors place a much greater tension on the landscape; the management programs, if they are to be effective, must account for these factors.

Hiking (day use) (in terms of normal behavioral pattern) is generally limited to the fringes of roadless areas, and backpacking usually extends further into the roadless area. The two activities generally are separated spatially, except along the trail in the fringe area. However, these two activities do interface at specific points of attraction located within the fringe. This is where specific action must be taken to reduce any conflict. Information, visitor use, and law enforcement programs may be necessary at those points where both types of participants may congregate. A more effective environmental and social program would be one that directs overnight use away from the point of concentration but allows all visitors to experience the particular attraction as *day users*. Also, the main trail and connecting trails could be designed to separate the two activities.[8]

HORSEBACK USE

The use of recreational stock (e.g., horses, mules) in roadless areas is increasing; much of this activity is provided through contracted outfitter services. Although the number of people who participate seems to be increasing, the total impact seems to be decreasing because of some new regulations on the recreational use of horses. The regulations were developed during the last decade because of the severe environmental impact of the horse on the resource area. This included the following:

1. Mechanical damage to vegetation, including root systems.
2. Trail erosion problems.
3. Depletion of grazing resources in many areas.
4. Introduction of exotic vegetation.
5. Aesthetic depreciation.
6. Litter.

The outfitted parties were the worst offenders, particularly those sponsored by a few conservation organizations.[9] A group of 20 people may have had as many as 100 horses for a 10-day pack trip through an area that was not durable enough to sustain that level of use. It was not until severe damage had occurred that management began to take action to reduce the effects of the horses.

There also is the social consideration of encounters between the traveler on foot and the horseman. The rider often avoided the hiker because of the possibility of the horse shying. On the other hand, hikers and other travelers on foot did not particularly appreciate the horseback riders because of the odor of the animals and their manure. Usually, the riding party was larger and carried more and bulkier equipment; they also required much more space at the attraction points. Thus, any management planning must consider the specific behavioral needs of both kinds of travelers and attempt to accommodate these needs while minimizing the conflict between the two.

Since these are dispersed-use areas, I would assume that very little management money will be spent on a per unit area basis. Furthermore, because of the costs, I would assume that expensive management strategies (such as dual trail systems, required permits, and maximum trail maintenance) would be given very little consideration except as a last resort. Based on these assumptions, the management strategy should be to encourage desirable patterns and levels of use – by offering a spectrum of hiking, backpacking, and horseback riding opportunities; by properly designing the specific sites (in this case, trails, primitive campgrounds, and so forth); and by informing the public about facilities and activities available to the user. These strategies, which basically reflect the management by design philosophy, have already been discussed by various agencies; even lengthy agency publications have been written about them. Yet these strategies are rarely practiced in the field. For some reason, the manager seems to revert to utilization of the more easily implemented (but more expensive, in many cases) overt types of controls. In reality, the visitor in dispersed-use areas is manipulated through management of access. Access refers to the ease in which one can enter or leave an area. If you increase access, you increase use. If you wish to direct use to certain points, increase access to these points. Conversely, if you wish to direct use away, decrease access. Differential access to and within an area will affect its attractiveness to various user groups. The manager can employ trail design to disperse use, concentrate it, or change it – whatever approach he feels is appropriate. Thus, the tools of management in dispersed-use areas are the access road (character, design, and location), trail head development, the recreational facilities along the road or at the trail head, the trail (character, design, and location), and the recreational facilities at various points along the trail. This must be coupled with a good informational program to make people aware of what is available. The "tools of management" fit together to provide a specific recreational opportunity and to communicate nonverbally and verbally to the user the type of experience being offered.

Answers to the problems of managing these dispersed-use areas should fit the difficulty of the problem; yet, sometimes we look for a more complex solution than may really be necessary. For example, it is not too difficult to understand why conflict occurs between hiker and horseman on the first two miles of the East Fork Trail. The trail meanders along a stream that is heavily used for fishing by the day-hiker. However, most parties of horseback riders start their trips to the high country from this access point because the manager chose to locate the horse facilities (corrals ramps, and so forth) at the same trail head. The problem is not people, but poor judgment on the part of the manager in location of facilities. The horseback rider simply goes where the facilities are located and then onto the nearest trail to the high country. The manager could separate the users by moving the horse facilities to another, convenient trail access which leads to the high country.

Let's look at another example. A trail into a roadless area was opened earlier than usual by having a trail crew remove the snow. This allowed the horseman and backpacker early access into the high country above the timberline where most of the snow had already melted. The visitors expressed their gratitude for opening the trail early. Within three years, severe compaction and erosion began to show up on parts of the trail, and there was a severe loss of vegetation at those places where people had camped during the early season.

Possibly, a limited permit system during the early season could have controlled the numbers and directed campers to more durable areas. However, a soil analysis indicated that the areas above timberline had a very shallow, heavy soil (which is highly compactible when wet). No other campsites were available near the timberline because of the lingering snow. Thus people had responded to a manmade stimulus – i.e., the cleared trail.

Before the snow removal program, very few backpackers (and no horseman) had actually crossed the snow-packed trail and camped in the high country. The snow-removal program, which was expensive in terms of direct costs and subsequent problems, was determined to be the cause and was discontinued. It was also decided that loss of vegetation and erosion of the soil would be monitored for extended periods of time to determine if further treatment would be necessary to renovate the depleted sites.

In another example, a trail into a roadless area was originally developed during the 1930s for monitoring forest fires and fire fighting by trail crews. It passed through large meadows, around high mountain lakes, and out of the area to a trail head that was located in another watershed. The area was being used for hiking—leave trailhead A, hike to the high lakes, and return to trailhead A—usually in day-long trips. Public feedback in the local district office indicated that many people were becoming dissatisfied with this area because of too many people on the trail and around the lakes. It was obvious that something had to be done. A simple solution would be to control the number of users through a permit system that would reduce undesirable social contact between groups; this actually was done. My feeling is that it was the poor design of the physical environs (the trail) that caused most of the problem, and the chosen solution had too many drawbacks to be effective. First, it was too expensive because of the cost of personnel involved in issuing the permits and then enforcing this regulation in the field. Second, by setting limits on the number of users, it reduced supply in the face of increasing demand. Yet the problem, as it is stated, is directly related to social encounters that affected the quality of experience. Third, unnecessary social contact (at the mountain lakes and on the trails) will continue because the trail is funneling people directly through the areas of greatest visitor concentration. In fact, the trail location contributes to the resulting concentration of people at the lakes. This increases not only the social contact but also the environmental impact caused by sheer numbers of people around the lakes (which generally is less durable as an environmental setting). Last, by going to a limited permit system, we are reducing the number of choices for the participant. We ultimately may have to reduce freedom of choice, but it is hoped that this would be a final alternative. In a recent study on river floating, most people could perceive many social and environmental problems that needed immediate management actions, but they felt a limit on freedom of choice to be the least popular alternative.[11]

A more desirable approach, both from the perspective of the manager and the user, would combine an improved information program with better trail design. The improved information program would reach the user prior to arrival at the area so that he would have knowledge of what is available and what to expect in terms of specific opportunities. Theoretically, this would shift some of the use to other places and reduce the number of "off-site" visitors. The new trail design would bypass any environmentally sensitive areas and points of known (or suspected) visitor concentrations; if possible, the new design would also conform to the normal travel behavior of the visitor.

Ideally, the design would fit these descriptive criteria:
1. There would be a loop trail, zoned one way, to bring the visitor near the attractions, but not directly through them.
2. Spur trails would be developed from the loop trail to the attractions.

3. The spur trails would exit from the primary trail near the halfway point of the loop trail so as to discourage the visitor from casually returning the *wrong* way on the one-way trail because it was the shorter route.

4. The main loop trail would offer a variety of visual experiences throughout to maintain the interest of the visitor. This would encourage a continuous flow pattern, and only those who wished to go to the lakes would seek that type of setting.

5. Many of the known or suspected attractions would be visually accessible from the main loop trail or from vistas near the trail. Then the visitor could enjoy the attractions without having to actually visit them.

6. Environmentally sensitive locations would be bypassed by the loop trail in order to discourage impact in those locations.

Possibly, an assessment of environmental durability around the lakes could be done. The *more* durable areas would be easily accessible via spur trails from the loop; the *less* durable ones would be made less accessible by increasing the length of the spur, possibly making it more of a physical challenge to the hiker. The least durable lake environments may be inaccessible by trail. If one wishes to visit this area, he must make his way cross-country.

This not only would satisfy the need to protect the quality of the environment but also would create a variety of roadless recreation experiences where previously there has been only one. Theoretically, larger numbers of people could be handled without loss of visitor satisfaction from too many encounters. Most important, freedom of choice would not be taken away from the individual; under the new management, more choices would become available.

Other criteria could be included in the design; in any event, this should indicate that there are more attractive techniques than simple overt control. Although the initial investment may be less, overt control programs are probably more expensive to implement than other, less restricted programs. In the dispersed-use areas, more emphasis must be placed on development of a modified, self-regulating system than on enforcement of agency regulations.

In another situation, horse riders and backpackers were attracted to several high mountain lakes at the head of a major drainage area. There was a divided trail along the boundary of the drainage area. Both horsemen and backpackers traveled the divide trail down to the lake basins below the divide. The divide trail began to show severe wear, mainly due to the use of horses. The vegetation around the lakes and in the adjacent wet meadows was rapidly deteriorating again because of the horse riding. Many backpackers had already complained about the environmental impact of the horses as well as the problems of odor and manure along the trail. Further investigation indicated that the backpacker was interested in a slower, more contemplative trip to the lakes, while the horseman was more interested in pushing ahead to get to the lakes.

One possible alternative would have been to close the drainage area to horse use. However, the manager had located a more direct route that potentially was more durable. The manager decided on developing a dual trail system. The valley trail was zoned for horseback riding, with spur trails that terminated at three different horse camps, which were located on durable sites below the timberline and within reasonable hiking distance of the lakes. The divide trail was zoned for travel by foot only. The lake attractions then were open for use by both types of participants. The only regulation that was needed was to zone the immediate area around the lakes as *no camping* zones so that one type of user could not monopolize the lakes by claiming it as a camping territory.

It seems obvious that a combination of management strategies is necessary to manage the dispersed-use activities. However, the less we depend on direct law enforcement programs while we emphasize informational and education programs and management by design, the more effective our management will be. This leaves the basic choice pattern to the participant, and manipulation of the visitor is easier yet more subtle. Some direct regulation may be necessary; but managing the dispersed-use activities completely through regulation removes some of the values (freedom of choice, spontaneity, lack of regulation) that should be maintained; plus, it is difficult and expensive to enforce regulations. A lack of regulation may be very important to many people. They may even participate in a way similar to one that would be achieved through regulations but would resent a dictation of participation style.

Dispersed-use activities can be offered within or adjacent to urban areas or in isolated rural areas. The problems that one encounters will vary with the local conditions. Thus, it may be more appropriate for the reader to solve a local problem. Try to identify the types of users concerned with that particular problem; the resource variables that it affects, and the history behind it (i.e., how long has this problem existed). Then give a detailed description of the problem. Develop two solutions—one emphasizing well-conceived regulations; the other, management by design. Based on the local conditions, what additional problems might arise in implementing these solutions? Which of the alternatives would you (as a user) prefer? Ask others which one they would choose. Managers have told me that a particular problem in their area could only be solved a certain way. Yet in the same conversation, they said that they personally would not like to participate in the area if that management strategy was implemented. Does there seem to be a contradiction in regard to the appropriateness of these managers' solutions?

DISPERSED RECREATIONAL ACTIVITIES (MOTORIZED)

Off-road vehicle use has never been seriously managed except in designated wilderness areas and a few designated roadless areas. Many of the problems now facing the manager have existed for a long time. The two primary management concerns are degradation of the environment through indiscriminate use and conflict between non-motorized and motorized users.

Environmental degradation from off-road vehicle use has increased drastically in the past decade.[1] Figures 17–2 and 17–3 show the types of physical damage and erosion that can result from vehicle use. This damage will most likely continue until specific management programs are developed to reduce the impact and possibly to renovate many of the rutted trails. Without renovation the erosion will continue even if the trail is rerouted. Thus, the manager's first step is to make a complete assessment of resource durability, especially concerning places of low durability—bogs, meadows, lakeshores, steep terrain, erosive soil types, and so forth. From these data, a base map of the area can be zoned according to durability to off-road vehicle use. If it is *not* durable—and there is no way to increase the durability—the off-road

Figure 17–2 Off-road vehicle use can cause severe loss of vegetation and subsequent soil erosion (photo by Alan Jubenville).

Figure 17–3 Closing of some off-road vehicle trails may be necessary (photo by Alan Jubenville).

vehicle trail should be removed or partially relocated to another, more durable portion of the landscape. Locating turnouts at points where the trail passes by such attractions as lakes or meadows allows the opportunity for people to see them without having to drive down to them. Even then, it might be desirable to have some type of natural barrier between the vehicle and the local attraction, to subtly say "stay on the trail."

Besides durability, the manager also should zone in relation to the activity and to the level of desired access into the area. Motorized and non-motorized use of a roadless area can potentially be conflicting unless the area is large enough so that the two activities can be separated. The conflict is not only from this direct confrontation but also from the noise pollution from the vehicles. Small areas may have to be zoned for one activity or possibly have limited access by using topographical features and vegetation to limit the noise level and to keep the motorist within specified corridors.

We should try to offer the motorist a satisfying experience and be willing at times to accept a certain amount of environmental degradation in order to achieve this objective. Realistically, the only way to eliminate the environmental degradation associated with off-road vehicle use is to eliminate off-road vehicles. To offer a satisfying experience to the motorist, the manager must develop scenic trails for motorized vehicles, stabilize or minimize resource damage, maximize visual experiences along the trail, allow opportunities to enjoy many of the attractions of the area (via some spur trail that discourages all but foot traffic), and limit vehicles to the off-road vehicle trails. Signs can be helpful but are not sufficient; disobedience of signs by a few vehicle users can be very disruptive in many areas.

If possible, the solution should fit the normal behavioral pattern of the off-road vehicle user. Otherwise, there may be great resistance to the management program; this resistance could effectively eliminate or at least stall its implementation. Figure 17–4 illustrates this point.

As shown in the figure, the existing trail was not planned, and much erosion is occurring on the steeper portions and at the Lake Creek crossing. In fact, there were several crossings because people would start a new one if the previous crossing became too rutted. The destination of the visitors was the two main lakes, and apparently, the trail developed because of easy access from Route 13, to the lakes. Many of the users recognized the problem of erosion but continued to use the trail.

The proposed solution to the problem was to develop a new trail leading through the spruce-fir forest zone and terminating near the lakes and then to have the visitors hike the remaining short distance. This would get the user close to his destination and eliminate environmental destruction in the sensitive alpine zone. Natural barriers should be used to keep vehicle use on the designated trail. Some stabilization work would have to be done, and the access point would have to be closed before natural revegetation could take place on the informal road; even then, it would be a slow process. Nearly all the users favored this strategy. However, this type of program must be vigorously followed with information and education and law enforcement to be fully effective. In addition, the designated trail should be marked so that there is no misunderstanding as to where vehicles are allowed.

Management by design to direct vehicle use with aid of natural barriers is very important. However, there are many areas in the United States, particularly on the Western plains, where it becomes impossible to manage the

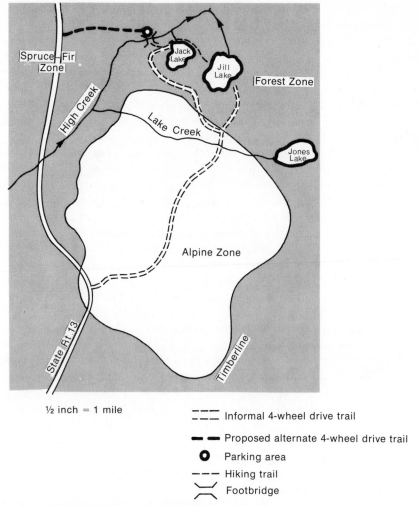

½ inch = 1 mile

‡‡‡ Informal 4-wheel drive trail

━ ━ Proposed alternate 4-wheel drive trail

O Parking area

━ ━ ━ Hiking trail

⁀⌣ Footbridge

Figure 17–4 Proposed relocation for an off-road vehicle trail.

vehicle use based strictly on trail design. It is a difficult problem because the motorist can drive almost anywhere across the plains. However, there are several alternatives that may help in directing off-road vehicle use to the more suitable locations:

1. *Developed and marked trails.* These tend to be more desirable because they tend to be less bumpy, less hazardous, and easier to find.

2. *Fencing.* Fencing, particularly in conjunction with agricultural uses, can subtly encourage or discourage particular use patterns. However, if access is very limited, there may be excessive damage to the fencing in order to gain entry.

3. *Signing.* Area information signs should show where vehicle use is allowed.

4. *Access points.* Access points into the area can take advantage of major physiographical features that may tend to limit use to a particular trail.

5. *Citizen participation in decision-making.* In order to be effective, you will need substantial support from the potential users on the proper course of action. This may require working closely with off-road vehicle clubs and other

interested groups in the area in order to develop a management plan. Theoretically, if they are willing to live with the plan, they will police members and nonmembers alike. The manager often finds this difficult to accept, or he has difficulty getting the cooperation of local clubs; however cooperation on all levels is important if the plan is to be effective.

6. *Law enforcement.* Enforcement of regulations is necessary; however, if the area is completely open, compliance with the off-road vehicle plan should be obtained through area planning, information, and cooperation. The less dependent one is on law enforcement, the more likely the plan will succeed.

Locate a local problem related to off-road vehicle use. Make an inventory of the soils, vegetation, and access. Designate management units and establish objectives for each unit. Then develop management strategies to accomplish these objectives. Use the preceding list of alternatives as a guide.

WINTER DISPERSED RECREATION ACTIVITIES

The primary dispersed winter activities are snowmobiling and cross-country skiing. These activities have not been managed well except in small areas where competition for winter landscape is high. Generally, the two are considered incompatible; yet both are conducted in similar terrain, which usually results in conflict over the same piece of real estate. To protect the integrity of each experience, it is necessary to separate them by zoning. This may not be needed in large roadless areas or in areas where use is low, but that type of situation is hard to find today. There are also behavioral differences between the snowmobiler and cross-country skier. The snowmobiler enjoys longer, faster trips (Fig. 17–5); the cross-country skier, shorter and more contemplative experiences.

Figure 17–5 Snowmobiling has become a prime winter sports activity.

Consequently, it is imperative to develop a basic management strategy before any major conflicts or safety problems occur. Once the patterns of use become established (including conflicts), they are difficult to change. Since they are two different uses of the same terrain, they should be separated through zoning. However, the zoning should follow certain guidelines, as suggested by Jubenville.

> By starting from separate trail heads and using natural barriers to separate the snowmobiler and cross-country skier, one has effectively zoned . . . without actually designating a particular location for a single use.
>
> The zones should have well-defined topographic boundaries to separate them physically, visually, and aurally.[8]

Safety is of great concern because of the hazards of winter conditions. The area should be monitored to ensure compliance with regulations to protect the visitor and the recreational experience. Thus, there is the dual responsibility to inform the public of possible safety hazards *and* to create the programs designed to reduce these hazards. Trails help to direct use and reduce the possibility of getting lost. They also can direct use away from avalanche zones, steep terrain, water crossings, thermal pools, and so forth. During potential avalanche periods, the manager should issue warnings or close the area to winter recreation.

Locate an area used by both cross-country skier and snowmobiler. Inventory the access, the developed facilities, and the areas where the two uses may overlap. Isolate and articulate the problems. What are the causes? List the steps you would take to maximize the experiences of both types of users yet minimize the potential conflicts between the two.

SELECTED READINGS

1. Balivin, M. F. 1970. *The Off-Road Vehicle and Environmental Quality* (2nd ed.). Washington, D.C.: The Conservation Foundation.
2. Banzhof, George, and Company. 1974. *United States Forest Service Survey for Use of Off-Road Vehicles.* Milwaukee: George Banzhof and Company.
3. Brockman, C. F., and L. C. Merriam, Jr. 1973. *Recreational Use of Wild Lands.* New York: McGraw-Hill Book Co.
4. Christianson, M. I. 1977. *Park Planning Handbook.* New York: John Wiley & Sons.
5. Cowgill, P. 1971. "Too Many People on the Colorado River," *National Parks and Conservation Magazine* 45(11):10.
6. Douglass, R. 1973. *Forest Recreation.* New York: Pergamon Press.
7. Jackson, R. 1971. "Zoning to Regulate On-Water Recreation," *Land Economics* 47(4):382.
8. Jubenville, A. 1975. *Outdoor Recreation Planning.* Philadelphia: W. B. Saunders Co.
9. Jubenville, A. 1975. "Wilderness and the Conservation Organization: A Time for Policy Appraisal?" *Environmental Conservation* 1(2):93.
10. Lucas, R. C. 1971. "Hikers and Other Trail Users," *Recreation Symposium Proceedings,* Northeast Forest Experiment Station.
11. Maxon, B. 1977. "The Perception of the Floating Experience by the Private Floater Compared with the Commercial Floater on the Snake River in Grand Teton National Park," unpublished master's thesis. University of Wyoming.
12. McCool, S. F., and J. W. Roggenbuck. 1974. "Off-Road Vehicle Use and Public Lands: A Problem Analysis," *The Institute for the Study of Outdoor Recreation and Tourism.* Logan, Utah: Utah State University.
13. Richard, W. E., Jr., and J. Brown. 1974. "Effects of Vehicles on Arctic Tundra," *Environmental Conservation* 1(1):55.
14. Stankey, G. H. 1973. *Visitor Perception of Wilderness Recreation Carrying Capacity.* U.S. Forest Service Research Paper INT-142.
15. Wilson, G. T. 1969. *Lake Zoning for Recreation: How to Improve Recreational Use of Lakes.* American Institute of Park Executives.

CHAPTER 18

Special Contemporary Management Problems

There are innumerable problems facing today's outdoor recreation manager. The type of problem and the conditions that caused them will vary according to the local situation. However, some of these important, contemporary problems are not unique. In this chapter, we will examine the problems of managing water-based recreation (motorized and non-motorized), wilderness recreation, and transportation systems at two levels—the specific problems unique to each use and the general problems (such as increased visitor participation) common to all.

WATER-BASED RECREATION

The manager of a water-based recreation area is faced with many different problems. Those associated with intensive waterfront development have been discussed in Chapter 16. Consequently, the emphasis of this chapter will be on the problems associated with surface use of the water—i.e., powerboating and river floating.

POWERBOATING

For many water-based recreation areas, powerboating is the primary use (Fig. 18–1). However, there are some major management problems associated with this activity, such as safety, conflicts with other uses and with fisheries, and littering.

Safety has become a major concern because of the increasing number of boating accidents, some of which are fatal. Lack of safety on the part of the powerboat user will affect not only himself but also the non-motorized boat user, swimmer, fisherman, and any casual water user. This type of boater can threaten the safety of other users either directly by its sheer speed and lack of maneuverability or indirectly through its wave action (for example, by swamping other boats and frightening inexperienced swimmers).

Conflict with other uses is another problem of powerboating, particularly when this conflict becomes a constant disruption of any non-powerboating

Figure 18–1 Powerboating is a primary activity on most large lakes and reservoirs.

experiences. If management does not respond to the situation at this point, social invasion and use succession will take place, forcing the other users to migrate to another recreation area. Unfortunately, in the typical sequence of events, the non-powerboat users retreat to increasingly more isolated locations while new roads and waterfront developments enable the powerboater to have even more opportunities than before. Some managers argue that this is the normal sequence of events, and it should not be disrupted. Others declare that the need for diversity of opportunity is a vital one, and that our incessant road building and waterfront development are socially, economically, and environmentally unhealthy. If the other users eventually run out of places to retreat to, a large segment of the potential user population will be dissatisfied because the type of recreational experience that they prefer is no longer available. Economically it also is desirable to maintain diversity in recreation in terms of services and equipment. The recreation marketplace should respond to changes in popular tastes and in management strategies. This might not be possible without a pre-existing diversity of services within the private sector. The changing picture in environment and energy also could affect the decision. Apparently, the early water-cooled engines added petroleum residues to the water and had a drastic polluting effect on the aquatic ecosystem.[3] The newer air-cooled engines have reduced this problem. However, we are not sure how to solve other problems such as the disruptive effects of motor noise and wave action on animal and plant life. For example, Yellowstone National Park does not permit motorized boating on the southeast branches of Yellowstone Lake because of its potentially disruptive effect on pelican rookeries and other terrestrial animal habitats; but what are the effects of any powerboating on underwater life?

Often, the real problem can be traced to the roads and developments that provide access for the powerboat user into new territories. Consequently, the manager must look toward area and regional planning to determine through well-planned access and development where certain uses should be encouraged or discouraged. Possibly, all surface waters in a given region could be zoned for specific recreational uses—the larger bodies of water for powerboating or multiple uses (including powerboating), the medium-size waters for recreational boating (small motorized crafts, as well as non-motorized uses), and the smaller bodies of water for only non-motorized uses. This would maintain and encourage a diversity of recreational uses with minimum disruption of the normal behavioral patterns.

Each body of water could be zoned for specific uses that are included in a regional zoning plan.[11] Most lakes can handle more than one use, even if powerboating is not allowed. The specific physiographic layout may facilitate setting up zones on surface waters. These boundaries may be natural (such as an island) or manmade (such as a breakwater). Temporary boundaries formed with ropes and floats, though less desirable, are functional if properly supervised and enforced.

Zoning by region and area may be the most effective management approach. However, good information and education programs are essential for the understanding and acceptance of such a program because of its controversial nature. Therefore, it also is mandatory that the zoning program have substantial support from the interested public. Even if the program has been accepted, it must be clearly understood by the public that it can be implemented with minimum disruption of use.

Physical design, along with zoning, can act as a nonverbal communication to encourage desired use patterns. However, signing *per se* will not be effective unless the nonverbal communication gives the same message. For example, a modern boat ramp with parking area can "say" that motorboating is allowed, even if the sign says "nonmotorized boating only"—it is encouraged to a degree by the physical design. Even with a good physical design, a certain amount of law enforcement is necessary in order to ensure compliance with safety regulations and zoning plan. Development and management of services such as concessions may be necessary but should basically fit zoning requirements.

The management objectives of a national, water-based recreation area supposedly encourage a variety of recreational uses. The situation is shown in Figure 18–2. However, the existing situation does not reflect the established management objectives. Powerboating is not limited in use except between the two islands. Also, canoeing, which was popular at the reservoir a few years ago, has become almost nonexistent. Recently, a young child drowned when the canoe that she and her parents were in was swamped with water and capsized from the wake of a powerboat in the south portion of the lake. Four major accidents, in which three people died, have occurred in the last two years involving powerboats; even the number of fishermen and swimmers who used to frequent Spruce and Bear Islands has decreased in the last few years. This problem still exists because management has been reluctant to take any action.

What would you do to alleviate this situation—change your objectives or management strategies? Make some assumptions about the regional situation in terms of demand and supply. Are they good ones? Based on these, think about possible solutions. If your objectives were valid initially, have situations changed sufficiently to dictate changing the original objectives? Before you change the objectives, try to develop a solution that will fit the original management objective (multiple reservoir uses). Then try to maintain the integrity of these uses in terms of normal behavioral patterns.

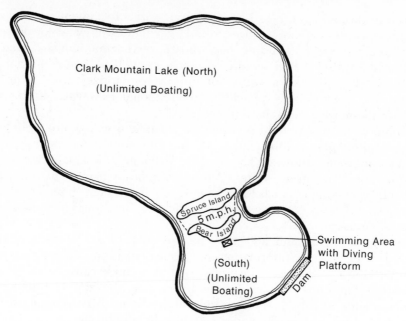

Figure 18–2   Layout of Clark Mountain Reservoir.

RIVER FLOATING

River floating is one of the most significant problems facing the outdoor recreation manager today, from the urban river to the whitewater system. Participation has increased dramatically on almost every river in the United States. Managers are having to quickly assess their own situation, implement stop-gap measures where problems exist, and then seek more satisfactory, long term solutions. The escalation of use is associated with economic and environmental problems and with social problems that include queuing at the launch sites, conflicts between users, reduced visitor satisfaction from encountering an excessive number of visitors, and on-water safety. Differences between landowner management objectives have also caused conflict between recreationists and landowners.

The environmental problems are many—from site degradation and subsequent erosion of launch sites (see Fig. 18–3) to pollution from human waste. The on-site environmental degradation at launch and takeout points is often severe, but it can be easily identified and solved by the manager. To protect the site, hardening (for heavily used portions) and site cultural treatments (for the lighter used portions) can be done without a major upgrading of the facilities that could attract even more people. Because of this fear of attracting more river floaters, some managers prefer *not* to stabilize the environmental deterioration if it is not having a major effect on water quality or on fishery production.

For the most part, the economic problems involve the use of concessioners to take visitors on commercial river float trips. Advertising and other promotional efforts have attracted large numbers of people to these trips, as illustrated in Figure 18–4. This allows more people to enjoy the river under relatively safe conditions, i.e., with an inspected craft and an experienced guide. In response to the rise in popular demand, many commercial float companies have come into existence during the last five years. In turn, this

Figure 18–3 Launch sites along rivers often show signs of continued heavy use.

capital has added immensely to the local and regional economies. However, because of increased social and environmental problems, managers are beginning to establish capacity limits; some are even reducing the present level of use. This is creating financial problems for some outfitters as well as conflicts between commercial and private floaters. On some rivers, the allocation of

Figure 18–4 River floating is becoming one of the more popular outdoor activities.

use favors commercial use as much as 86 to 92 per cent despite the high demand by private users as well.

The response of many of the managing agencies has not been to increase the number of access points but to improve the existing points to handle heavy loads, to establish a user capacity for the river in terms of days of use per year, and then to implement a permit system to schedule this traffic flow. This approach has allowed the manager to restore order in the face of the spiraling demand.

Usually the capacity limits are based on what is perceived as a desirable experience for the visitor, and potential environmental problems associated with the river recreational use. These capacity limits also may be the data that the manager will use in the development of specific management strategies. Yet there are problems in this type of approach. First, it is usually based on a nebulous term called the "quality of experience." Unfortunately, this term often is interpreted to mean *minimal social contact*. The "quality of experience" is relevant to the management objectives for a specific situation. If a high-density recreational river experience is the objective, excessive social contact may not detract from the quality of the experience. On the other hand, a whitewater experience in a wilderness area may dictate minimal social contact.

The environmental effects of floating may not be as severe as we believe them to be. The exceptions are isolated rivers on which the visitor spends an extended period of time in delicate ecosystems. These conditions may well justify the use of severe restrictions, but every river does not fall under that category—in fact, probably very few would. The environmental consequences are relative to the degree of change that we consider to be acceptable.

With this background description of the existing circumstances, let us determine a long range strategy for river management that can be adapted to any situation.

Management By Objectives. We need to establish objectives that are specific to each river or to each major segment of a river in terms of the type of experiences offered and the acceptable limit of environmental change. One cannot simply quote statutes, policy, or other agency guidelines as management objectives. They must be specifically stated for each segment of the river, including detailed criteria. In this way, one can reasonably judge the effectiveness of the management strategy in implementing the objectives.

The objectives should be incorporated into a system of river recreational opportunities on both a national and a regional basis. Ideally there would be a continuum of opportunities; at this point, it seems desirable to pinpoint and identify specific opportunities along that continuum. These could be used as models in the development of specific management plans for the following activities:

1. *Wilderness whitewater floating.* This would be the ultimate in terms of primitive and unconfined recreational use of the river. There would be limited access into the area; the maximum emphasis would be on the solitude and the maintenance of the pristine environment. The experience offers maximum challenge to the experienced whitewater user.

2. *Recreational whitewater floating.* The emphasis is on the floating skill and the thrill of the whitewater—not on the solitude or the pristine environment. However, separating the crafts while on the water does seem desirable in order to maintain certain levels of privacy and of streamside aesthetics.

3. *Scenic floating—natural area.* Scenic floating involves the leisurely enjoyment of the scenic landscape and natural attractions such as wildlife along the river. Reasonable access is developed with emphasis on day use and area protection from site degradation.

4. *Scenic-recreational floating.* Same emphasis as scenic floating; in addition, a certain amount of development and diversity of land uses is tolerated. Visual quality of the landscape is a major concern.

5. *Recreational floating.* Activity on the river is medium- to high-level density of use. The emphasis is on social interaction of the users as they float down the river, with little emphasis on the surrounding setting.

Management By Design. Managing a river system for recreational use so that it is essentially self-regulating is desirable for several reasons. Through proper physical design of the access we can encourage the types and levels of use that are compatible, socially and environmentally, with the objectives established for the area. This would allow the individual the opportunity to make the choice of whether or not to float. It could reduce the cost of management even though some direct action will still be necessary. The concept is not new but neither is it readily accepted by management. The river manager is falling into the same trap as that of the wilderness manager. The pattern begins with the rise in use. Then access is increased and improved to accommodate the increased use. As conflicts arise among users and between the users and the resource, we grasp for a magic number called the carrying capacity. This arbitrarily derived number is then used as the "cutoff point." Thus, first we promote increase in use by changing physical design and then try to limit it by setting up regulations.

Management by design employed to encourage specific patterns of use is not without drawbacks. Because of the physiography of the area, the number of well-known local attractions, and the lack of agency cooperation, it may be difficult to use this approach. In addition, enforcement of specific regulations concerning on-water use still may be required.

Access routes to the river direct people toward the through route—i.e., the river proper. Thus the river acts as a collector system. There is a concentration of use as one moves downstream along the river. Thus, the effects of access on the management of the river can only be measured downstream from a given access point and must be evaluated in terms of the additive effect on that river system. Without reasonable management of total access, there is no possible way of coping with specific on-water problems.

Cooperation. The landowners may have different objectives for their lands along the river, but each must realize that what he does in terms of land use, access, and so forth also will affect those downstream to him. Consequently, maximum cooperation and coordination are necessary if we are to effectively manage rivers with a diversity of landownership.

Innovative Regulations. Good management requires innovation in order to maximize the potential of the water resource. For example, a canyon on a major river was zoned to forbid overnight camping because of the sensitive riparian environment and the desire for solitude; yet it was barely possible to run the canyon segment in a long day. This meant that use would be concentrated on the river and at the campsites located around access points, since any boat would have to leave early in the morning to get through the canyon in a day. Since the manager felt that this trip should offer solitude, only six groups were allowed per day—all starting before 7:00 A.M. An inventory later indicated that several potential campsites were available outside the canyon, less than one-half mile from the river. Three small campgrounds were developed at this durable location where they could be maintained more easily. The floater-recreationist was required to portage his craft to the campsite. Rather than simply eliminate camping, this innovative approach was well received, and use levels were increased without sacrificing the desired solitude.

The Perfect System.   There are no perfect systems; we must be willing to settle for areas of inefficiency both in social satisfaction and in environmental effects. At the same time, the manager must develop long range monitoring programs in order to understand what is taking place. In terms of the natural environment, this can be done by identifying points of stress on the environment from recreational use and the level of durability of these points and then establishing criteria for acceptable limits of change.

As an example of a management problem, the Sargasso River is a top-rated canoe stream that is known throughout America. The most heavily used section of the river is owned by the state and is 23 miles long, starting at Indian City and ending at Pier Point. The water, which is somewhat fast, is generally appealing to the family. There are eight entrance points along the 23-mile stretch. Figure 18–5 shows a sketch of the area. Recreation use is beginning to reach crowded conditions. The "old-timers" have refused to canoe again on the stream until the congestion is relieved. Thus, the majority of visitors are "newcomers." Last year, some of the access points had to be hard-surfaced because of the heavy use. Stream banks are deteriorating badly in several places. As a point of interest, there were 491 canoes launched on the state portion of the river during the recent four-day, Fourth of July holiday weekend; some groups had as many as 23 canoes. One couple said they had to wait almost one and one-half hours to launch their canoe, and many other complaints and conflicts have been reported.

The original objective was to maintain a high-quality scenic-recreational canoe trail, but the situation seems to have degenerated into a low-quality offering. What is the problem? Conceptually, what types of programs might be useful in solving the problem? If there were no opportunities available to shift use to other rivers because of their inaccessibility what immediate action would you take? What additional information would you need to assist you in solving the problem?

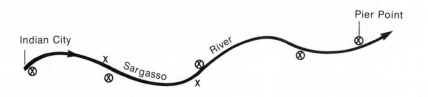

X Access points
O Campgrounds

Figure 18–5   Sketch of the Sargasso River area.

WILDERNESS RECREATION

Wilderness recreation is the extreme example of the dispersed type of activities. Theoretically, it epitomizes the primitiveness and challenge of outdoor recreation. Efforts to save the wilderness began with the administrative establishment of the Gila Wilderness and was re-emphasized by the Wilderness Act of 1964. Ironically, more recent efforts have resulted in a dramatic surge in wilderness recreation participation—an increase that is causing severe local damage and conflict.

The worst problem facing the wilderness manager has been the traditional approach of management toward the wilderness. Basically, there has been very little management. Since the Wilderness Act of 1964, agencies have become more involved with developing a system of *wilderness areas* and promoting these through informational programs. Yet when the visitors began to gather at the trail head, we assumed a "hands off" approach in our management strategy. Essentially, managing the wilderness has the same pitfalls as managing river floating. We promote overuse that results in more pressure to increase and improve access. After improved access quotas are imposed to reduce the impact caused by the overuse; yet we continue to develop expensive trail maintenance programs. Instead of these programs, the design, character, and level of maintenance of the trail could be used to encourage or discourage the levels and types of use established by the specific area management objectives.

Unfortunately, management has rarely established objectives that are specific to a particular wilderness area. The Wilderness Act lists only general guidelines for management; long range objectives should be established for each wilderness within the Wilderness Act guidelines. Lands adjacent to the wilderness should be coordinated to determine compatibility of objectives. Until this is accomplished, no effective management strategy can be developed or evaluated. Because of the lack of funds and the desire to maximize freedom of choice, the approach that is used should place the emphasis on management by design but include other management programs, such as information, safety, resource protection, and regulation enforcement. In order to implement this type of approach, one first must recognize that *wilderness,* as established under the Wilderness Act, is a unique concept that requires an active management program (primarily visitor management) to maintain the pristine environment and the primitive recreational opportunities. Once the manager recognizes this, there are several factors he must consider:

Coordination with Area Planning. What happens outside the wilderness area often affects the use within the area. The type of access road and its location, the type and location of recreational developments in relation to the wilderness access, and the alternative opportunities will determine the type and level of recreational use. This coordination also is predicated on the proper location of wilderness boundaries to protect the ecological integrity, to reduce visual intrusions, to manage vehicular intrusions, and to direct recreational trail use.[11]

System of Roadless Areas. In order to manage wilderness areas, there must be a system of roadless recreation experiences that permits shifting incompatible wilderness uses from one area to suitable substitute areas.[11] Such substitutes are essential if one is to obtain approval on the shifting of recreational use from the wilderness area. This shifting of use also requires an improved informational program that will alert the visitor to other opportunities. It would probably be a mistake to attempt to develop titles for these alternative roadless opportunities in hopes of attracting use away from the wilderness area, since that is not our intent. Our purpose is for the visitor to choose the level of roadless recreation that is most satisfying to him; in the process we must realize that many users will psychologically be forced out of the *wilderness* if the "purist" approach to access (recommended by Stankey[18] and Hendee et al.[6]) is adopted.

Develop Wilderness Area Objectives. This is essential to proper management. Each wilderness area should be inventoried and evaluated as to its existing use, its potential for recreational use, and the durability of the resource. Ideally, the objectives would conform to the potential for wilderness recreational opportunities and to the limitations of the resource. At the same time, the manager must recognize the influence of existing recreational use.

Innovative Management Strategy. This should focus on nonverbal communication techniques with the user to indicate the type of experience that is offered through control of access and trail design (i.e., challenge, primitive character, location, and so forth).[11] Some of the internal use problems in the wilderness area stem from an almost unanimous acceptance of the original trails (usually fire guard trails) with minimum rerouting. Until these trails are replanned and possibly relocated, we will continue to have social and environmental conflicts, since nearly all wilderness use is trail-oriented, particularly during the summer. For example, most trails are located so that they direct all use toward and through the primary attractions (lakes, meadows, and so forth); this causes unnecessary visitor contact at the attractions. The trails also encourage the visitor to return to the trail head via the same trail, increasing visitor contact on the trail. Usually the attractions are more sensitive to recreation use; yet we encourage all use to pass through these areas.

Although similar to the sample problems in Chapter 17, problems concerning the wilderness are often unique because of use levels, sensitivity of the environment, and legal mandate. Thus, you should develop a problem that is similar to the ones in Chapter 17 but with an emphasis on wilderness. If a wilderness area is not close by, look at problems associated with a roadless portion of a state park or similar property. Then imagine the area to be designated as a wilderness. Would you handle the problems differently than other roadless areas? Why?

TRANSPORTATION SYSTEMS

With the decline in availability of fossil fuels and the consequently higher prices for products such as gasoline, all managers should consider the effect of scarcity of energy resources on travel behavior and ultimately on participation in all forms of outdoor recreation. This may mean new forms of transportation and new systems by which the visitor can travel from his home to the recreational area, through the experience, and return. The prime considerations are:

Basic Philosophy of Management. There are two principles on which the development of a basic philosophy of recreation is based—movement of people and enhancement of the recreation experience. It is essential that we have a complete system to "collect" the visitors, move them through the recreation area, and then "deposit" them back into the main transportation system. We also should try to enhance the experience of the individual as he passes through the recreation area by designing the transportation system to fit the area management objectives and to complement the needs of the visitor.

Thus, as managers, we should ensure that our modes of transportation and routes are compatible both with area objectives (internal consistency) and with regional transportation systems. Through this type of coordination, we not only will ensure availability and maintenance of desired recreational opportunities but also will maintain flexibility of future options and changes in the regional transportation system.

Management Variables. The manager must consider variables that he can (and does) manipulate in order to provide the public with mass transportation, since both management concerns and energy shortage are moving us ever closer to that end. In certain recreation areas we are already providing mass public transportation (e.g., in the central valley in Yosemite National Park). The variables we should consider are:

a. *What.* The type of transportation and its design are important to the user. It must be attractive to the user in terms of his style of participation. For example, the staff of Yellowstone National Park have suggested a vehicle that would maximize viewing yet maintain privacy for the family even in a mass transit system—a bus-type unit with family compartments opening directly to the outside of the vehicle.

b. *Where.* This refers to the location of passenger service points. Probably the more service points within the recreation area, the more attractive it will be to the user because it would allow more flexibility in choosing stops. However, the agency must also consider the operating efficiency of the system in terms of the added costs. Perhaps it will be subsidized by public appropriations; even then, there are limitations to the service, and the response of the public will most likely reflect these inherent limitations.

c. *When.* "When" refers to frequency of service. There is no optimum level; the schedule should reflect the desires of the various users. An infrequent schedule most likely will not be considered as a reasonable trade-off for the average visitor; too frequent a schedule without sufficient patronage may prove too costly.

d. *How.* This refers to the policy and regulations governing use. Who will be allowed to use it? Baggage limitations? Pets?

e. *How much.* How much is this going to cost the user? The government?

The Future—Mass Transits. It appears that mass transits in many major park and recreation units are inevitable. How one prepares for such events and coordinates his actions with the public and private agencies will determine how successful the transition will be to the mass transit system. The attention given to management variables in relation to expectations of the user will determine the level of acceptance and participation in the mass transit. As a sample problem, attempt to measure people's reaction to a proposed mass transit system within a major park. What factors do they consider important in the development of that mass transit?

CONTEMPORARY PROBLEMS—A FINAL THOUGHT

Contemporary problems are basically caused by change in recreational use patterns brought about by administrative or legal mandate, change in recreational technology (snowmobiles, RV's, and so forth), environmental concerns, or scarcity of resources. Changes have occurred rapidly in the past decade or two and will probably escalate in the decade ahead. As recreation managers, we should try to balance human needs with resource durability and to use the problem-solving process to develop a management strategy to overcome problems brought about by change. Regardless of what happens, the manager should remain flexible and open-minded to change.

SELECTED READINGS

1. Cheek, N. H., Jr. 1976. "The Case for the Increased Regulation of Human Access to Parklands: Established Fact or Organizational Myth?" *Proceedings of the Recreation Management Institute.* College Station, Tex.: Texas A & M University.
2. Douglass, R. 1969. *Forest Recreation.* New York: Pergamon Press.
3. Frissell, S. S., and G. H. Stankey. 1972. "Wilderness Environmental Quality: Search for Social and Ecological Harmony," *Proceedings of the Society of American Foresters.*
4. Heinselman, M. L. 1966. "Vegetation in Wilderness Areas," *Trends* 3(1):23.
5. Helgath, S. F. 1975. "Trail Deterioration in the Selway-Bitterroot Wilderness," *U. S. Forest Service Research Note* INT-193.
6. Hendee, J. C., W. R. Catton, Jr., L. D. Marlow, and C. F. Brockman. 1968. *Wilderness Users of the Pacific Northwest: Their Characteristics, Values, and Management Preferences.* U.S. Forest Service Research Paper PNW-61.
7. Hendee, J. C., and R. W. Harris. 1970. "Forester's Perception of Wilderness Use Attitudes and Preferences," *Journal of Forestry* 68(12):759.
8. Hendee, J. C., and R. C. Lucas. 1973. "Mandatory Wilderness Permits: A Necessary Management Tool," *Journal of Forestry* 71(4):206.
9. Hendee, J. C., R. C. Lucas, and G. H. Stankey. 1977. *Wilderness Management.* U.S. Forest Service Monograph (to be published).
10. Hines, L. G. 1968. "The Measurement of the Benefits of Public Investment in National Parks," *The Canadian National Parks: Today and Tomorrow.* Nelson J. G., and R. C. Scace (eds.).
11. Jubenville, A. 1975. *Outdoor Recreation Planning.* Philadelphia: W. B. Saunders Co.
12. Jubenville, A. 1973. "Quasi-Wilderness," *Parks and Recreation,* July.
13. Lime, D. W., and C. A. Fasick. 1977. *Proceedings of the Symposium on River Recreation Management and Research.* U. S. Forest Service General Technical Report NC-28.
14. Lucas, R. C. 1973. "Wilderness: A Management Framework," *Journal of Soil and Water Conservation* 28(4):150.
15. Lucas, R. C. 1971. "Hikers and Other Trail Users," *Recreation Symposium Proceedings.* Doolittle, W. T., and R. E. Getty (eds.). Syracuse, N.Y.: U. S. Forest Service.
16. Neuzil, D. 1968. "Uses and Abuses of Highway Benefit-Cost Analysis: A Primer on Highway Economics for Park Officials, Conservationists, and Interested Citizens," *The Canadian National Parks: Today and Tomorrow.* Nelson, J. G., and R. C. Scace (eds.).
17. Shafer, E. L., G. H. Moeller, and R. E. Getty. 1974. *Future Leisure Environments.* U. S. Forest Service Research Paper NE-301.
18. Stankey, G. H. 1973. *Visitor Perception of Wilderness Recreation Carrying Capacity.* U. S. Forest Service Research Paper INT-141.
19. Stanley, G. H. 1971. "Myths in Wilderness Decision-Making," *Journal of Soil and Water Conservation* 26(5):183.
20. Warder, D. S., and A. Jubenville. 1975. "Perceptions and Management Preferences of Users As a Result of the Commercial Floating Experience on the Snake River within Grand Teton Park," University of Wyoming: Department of Recreation and Park Administration.

Habits and Requirements of Important Tree Species

CONIFERS

Species	Soil Requirements	Competitive Ability	Natural Regeneration	Wind-firmness	Insect Suscepti-bility	Disease Suscepti-bility
Bald-cypress	Deep, fine, sandy loam with plenty of moisture and good drainage best. Permanent swamps within climatic range	Low	Poor and uncertain because of soil moisture fluctuations	Moderately windfirm	Low	Low, except in old age
Douglas-fir	Not exacting, but soil must be moderately moist	Intermediate to low	Fairly generous if surface soil does not dry out; otherwise irregular and uncertain	Moderately windfirm to windfirm	Low	Low, except after 150 years
Fir, balsam	Moist well-drained sandy loams best. Also moist but well-drained clay and organic soil	High	Generous in variety of seed beds and stand densities	Low to moderate windfirmness	Moderate to high. Spruce budworm and balsam woolly aphid worst enemies	High. Rot is bad after trees attain 10″ d.b.h.
Fir, grand	Deep alluvial soils best	High	Generous on protected sites	Moderately windfirm	Low. Occasionally attacked by spruce budworm	High. Trunk rot common in trees over 12″ d.b.h.
Fir, white	Northerly exposure on deep, moist well-drained gravel or sandy loam best	High	Generous and frequent on protected sites	Moderately windfirm	Low. Occasionally attacked by spruce budworm	High. Trunk rot common
Hemlock, eastern	A variety of soils in cool, moist situations	High	Generous and frequent on moist, shaded humus; poor on exposed sites	Moderately windfirm to windfirm	Low	Low
Hemlock, western	Moist, porous soil	High	Generous on a moist, protected site	Moderately windfirm	Moderate. Occasional severe attack by hemlock looper	Low until old age
Incense-cedar	Moist loam	High	Generous in moist seed bed	Windfirm	Low	Moderate to high
Juniper, one-seed	Dry, gravelly soils	Intermediate	Sparse and slow	Windfirm	Low	Low

*From Westveld, R. H. 1958. *Forestry in Farm Management.* New York: John Wiley & Sons, Inc. pp. 284–295. Copyright © 1958 by John Wiley & Sons, Inc. Reprinted by permission of John Wiley & Sons, Inc.

Habits and Requirements of Important Tree Species

Conifers (*Continued*)

Species	Soil Requirements	Competitive Ability	Natural Regeneration	Wind-firmness	Insect Suscepti-bility	Disease Suscepti-bility
Juniper, Rocky Mountain	Gravelly or sandy soil	Intermediate	Generally slow and uncertain	Windfirm	Low	Low
Larch, western	Deep, moist soils best. Will grow on dry gravels	Low	Generous at intervals of several years on exposed mineral soil	Windfirm	Low	Low
Pine, Austrian	Ill-defined but best on sandy loam	Intermediate to low	Unknown to date, only planted	Windfirm	Low	Low
Pine, eastern white	Moist, sandy loams best	Intermediate	Moderate to generous on moderately open sites relatively free of litter and vegetation	Windfirm	Moderate to high. White pine weevil worst. Pales weevil sometimes attacks seedlings	High, if currant or gooseberry bushes are near by; otherwise low
Pine, jack	Dry sands	Low	Profuse on moderately open site if a sufficient number of cones open	Windfirm to moderately windfirm	Moderate. Sawflies and spruce budworm sometimes troublesome	Low
Pine, loblolly	Moist to wet soils of various textures	Intermediate	Profuse and frequent on most seed beds	Moderately windfirm to windfirm	Low	Moderate. Rusts are troublesome
Pine, lodgepole	A variety of soils, excepting those of limestone origin	Low	Profuse in open. Maintenance of some canopy desirable to prevent overstocking	Moderately windfirm to windfirm	High	Low
Pine, longleaf	Sands, some of which are underlain by hardpan, causing water to stand on the surface during wet seasons	Very low	Abundant at intervals of several years if litter and vegetation are not heavy	Windfirm	Low, except turpentined trees which may be attacked by turpentine borer	Low, except during seedling stage, when brown-spot needle blight is sometimes serious
Pine, pitch	Sandy and sandy loam soils	Low	Profuse on an open site with mineral soil exposed	Windfirm except in late life, when it is easily windthrown	Low	Low

CONIFERS (*Continued*)

Species	Soil Requirements	Com-petitive Ability	Natural Regeneration	Wind-firmness	Insect Suscepti-bility	Disease Suscepti-bility
Pine, ponderosa	A variety of soils which in general are dry	Low	Best in openings. Generally repro-duces sparingly, requiring 15 to 20 years to produce full stocking	Windfirm to moderately windfirm	Moderate. Western pine beetle some-times serious	Moderate. Western red rot and mistletoe worst of-fenders
Pine, red	Sandy, relatively dry soil	Low	In open fairly good during years of good seed crops which occur every 3 to 5 years	Windfirm	Low	Low
Pine, Scotch	Sandy soils	Low	Unknown	Windfirm	Low	Low
Pine, shortleaf	Chiefly dry uplands but found also on moist soils in mix-ture with other species	Interme-diate	Best on moder-ately open sites where mineral soil is exposed	Windfirm	Low	Low
Pine, slash	Moist to wet soils	Interme-diate	Profuse on a variety of sites protected from fire	Moderately windfirm. Dense young stands often have poor root systems	Low	Moderate. Rusts sometimes serious
Pine, sugar	Moist loam best	Low	Irregular and rather poor. Requires a rela-tively open, moist, mineral soil seed bed	Windfirm	Frequently attacked by mountain pine beetle	White pine blister rust a threat
Pine, Virginia	Sandy loam best. Will tolerate the driest sands	Very low	Easily regener-ates abundantly on open sites on exposed mineral soil	Moderately windfirm ex-cept in late mature and over-mature stages	Low	Low
Pine, western white	Deep, moist loams and sandy loams. Poor development on dry soils	Interme-diate	Fairly good on moist mineral soil (especially a burned sur-face) if site is relatively open	Moderately windfirm	Moderate attacks by mountain pine beetle common	White pine blister rust a threat
Pinyon	A variety of well-drained soils	Low	Fair in open	Windfirm	Low	Low

Habits and Requirements of Important Tree Species

CONIFERS (*Continued*)

Species	Soil Requirements	Competitive Ability	Natural Regeneration	Wind-firmness	Insect Susceptibility	Disease Susceptibility
Redcedar, eastern	Light loam of limestone origin best. Will grow on dry infertile soil if alkaline or only slightly acid	Intermediate	Fairly good unless stand is dense. Seedlings usually do not appear until second year after seed's maturity	Windfirm	Low	Low. Cedar apple rust, which usually does no serious damage to the cedar, damages apple trees severely
Redcedar, western	Moist soil	High	Generous if surface soil does not dry out	Moderately windfirm	Low	Low
Redwood	Deep, moist loams best. (Dry atmosphere is more of a limiting factor)	High	Only moderately good (low percentage of seed germinates) on moist mineral soil	Windfirm	Low	Low
Spruce, black	Moist, well-drained sands and sandy loams best. Tolerates cold, wet, poorly drained, peat, muck, and mineral soil	High	Little known, but moist soil believed essential	Shallow root system makes it easily windthrown	Generally low. Occasionally some danger of spruce budworm	Low
Spruce, Norway	Moist, well-drained loams and sandy loams	High	Unknown. (An exotic that has been propagated artificially)	Moderately windfirm	Low. Some damage by white pine weevil	Low
Spruce, red	Moist, well-drained loams and sandy loams best. Tolerates wet sites	High	A moist, mineral-soil seed bed on a moderately open site best	Shallow root system makes it easily windthrown	Moderate. Spruce budworm, eastern spruce bark beetle are worst enemies	Low
Spruce, Sitka	Moist, well-drained loams best	High	A moist, preferably shaded, mineral-soil seed bed	Shallow root system makes windthrow common	Generally low. Some damage by Sitka spruce weevil and spruce aphid	Low

CONIFERS (*Continued*)

Species	Soil Requirements	Com-petitive Ability	Natural Regeneration	Wind-firmness	Insect Suscepti-bility	Disease Suscepti-bility
Spruce, white	Moist, well-drained sandy loams and loams best, but will tolerate a wet site	High	A moist mineral-soil seed bed on a moderately open site best	Shallow root system makes it easily wind-thrown	Moderate. Spruce bud-worm, east-ern spruce bark beetle are worst enemies	Low
Tamarack	Moist, well-drained soils best, but will tolerate a wet site, either organic or mineral soil	Low	Little known but an open moist seed bed seems best	Windfirm	High. Severe widespread damage by larch sawfly in some localities, especially in Lake States	Low
White-cedar, Atlantic	Sandy soil in fresh-water swamps and bays, wet depres-sions or stream banks	High	Generous when soil moisture is abundant, ex-cept in dense stands of old cedar	Moderately windfirm	Low	Low
White-cedar, northern	Limestone soils best, but grows on many moist to wet soils, organic or mineral	High	Generous in moist seed bed	Moderately windfirm	Low	Low, except in old age
White-cedar, Port Orford	Sandy loam and loams with an abundance of moisture	High	Generous in moist seed bed	Moderately windfirm	Low	Low

HARDWOODS

Species	Soil Requirements	Com-petitive Ability	Natural Regeneration	Wind-firmness	Insect Suscepti-bility	Disease Suscepti-bility
Ash, black	Moist to wet soil, either organic or mineral	Interme-diate	Little known; a moist to wet mineral soil probably best	Moderately windfirm	Generally low. Some damage by oyster-shell scale	Low
Ash, blue	Well-drained to dry uplands	Interme-diate	Little known	Windfirm	Low	Low
Ash, green	Similar to white ash					

Habits and Requirements of Important Tree Species

Hardwoods (*Continued*)

Species	Soil Requirements	Competitive Ability	Natural Regeneration	Wind-firmness	Insect Suscepti-bility	Disease Suscepti-bility
Ash, white	Deep, moist, fertile loams and sandy loams best	Interme-diate	Reproduces well and frequently if site is moder-ately open	Windfirm	Generally low, but sometimes severely in-fested with oyster-shell scale or forest tent caterpillar	Low
Aspen, big-tooth	Similar to quaking aspen except that it attains 10″ to 12″ d.b.h. before rot is severe.					
Aspen, quaking	Not exacting. Grows on almost any well-drained soil within its cli-matic range	Low	Profuse, chiefly from suckers when parent trees are cut. Open site re-quired for seed-ling reproduc-tion	Windfirm until butt becomes decayed	Generally low. Some severe local damage by spring cankerworm	High. Rot is common in trees over 6″ d.b.h.
Basswood, American	Moist, well-drained, fertile loams and sandy loams	Interme-diate to high	Seedling regener-ation generally poor. Sprouts prolifically. To secure seedling reproduction artificial propa-gation seems best. Seed must be treated	Windfirm	Low	Moderate. Trees over 15″ d.b.h. frequently contain butt rot
Beech, American	Not exacting. Grows best on moist, well-drained sandy loams, but does fairly well on dry, sandy loams and relatively wet loams, sandy loams, and silt loams	Very high	Seedling repro-duction only fair; limiting factors not well known. Pro-duces some suckers	Windfirm	Low	Rot is greatest hazard. Canker sometimes troublesome
Birch, gray	Not exacting. Dry sands and moist sandy loams	Low	Prolific only on an open site with exposed mineral soil	Moderately windfirm	High to gypsy moth	High. Rot chief enemy, at early age
Birch, paper	Not exacting but prefers a cool, moist mineral soil	Low	Prolific only on an open site with mineral soil exposed	Moderately windfirm	High to gypsy moth and some-times to bronze birch borer	High. Rot chief enemy

HARDWOODS (*Continued*)

Species	Soil Requirements	Competitive Ability	Natural Regeneration	Wind-firmness	Insect Susceptibility	Disease Susceptibility
Birch, river	Moist to wet sandy loams and silt loams, especially along streams	Low	Poorly known, but apparently not exacting. Ample moisture probably chief requirement	Moderately windfirm	High to gypsy moth	Moderate. Rot chief enemy
Birch, sweet	Deep, moist, well-drained sandy loams and loams	Low	A moist mineral-soil seed bed on an open site is best	Windfirm	Moderate	Moderate to low
Birch, yellow	Moist, cool, well-drained sandy loams and loams	Intermediate	Moist seed bed, either mineral or organic soil, on an open site	Windfirm	Moderate. Bronze birch borer sometimes troublesome	Moderate; rot, cankers, and birch die-back chief enemies
Boxelder	Moist, sandy loams and loams, especially along streams	Intermediate	Not exacting	Windfirm	Low, except where the gypsy moth occurs	Moderate; rot is chief enemy
Buckeye, Ohio and yellow	Moist loams	Intermediate	Little known	Windfirm	Low	Low
Butternut	Moist loams best, but grows fairly well on relatively dry rocky soils of limestone origin	Low	A moist, relatively open site covered by leaf litter is best. Seldom reproduces generously	Windfirm	Low	Low
Catalpa, hardy	Deep, moist, fertile, well-drained loam or silt loam best, but grows quite well on a variety of moist loams	Low	Not well known. Probably a moist mineral soil in open is best	Windfirm	Moderate. Damage by catalpa sphinx sometimes severe	Moderate. Rot, coming in through branch wounds, chief hazard
Cherry, black	Moist, fertile, well-drained sandy loams and loams	Intermediate	Reproduction is generous on a moist seed bed on a relatively open site	Windfirm	Low	Moderate. Sprouts very subject to decay
Cherry, pin	Not exacting, but prefers moist sandy loams	Low	Profuse on an open site	Windfirm	Low	High. Rot is chief enemy at an early age

Habits and Requirements of Important Tree Species

Hardwoods (*Continued*)

Species	Soil Requirements	Competitive Ability	Natural Regeneration	Wind-firmness	Insect Susceptibility	Disease Susceptibility
Cottonwood, eastern	Moist alluvial soils best, but it grows quite well on relatively dry soils	Low	A moist mineral-soil seed bed on an open site. Seedling reproduction is uncertain and irregular	Moderately windfirm	Low	Moderate to high. Decay starts in trunk at relatively early age
Cucumbertree	Deep, moist friable loam	Intermediate	Unknown	Windfirm	Low	Low
Dogwood, flowering	Deep, moist loams	High	Not exacting, but is best on a moist protected site	Windfirm	Low	Low
Elm, American	Deep, moist, well-drained loams best but grows well on wet and relatively dry sandy loams and loams	High	Frequent and generous in a moist seed bed	Windfirm on drier sites; only moderately on wet sites	High. Damage by elm leaf beetle often high	Low, except where Dutch elm disease threatens
Elm, Chinese	Not exacting. Moist, well-drained sandy loams best	Intermediate	Unknown. Propagated artificially in United States	Windfirm	Same as American elm	Low
Elm, rock	Relatively dry, gravelly soils	Intermediate	Generally poor, owing to undetermined factors	Moderately windfirm	Same as American elm	Low
Elm, slippery	Fertile, well-drained loams, particularly those of limestone origin preferred	High	Similar to American elm, but not so prolific	Windfirm	Same as American elm	Low
Hackberry	Moist alluvial loams, but grows quite well on moist upland loams	Intermediate	Little known, but apparently not exacting	Windfirm	Low	Low
Hickories	Moist bottomlands best, but grows quite well on a variety of moist, well-drained sandy and clay loams	Intermediate to low	Not well known. Reproduces moderately well on a moist site if nuts become covered	Windfirm	Moderate. Hickory bark beetle sometimes troublesome	Low
Holly	Deep, moist, bottomland loams best	High	Not well known, but apparently slow and uncertain under any conditions	Windfirm	Low	Low

HARDWOODS (*Continued*)

Species	Soil Requirements	Competitive Ability	Natural Regeneration	Wind-firmness	Insect Suscepti-bility	Disease Suscepti-bility
Honey-locust	Moist bottomland loams best, but grows satisfactorily on relatively dry sites	Low	A moist, open seed bed favors abundant re-production	Windfirm	Low	Low
Hophorn-beam, eastern	Moist, well-drained sandy loams and loams	High	Not well known, but apparently not exacting	Windfirm	Low	Low
Hornbeam, American	Moist, well-drained loams and sandy loams	High	Not exacting. Generous repro-duction on a variety of sites	Windfirm	Low	Low
Locust, black	Moist loams and sandy loams with permeable subsoil best	Low	Profuse in open on a variety of seed beds. Sucker repro-duction often abundant	Windfirm	Moderate. Locust borer frequently troublesome	Low
Magnolia, southern	Moist to wet sandy loams and loams in bottomlands and hammocks	Interme-diate	Unknown	Windfirm	Low	Low
Maple, mountain and striped	Moist, well-drained sandy loams and loams	High	Not exacting. Nearly any type of seed bed on open or closed site	Windfirm	Low	Low
Maple, red	Wet, bottomland loams and sandy loams best, but grows well on a variety of soils in-cluding those only moderately moist to relatively dry	High	Reproduces gen-erously on a variety of sites	Moderately windfirm	Low	Moderate. Cankers rather com-mon in early life. Rot likely to infect middle-aged trees
Maple, silver	Wet to moist bot-tomland loams and sandy loams	High	Similar to red maple	Moderately windfirm	Low	Moderate. Rot is chief enemy in middle life
Maple, sugar	Moist, fertile, well-drained sandy loams, clay loams, and loams	Very high	Reproduces abun-dantly wherever there is a source of seed. One of the most pro-lific reproducers in the U. S.	Windfirm	Low, except that sugar maple borer can be serious in sugar orchards	Low, except in early life when cankers are prevalent in some localities

Habits and Requirements of Important Tree Species

Hardwoods (*Continued*)

Species	Soil Requirements	Competitive Ability	Natural Regeneration	Wind-firmness	Insect Suscepti-bility	Disease Suscepti-bility
Mulberry, red	Moist, fertile, friable bottomland loams best, but grows quite well on upland loams	Low	Little known but appears to reproduce quite well on a relatively open moist site	Windfirm	Low	Low
Oaks (all species) [1]	Vary widely from poorly drained clays and clay loams in bottomland to dry upland sands and clays	Low to intermediate	Oaks reproduce rather sparingly from seed because acorns are likely to dry out before germination. A seed bed that is partially protected by a tree canopy and by a leaf litter, thus preventing excessive drying out of the acorns, is essential for regeneration of oaks from seed	Oaks, except some of the swamp species which are only moderately windfirm, are windfirm	Oaks are relatively free from insect attacks, although locally the June beetle and the golden oak scale cause some damage. In New England gypsy moth is serious	Oaks, especially in the New England and adjacent states, are damaged by cankers. Oak wilt is serious in some parts of Middle West. Except as noted for the individual species, the oaks have low susceptibility to other diseases
Oaks (inferior value) bear blackjack bluejack turkey	Dry uplands, from sands to loams	Low to intermediate				High susceptibility to rot at early age
Oaks (intermediate value) upland chinkapin post scarlet southern red	Dry, sandy loams, loams and silt loams					Scarlet and post oak particularly high susceptibility to decay at early age

[1] Since the oaks vary so widely in commercial value, they are divided here into three broad groups in order that the informational details may be given in proportion to the importance of the species. The first group is the inferior oaks; the second, the species of intermediate value; and the third, those of high value. The last two groups are divided into upland and bottomland species.

Hardwoods (*Continued*)

Species	Soil Requirements	Com-petitive Ability	Natural Regeneration	Wind-firmness	Insect Suscepti-bility	Disease Suscepti-bility
bottom-land laurel live pin shingle water willow	Moist to wet loams and sandy loams. Pin and shingle oak also on moist uplands. Live oak tolerates dry sands and flooded sites also					
Oaks (high value) upland black bur chestnut northern red white	Moist, well-drained loams and clay loams. Bur oak also moist to wet bottomland loams. Chestnut oak toler-ates dry rocky soils	Interme-diate except north-ern red and white oak which tend toward high			White oak has high sus-ceptibility to browntail moth	
bottom-land Nuttall overcup Shumard swamp chestnut swamp red swamp white	Moist to wet silt loams and clays	All low except swamp red oak which is inter-mediate				
Osage-orange	Moist, well-drained bottomland loams and silt loams, but grows well on a variety of moist upland loams and sandy loams	Low	Little known. Largely propa-gated artificially	Windfirm	Low	Low
Persimmon	Not exacting, toler-ating dry, infertile, eroded soils, but making best growth on moist loams and sandy loams	Low	Reproduces well on an open site with mineral-soil seed bed	Windfirm	Low	Low, except where per-simmon wilt threatens
Poplar, balsam	Wet, poorly drained loams and clay loams, especially along streams	Low	Little known. Apparently re-quires a mineral soil on an open site	Moderately windfirm	Low, except for occa-sional at-tacks by canker-worms	Moderate. Rot is chief enemy

ORNAMENTAL PLANTS FOR PROBLEM AREAS OF THE WEST

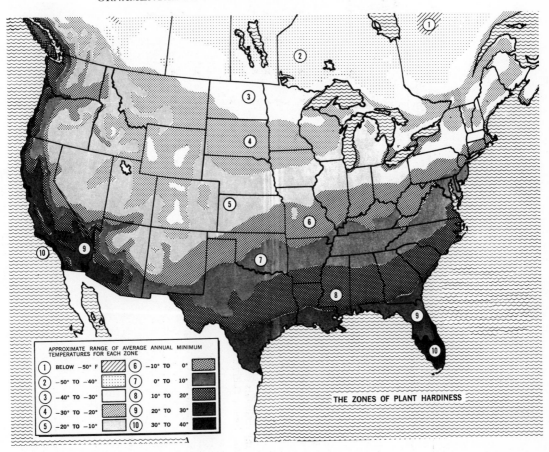

APPROXIMATE RANGE OF AVERAGE ANNUAL MINIMUM
TEMPERATURES FOR EACH ZONE

①	BELOW −50° F		⑥	−10° TO	0°	
②	−50° TO −40°		⑦	0° TO	10°	
③	−40° TO −30°		⑧	10° TO	20°	
④	−30° TO −20°		⑨	20° TO	30°	
⑤	−20° TO −10°		⑩	30° TO	40°	

THE ZONES OF PLANT HARDINESS

*Yearbook of Agriculture. 1972. *Landscape for Living*. Washington, D.C.: U.S. Department of Agriculture, front cover and pp. 156–164.

Common name	Annual rainfall		Adaptability to:					Salt or alkaline soils	Altitude requirement	Shade
	Less than 10"	10"–20"	Zones					pH–8.0+	ft.+	
			III	IV	V	VI	VII			
Trees (Evergreen)										
Arborvitae, Eastern		X			X	X	X			X
Arborvitae, Oriental		X		X	X	X				X
Cypress, Arizona		X				X				X
Fir, White		X		X	X		X	X	3,000	X
Juniper, Alligator	X	X				X	X			
Juniper, Oneseed		X		X	X	X	X	X		
Juniper, Redberry		X				X	X			
Juniper, Redcedar (many cultivars)		X	X	X	X	X	X			X
Juniper, Rocky Mountain (many cultivars)	X	X	X	X	X	X				X
Larch, Siberian		X	X				X			
Pine, Aleppo		X				X	X			
Pine, Austrian		X		X	X	X	X			
Pine, Bristlecone		X		X	X					
Pine, Colorado Pinyon		X		X	X	X	X	X	4,000	
Pine, Limber		X		X	X			X		
Pine, Ponderosa		X	X	X	X	X	X	X		X
Pine, Scotch		X	X	X	X	X	X			
Pine, Swiss Mountain (mugo)		X		X	X	X				
Spruce, Black Hills		X	X	X	X					X
Spruce, Colorado		X	X	X	X				3,000	X
Spruce, Engelmann		X		X	X				3,000	X
Shrubs (Evergreen)										
Juniper, Common		X		X	X	X	X			X
Juniper, Creeping		X		X	X	X	X			X
Juniper, Meyer Singleseed		X		X	X	X				
Juniper, Pfitzer Chinese		X	X	X	X	X				

Appendix B (Continued)

Juniper, Savin 'Tamarix'						x		x	x	x	x		x
Pine, Mugho Swiss Mountain						x		x	x	x	x		
Trees (Broadleaf)													
Albizzia, Silktree (Mimosa)									x	x	x		
Ash, Green						x		x	x	x	x		
Ash, European Mountain								x	x	x	x		
Birch, Cutleaf Weeping								x	x	x	x		
Buckeye								x	x	x	x+		
Cottonwood						x		x	x	x	x		
Crabapple, Flowering						x		x	x	x	x		
Elm, Lacebark Chinese									x	x	x		
Elm, Siberian					x		x	x	x	x	x		
Hackberry, Common					x		x	x	x	x	x		
Honeylocust (thornless)								x	x	x	x		
Jujube, Common									x	x	x		
Linden, American								x	x	x	x		
Linden, Littleleaf							x	x	x	x	x		
Locust, Black							x	x	x	x	x		
Maple, Amur						x		x	x	x	x		
Maple, Manchurian								x	x	x	x		
Maple, Norway						x		x	x	x	x		
Maple, Silver							x	x	x	x	x		
Maple, Sugar								x	x	x	x		
Maple, Tatarian						x		x	x	x	x		
Mulberry, Russian						x		x	x	x	x		
Oak, Bur							x		x	x	x		
Oak, Live (sometimes evergreen)									x	x	x		
Oak, Northern Red							x			x	x		
Oak, Pin									x	x	x		
Pecan									x	x	x		
Redbud, Eastern									x	x	x		
Russian-Olive						x		x	x	x	x		x
Sweetgum, American									x	x	x		
Sycamore							x		x	x	x		
Walnut, Black								x	x	x	x		

4,000

Appendix B (*Continued*)

Common name	Annual rainfall		Adaptability to: Zones					Salt or alkaline soils pH–8.0+	Altitude requirement ft.+	Shade
	Less than 10"	10"–20"	III	IV	V	VI	VII			
Shrubs (Broadleaf)										
Adina (Adina rubella)		x				x	x			
Almond, Flowering		x				x	x			
Almond, Prairie (Prunus triloba x P. pedunculata)		x	x	x	x	x				
Almond, Russian		x	x	x	x	x				
Amorpha, Indigobush		x		x	x	x	x			
Apacheplume	x	x		x	x	x	x			
Beautybush		x			x	x	x	x		
Bitterbrush, Antelope	x	x		x	x	x	x	x	4,000	
Bluebeard (Caryopteris sp.)		x		x	x	x				
Buckthorn, Common		x	x	x	x	x				
Buckthorn, Dahurian		x	x	x	x	x				
Buckthorn, Rock		x	x	x	x	x				
Buffaloberry		x								
Butterflybush		x			x	x	x			
Ceanothus, Inland	x	x			x	x	x			
Chaste-tree		x				x	x			
Cherry, Manchu		x	x	x	x	x				
Chokecherry, Western 'Schubert'		x	x	x	x	x	x			
Cinquefoil, Bush		x		x	x	x		x	4,000	
Cliffrose, Stansbury		x		x	x	x			4,000	
Coralberry		x			x	x	x			
Cotoneaster, European		x		x	x	x				
Cotoneaster, Hedge		x	x	x	x	x	x			
Cotoneaster, Multiflora		x			x	x				
Cotoneaster, Peking		x	x	x	x	x	x			
Cotoneaster, Sungari Redbead		x	x	x	x	x		x		
Crapemyrtle		x			x	x	x			

Appendix B (*Continued*)

	1	2	3	4	5	6	7	8	9
Desertwillow	x	x				x	x		x	
Dogwood, Colorado Redosier		x		x	x				
Dogwood, Siberian		x		x	x				
Elderberry, Blueberry		x		x	x	x	x		
Elderberry, European Red 'Redman'		x		x	x	x	x		
Euonymus, European		x		x	x	x	x		x
Euonymus, Winterberry		x		x	x	x	x		x
Firethorn, Laland		x			x	x	x		
Fontanesia, Fortune	x	x				x	x	x	
Forestiera, New Mexican	x	x		x	x	x	x	x	
Forsythia, Border		x			x	x	x		
Forsythia, Fortune Weeping		x			x	x	x		
Goldraintree		x				x	x		
Greasewood	x	x		x	x	x	x	x	
Hawthorn, Cockspur		x	x	x					
Hawthorn, Downy		x		x	x	x			
Hawthorn, English		x			x	x			
Hawthorn, Russian		x		x	x	x			
Honeysuckle, Amur		x			x	x	x		
Honeysuckle, 'Arnold Red', 'Cardinal', 'Carlton', 'Valentia'		x	x	x	x	x			
Honeysuckle, Winter		x			x	x	x		
Honeysuckle, Zabel Blueleaf		x		x	x	x	x		
Leadplant	x	x		x	x	x	x	x	
Lilac, Early		x	x	x	x				
Lilac, French Hybrids		x		x	x	x	x		
Lilac, Hungarian		x		x	x	x			
Lilac, Japanese Tree		x	x	x	x	x	x		
Lilac, Late		x		x	x				
Lilac, Persian		x	x	x	x	x	x		
Mockorange, Lewis		x		x	x				
Mockorange, Sweet		x			x	x	x		
Mockorange, Virginalis		x			x	x	x		
Mountainmahogany, Douglas	x	x		x	x			4,000	
Nandina		x				x	x		x
Peach, Flowering		x			x	x	x		
Peashrub, Globe Russian		x	x	x	x				
Peashrub, Pygmy		x	x	x	x				

Appendix B (Continued)

	Adaptability to:										
	Annual rainfall		Zones					Salt or alkaline soils	Altitude require-ment	Shade
Common name	Less than 10"	10"–20"	III	IV	V	VI	VII	pH–8.0+	ft.+	
Peashrub, Siberian		x	x	x	x					
Perovskia, Russiansage		x		x	x	x				
Plum, Cistena		x	x	x	x					
Plum, Flowering		x	x	x	x					
Plum, Newport		x		x	x	x				
Privet, European		x		x	x	x	x			x
Quince, Flowering		x			x	x	x			
Quince, Japanese Flowering		x			x	x				
Rabbitbrush	x	x	x	x	x	x				
Rose, Austrian Copper		x	x	x	x			x		
Rose, 'Harison's Yellow'		x	x	x	x					
Rose, Hybrid Tea		x		x	x	x	x			
Rosewood, Arizona	x	x				x	x			x
Sagebrush	x	x		x	x	x	x	x		
Saltbush	x	x	x	x	x	x	x	x		
Serviceberry, Allegany		x	x	x	x					
Serviceberry, Saskatoon		x	x	x	x					
Serviceberry, Shadblow		x	x	x	x					
Shrubalthea		x				x	x			
Sibirea, Smooth		x		x	x					
Smoketree, Common		x		x	x	x	x			
Snowberry	x	x	x	x	x	x				
Spirea, Mongolian		x		x	x	x	x			
Spirea, Nippon		x		x	x	x	x			
Spirea, Sargent		x	x	x	x	x				
Spirea, Threelobe		x	x	x	x	x				
Spirea, Vanhoutte		x	x	x	x	x	x			
Sumac, Skunkbush		x	x	x	x	x	x			

Appendix B (*Continued*)

Plant	1	2	3	4	5	6	7	8	9	10
Sumac, Staghorn			×						×	
Tamarix, Amur		×	×			×			×	
Tamarix, Kashgar		×	×						×	
Viburnum, Common Snowball				×	×	×			×	
Viburnum, European Cranberrybush				×	×	×			×	
Viburnum, Koreanspice				×	×	×			×	
Viburnum, Manchurian				×	×	×			×	
Viburnum, Nannyberry					×	×			×	
Viburnum, Wayfaring Tree						×			×	

Plants for the Desert Southwest

Plant	1	2	3	4	5	6	7	8	9	10
Agave		×	×						×	×
Boojam Tree		×	×						×	×
Brittlebush		×	×						×	×
Broom Baccharis		×	×						×	×
Cacti (many types)		×	×		×				×	×
Catclaw		×	×						×	×
Creosotebush		×	×						×	×
Hackberry, Spiny		×	×			×			×	×
Jojoba		×	×				×		×	×
Mesquite		×	×			×			×	×
Ocotillo		×	×						×	×
Paloverde		×	×						×	×
Sotol		×	×						×	×
Tesota		×	×		×				×	×
Yucca (many types)		×	×						×	×

Vines

Plant	1	2	3	4	5	6	7	8	9	10
Clematis, Drummond			×		×	×			×	
Clematis, Jackman				×	×	×			×	
Grape (use the native species in each zone)	×		×	×		×			×	
Honeysuckle, Dropmore Scarlet Trumpet				×	×	×			×	
Honeysuckle, Everblooming					×	×			×	
Ivy, Engelmann	×				×	×			×	
Monkshoodvine			×	×		×			×	
Moonseed, Asiatic	×								×	
Rose, Climbing (Grecian and Chinese)					×	×			×	
Silkvine (Grecian and Chinese)			×			×			×	

INDEX

Page numbers in *italics* refer to illustrations; page numbers followed by (t) indicate tables.